LEAVES FROM THE NOTEBOOK
OF A TAMED CYNIC

Leaves
From the Notebook
of a Tamed Cynic

REINHOLD NIEBUHR

Westminster/John Knox Press
LOUISVILLE, KENTUCKY

To
my friends
and former co-workers
in
Bethel Evangelical Church
Detroit, Michigan

Copyright © 1929; renewed 1957 by Reinhold Niebuhr. Foreword by Martin E. Marty copyright © 1980 by Harper & Row; reprinted by permission of Harper & Row, Publishers, Inc.

Published by Westminster/John Knox Press
Louisville, Kentucky

PRINTED IN THE UNITED STATES OF AMERICA
4   6   8   9   7   5   3

Library of Congress Cataloging-in-Publication Data

Niebuhr, Reinhold, 1892-1971.
    Leaves from the notebook of a tamed cynic / Reinhold Niebuhr.
        p.   cm.
    Reprint. Previously published: San Francisco : Harper & Row, 1980, © 1929. (Harper's ministers paperback library).
    ISBN 0-664-25164-1

    1. Niebuhr, Reinhold, 1892-1971 — Diaries.   2. Clergy — Michigan — Detroit — Diaries.   3. Church work with the poor — Michigan — Detroit.
    4. Church and social problems — Michigan — Detroit.
    5. Clergy — Office.   6. Detroit (Mich.) — Church history — 20th century.
    I. Title
    [BX4827.N5A34   1990]
    280 ' .4 ' 092 — dc20   90-35060
    [B]   CIP

Foreword

Hundreds of thousands of Americans have been Christian ministers or priests through the past five centuries. Thousands of them left a record of their musings in the form of autobiographies, memoirs, and reflections. Only two or three of these have attained the status of a classic. Reinhold Niebuhr's modest collection of fragments is one that has. Two generations of laity have used the book in order to gain some sense of life behind the curtains at the parsonage, some feeling for the nuances of the pastoral heart. And two generations of clergy have grasped *Leaves from the Notebook of a Tamed Cynic* as a manual of arms, a book of consolation, an example for imitation.

In its favor, this book has the weight of the author's reputation. Niebuhr and his brother, H. Richard, have come to be regarded as the two most notable homegrown American theologians of this century. When religious editors polled leaders to see whose faces might be chipped in a foursome on an American religious Mt. Rushmore, Niebuhr was in that select group. But the fame of an author, by itself, will not move people as *Leaves* has. Niebuhr himself wrote some forgettable books; they gather dust as this little work now sees its fourth incarnation. What are the sources of its power, its charm?

Certainly the moment of its production was decisive in American religious history, and the transitions it describes are similar to those many religious leaders have had to make before and since. Niebuhr here is the small-town member of a provincial church body finding his way in the jostling metropolis of Detroit, cutting a path beyond parochialism into ecumenical and interfaith relations. No one prepares a ministry-bound child for such transitions, and theological schools can at best talk about them from a distance. Here is someone nurtured in conservative Protestantism having to deal with labor leaders, civic professionals, and men and women who share little of his regard for the cross of Jesus Christ. Others who have had to learn this bifocality have found Niebuhr a faithful and reliable guide. He had to pick and choose in the face of ideologies and urban discontents, and while all his choices may not be attractive today, his developing skill at determining how to choose a course is something that readers find exemplary.

Another asset of this book is its ability to convey the loyalties and struggles of a man who was, in the language of his later colleague Paul Tillich, "on the boundary." The shapers of American theology in the Protestant camp were, until recently, people who spent much of their career in the parish ministry. Jonathan Edwards served in Northampton and among the Stockbridge Indians; Horace Bushnell shaped the concept of Christian nurture from a Connecticut pulpit; the most notable social prophet among the American clergy, Walter Rauschenbusch, formed his vision in New York's Hell's Kitchen slum. And Niebuhr spent thirteen years in a tiny but growing parish in industrial Detroit.

He never forgot what he learned there. Niebuhr could be diffident or even self-derisive about how little epistemology he learned at Yale or how little formal theology he imparted at Union Theological Seminary, the site of his subsequent career. But he always felt competent to deal with the empirical religious and social scene, thanks to the parish work he employed to engender this collection of *Leaves*. In a sparse and succinct "Intellectual Autobiography," he noted that the Detroit facts "determined my development more than any books which I have read." And in 1939 he told readers of *The Christian Century*: "Such theological convictions which I hold today began to dawn upon me during the end of a pastorate in a great industrial city." At Union, "the gradual unfolding of my theological ideas [came] not so much through study as through the pressure of world events," events filtered through the windows of his study and church in Detroit.

Let the late and great theologian then be shy, let him mumble about *Leaves* as he blushingly presents them to the publisher who dragged him into rewriting a first paperback edition. He was not the best judge of the use to which the book can be put. On these pages we see a minister learning the limits of moralism—his peoples' and his own. Here are glimpses of his reaction to formalism and liturgy, along with compensatory statements about what common rites and gestures meant to the people who made up the congregation. One gains from *Leaves* a sense of Niebuhr's growing confidence as he found power in the preached Word, courage to face up to ethical problems, and a sense that he was fabricating an outlook that might help him meet societal problems.

Forewords permit foreworders to comment autobiographically about the books they are helping to present. In this case, there is no shy mumbling, no blush of embarrassment, as I confess that Niebuhr was (and remains) a hero and model to me. His theology, for all its limits—and who more than Niebuhr was aware of his limits and taught us about ours?—still speaks with power, despite vast changes in cultural contexts. Niebuhr was engaged with the culture as few clerics have been, and that engagement seemed and seems urgent to me. And like him, I carried advanced theological training into what to my peers looked like the exile of parishes. The paperback came out in 1956, just when I was called to start a new parish. When the sermonizing impulse grew weak and the words seemed sterile, it gave me confidence to know that Niebuhr had also known dry periods. As one who liked but also did not like to make pastoral calls, I appreciated knowing of similar Niebuhrian reluctances when the weather gave him the least excuse. Then I took courage from his own irresponsibility. There may have been days when other great books on ministry spoke to me more systematically: Georges Bernanos's *The Diary of a Country Priest* has literary values to which *Leaves* does not aspire; Richard Baxter's *The Reformed Pastor* has an integrity which this chopped-up notebook cannot embody.

But I shall ever recall the sense of coincidence between the author's experience and my own on many days, and am sure that another generation will also find it. Among these, thanks in part to Niebuhr, was an observation he could not resist, one that so many of us came to share: "I am really beginning to like the ministry." He found he liked his and helped others like theirs. So it is good to have this bundle of *Leaves* in hand again, as a new cohort of laypeople eavesdrops on, and ministers plunder, his notions about the frustrations and enjoyments of ministry in a time when the questions of morale and knowledge are again urgent.

MARTIN E. MARTY
Fairfax M. Cone Distinguished Service Professor at The University of Chicago;
Formerly Pastor of The Lutheran Church of the Holy Spirit

Preface–1956

An author is naturally embarrassed to have a book, first published more than a quarter century ago, re-issued and presumably reaching some new readers who will be astounded by the dated character of the observations in the book. My own embarrassment is the more acute because these autobiographical notes are more than ordinarily dated. They were prompted by the experiences of a young minister serving his first parish in the growing city of Detroit. Some of the observations may have a faint historical significance inasfar as they throw light upon the social climate of a large urban center, the seat of the growing automobile industry in a day in which the unions, which now dominate the picture, were still unheard of.

But the notes are not primarily a social document. As the self-revelations of a young parson they freely express the then typical notions of liberal Protestantism before the whole liberal world view was challenged by world events. Of course they were written after the first world war. But that war did not essentially challenge the liberal culture of America. It required a depression and another world war to corrode an optimism in America which was lost in Europe after the first world war. There are some indications in these notes of uneasiness about the general religious presuppositions which informed a youthful ministry. But on the whole there are no serious evidences of a revolt which occurred in the soul of the author and of many of his contemporaries, only a few years after the book was published. Thus indisputable evidence is offered for the fact that we are all, whatever our pretensions, the children of our day and hour. What we think of man and God, of sin and salvation, is partly prompted by the comparative comforts or discomforts in which we live. It is a very sobering reflection on the lack of transcendence of the human spirit over the flux of historical change.

Perhaps too much has been said about the embarrassment of the author because of the "dated" character of his views. The notes are primarily a record of the experiences of a young minister and they will have interest primarily to other young ministers. I have no embarrassment about the fact that the notes reveal the satisfaction which one may have in preaching the gospel and "tending the flock" in a local parish. And I hope that they may also reveal some of the variegated problems and issues which confront the Christian ministry. After a quarter of a century in academic life, I can still understand why I was so reluctant to leave the local parish. Academic life seems highly specialized in comparison with the life of a parish priest meeting human problems on all levels of weal and woe, and trying to be helpful in fashioning a "community of grace" in the barren anonymity of a large city.

I regret the immaturity with which I approached the problems and tasks of the ministry but I do not regret the years devoted to the parish.

REINHOLD NIEBUHR

Preface and Apology

Most of the reflections recorded in these pages were prompted by experiences of a local Christian pastorate. Some are derived from wider contacts with the churches and colleges of the country. For the sake of giving a better clue to the meaning of a few of them, it may be necessary to say that they have as their background a pastorate in an industrial community in which the natural growth of the city made the expansion of a small church into a congregation of considerable size, in a period of thirteen years, inevitable. By the time these lines reach the reader the author will have exchanged his pastoral activities for academic pursuits.

It must be confessed in all candor that some of the notes, particularly the later ones, were written after it seemed fairly certain that they would reach the eye of the public in some form or other. It was therefore psychologically difficult to maintain the type of honesty which characterizes the self-revelations of a private diary. The reader must consequently be warned (though such a warning may be superfluous) to discount the unconscious insincerities which no amount of self-discipline can eliminate from words which are meant for the public.

The notes which have been chosen for publication have been picked to illustrate the typical problems of a modern minister in an industrial and urban community and what seem to be more or less typical reactions of a young minister to such problems. Nothing new or startling was attempted in the pastorate out of which these reflections grew. If there is any justification for their publication, it must lie in the light they may throw upon the problems of the modern church and ministry rather than upon any possible solutions of these problems.

The book is published with an uneasy conscience, the author half hoping that the publishers would make short shrift of his indiscretions by throttling the book. Some of the notes are really too inane to deserve inclusion in any published work, and they can be justified only as a background for those notes which deal critically with the problems of the modern ministry. The latter are unfortunately, in many instances, too impertinent to be in good taste, and I lacked the grace to rob them of their impertinence without destroying whatever critical value they might possess. I can only emphasize in extenuation of the spirit which prompted them, what is confessed in some of the criticisms, namely, that the author is not unconscious of what the critical reader will himself divine, a tendency to be most critical of that in other men to which he is most tempted himself.

The modern ministry is in no easy position; for it is committed to the espousal of ideals (professionally, at that) which are in direct conflict with the dominant interests and prejudices of contemporary civilization. This conflict is nowhere more apparent than in America, where neither ancient sanctities nor new social insights tend to qualify, as they do in Europe, the heedless economic forces of an industrial era.

Inevitably a compromise must be made, or is made, between the rigor of the ideal and the necessities of the day. That has always been the case, but the resulting compromises are more obvious to an astute observer in our own day than in other generations. We are a world-conscious generation, and we have the means at our disposal to see and to analyze the brutalities which characterize men's larger social relationships and to note the dehumanizing effects of a civilization which unites men mechanically and isolates them spiritually.

Our knowledge may ultimately be the means of our redemption, but for the moment it seems to rob us of self-respect and respect for one another. Every conscientious minister is easily tempted to a sense of futility because we live our lives microscopically while we are able to view the scene in which we labor telescopically. But the higher perspective has its advantages as well as its dangers. It saves us from too much self-deception. Men who are engaged in the espousal of ideals easily fall into sentimentality. From the outside and the disinterested perspective this sentimentality may seem like hypocrisy. If it is only sentimentality and self-deception, viewed at closer range, it may degenerate into real hypocrisy if no determined effort is made to reduce it to a minimum.

It is no easy task to deal realistically with the moral confusion of our day, either in the pulpit or the pew, and avoid the appearance, and possibly the actual peril, of cynicism. An age which obscures the essentially unethical nature of its dominant interests by an undue preoccupation with the application of Christian principles in limited areas, may, as a matter of fact, deserve and profit by ruthless satire. Yet the pedagogical merits of satire are dubious, and in any event its weapons will be foresworn by an inside critic for both selfish and social reasons. For reasons of self-defense he will be very gentle in dealing with limitations which his own life illustrates.

But he will be generous in judgment for another reason. His intimate view of the facts will help him to see that what an outside critic may call hypocrisy may really be honest, because unconscious, sentimentality and self-deception. When virtues are used to hide moral limitations the critic ought not to be too sure that the virtues are bogus. Sometimes they are. But sometimes they merely represent the effort of honest but short-sighted men to preserve the excellencies of another day long after these have ceased to have relevancy for the problems of our own day; or sometimes they spring from efforts to apply the Christian ideal to limited and immediate areas of conduct where application is fairly easy. In such cases no one can be absolutely sure whether it is want of perspective or want of courage which hinders the Christian idealist from applying his ideals and principles to the more remote and the more difficult relationships.

That the ministry is particularly tempted to the self-deceptions which afflict the moral life of Christians today is obvious. If it is dangerous to entertain great moral ideals without attempting to realize them in life, it is even more perilous to proclaim them in abstract terms without bringing them into juxtaposition with the specific social and moral issues of the day. The minister's premature satisfaction in the presentation of moral ideals is accentuated by the fact that he is a leader in a community in which appreciative attitudes are on the whole more prevalent than critical ones. The minister is therefore easily fooled by extravagant conceptions of his own moral stature, held by admiring parishioners. If he could realize how much of this appreciation represents transferred religious emotion he could be more realistic in analyzing himself. And if he could persuade himself to speak of moral ideals in terms of specific issues and contemporary situations, he would probably prompt currents of critical thought which would destroy the aura which invests his person with premature sanctity.

If a minister wants to be a man among men he need only to stop creating devotion to abstract ideals which every one accepts in theory and denies in practice, and to agonize about their validity and practicability in the social issues which he and others face in our present civilization. That immediately gives his ministry a touch of reality and potency and robs it of an artificial prestige which it can afford to dispense with, and is bound to be stripped of, the kind of prestige which is the prerogative of priests and professional holy men.

The number of ministers who are perfectly realistic about

their tasks and who are sincerely anxious to help the modern generation find itself, not only in the intricate problems of the personal life but in the moral and social complexities of an industrial society, is much larger than the critics outside of the church are able to know and willing to concede. If I have any regrets, it is that these pages, preoccupied with criticism, deal inadequately with such men and fail to discharge my debt of gratitude to them. It is comparatively easy for professors, secretaries and even bishops to criticise the man in a local situation from the perspective and the safety (relative, of course) which an irresponsible itinerancy supplies.

No amount of pressure from an itinerant "prophet" can change the fact that a minister is bound to be a statesman as much as a prophet, dealing with situations as well as principles. In specific situations, actions must be judged not only in terms of absolute standards but in consideration of available resources in the lives of those whom the minister leads.

It may be well for the statesman to know that statesmanship easily degenerates into opportunism and that opportunism cannot be sharply distinguished from dishonesty. But the prophet ought to realize that his higher perspective and the uncompromising nature of his judgments always has a note of irresponsibility in it. Francis of Assisi may have been a better Christian than Pope Innocent III. But it may be questioned whether his moral superiority over the latter was as absolute as it seemed. Nor is there any reason to believe that Abraham Lincoln, the statesman and opportunist, was morally inferior to William Lloyd Garrison, the prophet. The moral achievement of statesmen must be judged in terms which take account of the limitations of human society which the statesman must, and the prophet need not, consider.

Having both entered and left the parish ministry against my inclinations, I pay my tribute to the calling, firm in the conviction that it offers greater opportunities for both moral adventure and social usefulness than any other calling if it is entered with open eyes and a consciousness of the hazards to virtue which lurk in it. I make no apology for being critical of what I love. No one wants a love which is based upon illusions, and there is no reason why we should not love a profession and yet be critical of it.

REINHOLD NIEBUHR

Leaves from the Notebook of a Tamed Cynic

1915

There is something ludicrous about a callow young fool like myself standing up to preach a sermon to these good folks. I talk wisely about life and know little about life's problems. I tell them of the need of sacrifice, although most of them could tell me something about what that really means. I preached a sermon the other day on "The Involuntary Cross," using the text of Simon the Cyrene bearing the cross of Jesus. A good woman, a little bolder than the rest, asked me in going out whether I had borne many crosses. I think I know a little more about that than I would be willing to confess to her or to the congregation, but her question was justified.

Many of the people insist that they can't understand how a man so young as I could possibly be a preacher. Since I am twenty-three their reaction to my youth simply means that they find something incompatible even between the ripe age of twenty-three and the kind of seasoned wisdom which they expect from the pulpit. "Let no one despise thy youth," said Paul to Timothy; but I doubt whether that advice stopped any of the old saints from wagging their heads. I found it hard the first few months to wear a pulpit gown. Now I am getting accustomed to it. At first I felt too much like a priest in it, and I abhor priestliness. I have become reconciled to it partly as a simple matter of habit, but I imagine that I am also beginning to like the gown as a kind of symbol of authority. It gives me the feeling that I am speaking not altogether in my own name and out of my own experience but by the authority of the experience of many Christian centuries.

Difficult as the pulpit job is, it is easier than the work in the organizations of the congregation. Where did anyone ever learn in a seminary how to conduct or help with a Ladies Aid meeting? I am glad that mother has come to live with me and will take care of that part of the job. It is easier to speak sagely from the pulpit than to act wisely in the detailed tasks of the parish. A young preacher would do well to be heard more than he is seen.

1915

I am glad there are only eighteen families in this church. I have been visiting the members for six weeks and haven't seen all of them yet. Usually I walk past a house two or three times before I summon the courage to go in. I am always very courteously received, so I don't know exactly why I should not be able to overcome this curious timidity. I don't know that very much comes of my visits except that I really get acquainted with the people.

Usually after I have made a call I find some good excuse to quit for the afternoon. I used to do that in the days gone by when I was a book agent. But there was reason for it then. I needed the afternoon to regain my self-respect. Now it seems to be pure laziness and fear. The people are a little discouraged. Some of them seem to doubt whether the church will survive. But there are a few who are the salt of the earth, and if I make a go of this they will be more responsible than they will ever know.

1915

Now that I have preached about a dozen sermons I find I am repeating myself. A different text simply means a different pretext for saying the same thing over again. The few ideas that I had worked into sermons at the seminary have all been used, and now what? I suppose that as the years go by life and experience will prompt some new ideas and I will find some in the Bible that I have missed so far. They say a young preacher must catch his second wind before he can really preach. I'd better catch it pretty soon or the weekly sermon will become a terrible chore.

You are supposed to stand before a congregation, brimming over with a great message. Here I am trying to find a new little message each Sunday. If I really had great convictions I suppose they would struggle for birth each week. As the matter stands, I struggle to find an idea worth presenting and I almost dread the approach of a new sabbath. I don't know whether I can ever accustom myself to the task of bringing light and inspiration in regular weekly installments.

How in the world can you reconcile the inevitability of Sunday and its task with the moods and caprices of the soul? The prophet speaks only when he is inspired. The parish preacher must speak whether he is inspired or not. I wonder whether it is possible to live on a high enough plane to do that without sinning against the Holy Spirit.

12

1916

Visited old Mrs. G. today and gave her communion. This was my first experience with communion at the sick bed. I think there is a good deal of superstition connected with the rite. It isn't very much different in some of its aspects from the Catholic rite of extreme unction. Yet I will not be too critical. If the rite suggests and expresses the emotion of honest contrition it is more than superstition. But that is the difficulty of acting as priest. It is not in your power to determine the use of a symbol. Whether it is a blessing or a bit of superstition rests altogether with the recipient.

I must admit that I am losing some of the aversion to the sacraments cultivated in my seminary days. There is something very beautiful about parents bringing their child to the altar with a prayer of thanksgiving and as an act of dedication. The trouble is that the old ritual in the book of forms does not express this idea clearly. I have to put the whole meaning of the sacrament as I see it into the prayer. Perhaps I can use my own form later on, if I get the confidence of the people.

Incidentally Mrs. G. gave me a shock this afternoon. After the service was completed she fished around under her pillow and brought forth a five dollar bill. That was to pay me for my trouble. I never knew this fee business still existed in such a form in Protestantism. I knew they were still paying for baptism in some denominations, ours included. But this is a new one. The old lady was a little hurt, I think, by my refusal. I think she imagined that pity prompted my diffidence. She insisted that she was quite able to pay. I'd better get started on this whole fee question and make an announcement that I won't accept any fees for anything. I think I'll except weddings however. Every one takes fees for them. It will just make a scene when the groom or best man slyly crosses your palm with a bill and you make a righteous refusal. They never will understand. Marriage is not a sacrament anyway. Then, too, it's fun getting a little extra money once in a while. But isn't marriage a sacrament?

1916

Doesn't this denominational business wear on one's nerves? If I were a doctor people would consult me according to the skill I had and the reputation I could acquire. But being a minister I can appeal only to people who are labeled as I am. Yesterday that professor I met asked me what denomination I belonged to. Being told, he promptly pigeonholed me into my proper place and with a superior air assumed that my mind was as definitely set by my denominational background as is that of an African Hottentot by his peculiar environment.

Perhaps if I belonged to a larger denomination this wouldn't irk me so much. I suffer from an inferiority complex because of the very numerical weakness of my denomination. If I belonged to a large one I might strut about and claim its glory for myself. If I give myself to religion as a profession I must find some interdenominational outlet for my activities. But what? Secretaries and Y.M.C.A. workers are too inarticulate. They deal too much with machinery and too little with ideas. I don't want to be a chauffeur. Does that mean that I am a minister merely because I am a fairly glib talker? Who knows?

But let us not be too cynical and too morbidly introspective. I may find something worth saying in time and escape the fate of being a mere talker. At any rate I swear that I will never aspire to be a preacher of pretty sermons. I'll keep them rough just to escape the temptation of degenerating into an elocutionist. Maybe I had better stop quoting so much poetry. But that is hardly the point. Plenty of sermons lack both beauty and meaning.

1916

The young fellows I am trying to teach in Sunday school don't listen to me attentively. I don't think I am getting very close to where they live. Or perhaps I just haven't learned how to put my message across. I am constantly interrupted in my talk by the necessity of calling someone to order. It is a good thing that I have a class like that. I'll venture that my sermons aren't getting any nearer to the people, but the little group of adults I am speaking to in the morning service are naturally more patient or at least more polite than these honest youngsters, and so I have less chance to find out from them how futile I am. But that doesn't solve the problem of how to reach those fellows.

1916

I had a letter from Professor L—— today suggesting that I return to college and prepare myself for the teaching profession. A year ago I was certain that I would do that. Now I am not so sure. Nevertheless the academic life has its allurements. It is really simpler than the ministry. As a teacher your only task is to discover the truth. As a preacher you must conserve other interests besides the truth. It is your business to deal circumspectly with the whole religious inheritance lest the virtues which are involved in the older traditions perish through your iconoclasm. That is a formidable task and a harassing one; for one can never be quite sure where pedagogical caution ends and dishonesty begins.

What is particularly disquieting to a young man in the ministry is the fact that some of his fine old colleagues make such a virtue of their ignorance. They are sure that there is no Second Isaiah and have never heard that Deuteronomy represents a later development in the law. I can't blame them for not having all the bright new knowledge of a recent seminarian (not quite as new as the seminarian imagines); but the ministry is the only profession in which you can make a virtue of ignorance. If you have read nothing but commentaries for twenty years, that is supposed to invest you with an aura of sanctity and piety. Every profession has its traditions and its traditionalists. But the traditionalists in the pulpit are much more certain than the others that the Lord is on their side.

1917

Next week we are going to hold our first every member canvass. They expect me to preach a sermon which will prepare the good people to give generously. I don't mind that. Most people give little enough for the church or for anything else not connected with their own pleasures. But I don't see how you can preach a sermon adequate to the needs of the moment without identifying the church with the kingdom of God too unqualifiedly. And meanwhile you are drawing your salary from the church and remembering that if the canvass is a success there may be an increase in salary next year. It isn't easy to mix the business of preaching with the business of making a living and maintain your honesty and self-respect.

Of course every laborer is worthy of his hire. But you notice that Paul, who insisted on that point, nevertheless prided himself on his independence. He wanted "not yours but you." But let us not be too squeamish. There is old J.Q. It would do his soul good if he loosened up a bit. One might say to him, "I want yours so that I can get you."

1918

After a Trip Through the War Training Camps.

I hardly know how to bring order out of confusion in my mind in regard to this war. I think that if Wilson's aims are realized the war will serve a good purpose. When I talk to the boys I make much of the Wilsonian program as against the kind of diplomacy which brought on the war. But it is easier to talk about the aims of the war than to justify its methods.

Out at Funston I watched a bayonet practice. It was enough to make me feel like a brazen hypocrite for being in this thing, even in a rather indirect way. Yet I cannot bring myself to associate with the pacifists. Perhaps if I were not of German blood I could. That may be cowardly, but I do think that a new nation has a right to be pretty sensitive about its unity.

Some of the good old Germans have a hard time hiding a sentiment which borders very closely on hatred for this nation. Anyone who dissociates himself from the cause of his nation in such a time as this ought to do it only on the basis of an unmistakably higher loyalty. If I dissociated myself only slightly I would inevitably be forced into the camp of those who romanticize about the Kaiser. And the Kaiser is certainly nothing to me. If we must have war I'll certainly feel better on the side of Wilson than on the side of the Kaiser.

What makes me angry is the way I kowtow to the chaplains as I visit the various camps. Here are ministers of the gospel just as I am. Just as I they are also, for the moment, priests of the great god Mars. As ministers of the Christian religion I have no particular respect for them. Yet I am overcome by a terrible inferiority complex when I deal with them. Such is the power of a uniform. Like myself, they have mixed the worship of the God of love and the God of battles. But unlike myself, they have adequate symbols of this double devotion. The little cross on the shoulder is the symbol of their Christian faith. The uniform itself is the symbol of their devotion to the God of battles. It is the uniform and not the cross which impresses me and others. I am impressed even when I know that I ought not be.

What I dislike about most of the chaplains is that they assume a very officious and also a very masculine attitude. Ministers are not used to authority and revel in it when acquired. The rather too obvious masculinity which they try to suggest by word and action is meant to remove any possible taint which their Christian faith might be suspected to have left upon them in the minds of the he-men in the army. H—— is right. He tells me that he wants to go into the army as a private and not as a chaplain. He believes that the war is inevitable but he is not inclined to reconcile its necessities with the Christian ethic. He will merely forget about this difficulty during the war. That is much more honest than what I am doing.

1918

I can see one element in this strange fascination of war which men have not adequately noted. It reduces life to simple terms. The modern man lives in such a complex world that one wonders how his sanity is maintained as well as it is. Every moral venture, every social situation and every practical problem involves a whole series of conflicting loyalties, and a man may never be quite sure that he is right in giving himself to the one as against the other. Shall he be just and sacrifice love? Shall he strive for beauty and do it by gaining the social privileges which destroy his sense of fellowship with the underprivileged? Shall he serve his family and neglect the state? Or be patriotic to the detriment of the great family of mankind? Shall he be diligent at the expense of his health? Or keep healthy at the expense of the great cause in which he is interested? Shall he be truthful and therefore cruel? Or shall he be kind and therefore a little soft? Shall he strive for the amenities of life and make life less robust in the process? Or shall he make courage the ultimate virtue and brush aside the virtues which a stable and therefore soft society has cultivated?

Out of this mesh of conflicting claims, interests, loyalties, ideals, values and communities he is rescued by the psychology of war which gives the state at least a momentary priority over all other communities and which makes courage the supreme virtue. I talked to a young captain at camp last week who told me how happy he was in the army because he had "found himself" in military service. Our further conversation led me to suspect that it was this simplification of life which had really brought him happiness; that and his love of authority.

Unfortunately, all these momentary simplifications of the complexities of life cannot be finally satisfying, because they do violence to life. The imperiled community may for a moment claim a kind of unqualified loyalty which no community or cause has the right or ability to secure in normal times. But judgment returns to sobriety as events become less disjointed and the world is once more revealed in all its confusion of good in evil and evil in good. The imperiled community was threatened because of its vice as much as because of its virtue, and the diabolical foe reassumes the lineaments of our common humanity. Physical courage is proved unequal to the task of ennobling man without the aid of other virtues, and the same men who have been raised to great heights by the self-forgetfulness of war have been sunk into new depths of hatred. There is only momentary peace in an all-consuming passion, except it be a passion for what is indubitably the best. And what is the best?

1919

We had a great Easter service today. Mother made the little chapel look very pretty, working with a committee of young women. It takes real work to decorate such a little place, and make it really inviting. We received our largest class of new members into the church thus far, twenty-one in all. Most of them had no letters from other churches and yet had been reared in some church. We received them on reaffirmation of faith.

This matter of recruiting a membership for the church is a real problem. Even the churches which once believed a very definite conversion to be the sine qua non of entrance into the fellowship of the church are going in for "decision days" as they lose confidence in the traditional assumption that one can become a Christian only through a crisis experience. But if one does not insist on that kind of an experience it is not so easy to set up tests of membership. Most of these "personal evangelism" campaigns mean little more than an ordinary recruiting effort with church membership rather than the Christian life as the real objective. They do not differ greatly from efforts of various clubs as they seek to expand their membership.

Of course we make "acceptance of Jesus as your savior" the real door into the fellowship of the church. But the trouble is that this may mean everything or nothing. I see no way of making the Christian fellowship unique by any series of tests which precede admission. The only possibility lies in a winnowing process through the instrumentality of the preaching and teaching function of the church. Let them come in without great difficulty, but make it difficult for them to stay in. The trouble with this plan is that it is always easy to load up your membership with very immature Christians who will finally set the standard and make it impossible to preach and to teach the gospel in its full implications.

1919

What a picture that is of Wilson, Lloyd George and Clemenceau settling the fate of the world in Paris! Wilson is evidently losing his battle. He would have done better to stay at home and throw bolts from Olympus. If you have honest and important differences of opinion with others, it is better to write letters than to put your feet under the same table with them. Compromises are always more inevitable in personal contact than in long distance negotiation.

What seems to be happening at Paris is that they will let Wilson label the transaction if the others can determine its true import. Thus realities are exchanged for words. There will be "no indemnities" but of course there will be reparations; and, since the damage was great, the reparations may be made larger than any so-called indemnity of the past. There will be "no annexations" but there will be mandates.

Wilson is a typical son of the manse. He believes too much in words. The sly Clemenceau sneaks new meanings into these nice words, in which task he is probably ably helped by Mr. Lloyd George, who is an admirable go-between, being as worldly wise as M. Clemenceau and as evangelical as Mr. Wilson. Yet who knows? Time may yet give Mr. Wilson the victory. Words have certain meanings of which it is hard to rob them, and ideas may create reality in time. The league of nations may be, for the time being, merely a league of victors but it will be difficult to destroy the redemptive idea at the heart of it completely. Realities are always defeating ideals, but ideals have a way of taking vengeance upon the facts which momentarily imprison them.

On the other hand, it is always possible that diabolical facts will so discredit the idea which they ostensibly incarnate that they will necessitate the projection of a new idea before progress can be made.

1919

Visited Miss Z. at the hospital. I like to go now since she told me that it helps her to have me pray with her. I asked the doctor about her and he says her case is hopeless. Here faith seems really to be functioning in lifting the soul above physical circumstance. I have been so afraid of quackery that I have leaned over backwards trying to avoid the encouragement of false hopes. Sometimes when I compare myself with these efficient doctors and nurses hustling about I feel like an ancient medicine man dumped into the twentieth century. I think they have about the same feeling toward me that I have about myself.

It must be very satisfying to deal as an exact scientist with known data upon which to base your conclusions. I have to work in the twilight zone where superstition is inextricably mixed up with something that is—well, not superstition. I do believe that Jesus healed people. I can't help but note, however, that a large proportion of his cures were among the demented. If people ask me, I tell them that religion has more therapeutic value in functional than in organic diseases. But I don't know whether I am altogether honest about this at the bedside. I am still praying for health with Miss Z. But of course I don't leave it at that. I am trying to prepare her for the inevitable and I think I have helped her a little in that respect.

1919

This sickness of Miss Z.'s is getting on my nerves. I can't think of anything for the rest of the day after coming from that bed of pain. If I had more patients I suppose I would get a little more hardened. Talk about professionalism! I suppose men get professional to save their emotional resources. Here I make one visit in an afternoon and get all done up. Meanwhile the doctor is making a dozen. He is less sentimental, but probably does more good.

1920

I am really beginning to like the ministry. I think since I have stopped worrying so much about the intellectual problems of religion and have begun to explore some of its ethical problems there is more of a thrill in preaching. The real meaning of the gospel is in conflict with most of the customs and attitudes of our day at so many places that there is adventure in the Christian message, even if you only play around with its ideas in a conventional world. I can't say that I have done anything in my life to dramatize the conflict between the gospel and the world. But I find it increasingly interesting to set the two in juxtaposition at least in my mind and in the minds of others. And of course ideas may finally lead to action.

A young woman came to me the other day in —— and told me that my talk on forgiveness in the C—— Church of that town several months ago has brought about a reconciliation between her mother and sister after the two had been in a feud for five years. I accepted the news with more outward than inward composure. There is redemptive power in the message! I could go on the new courage that came out of that little victory for many a month.

I think I am beginning to like the ministry also because it gives you a splendid opportunity to have all kinds of contacts with people in relationships in which they are at their best. You do get tired of human pettiness at times. But there is nevertheless something quite glorious about folks. That is particularly true when you find them bearing sorrow with real patience. Think of Mrs. —— putting up with that drunkard of a husband for the sake of her children—and having such nice children. One can learn more from her quiet courage than from many a book.

1920

Good old Gordon came to me today to advise me that so-and-so might join the church but that he had been told that I talked considerably on political issues and he did not like politics in church. I told my friend that I did not like political lectures in a worship service myself, but that every religious problem had ethical implications and every ethical problem had some political and economic aspect. We had quite a nice chat about it, though my explanation did not seem altogether satisfactory. Gordon suggested that I seemed unable to get as many "prominent" people into the church as I ought. I told him that we had some very nice people in our church, but that I had no particular desire or ability to cater to "prominent" people, especially since there are plenty of churches who seem to serve this class quite well.

This is as close as I have come to having the freedom of the pulpit challenged, except of course by the tacit challenge of an occasional defection from the ranks. The problem of the freedom of the pulpit is a real one. But I am convinced that the simplest way to get liberty is to take it. The liberty to speak on all vital questions of the day without qualifying the message in a half dozen ways adds sufficient interest to the otherwise stodgy sermon to attract two listeners for every one who is lost by having some pet prejudice disarranged. But that generalization is hardly justified by my meager experience.

1920

I had a great discussion in my young men's class this morning. Gradually I am beginning to discover that my failure with the class was due to my talking too much. Now I let them talk and the thing is becoming interesting. Of course it isn't so easy to keep the discussion steered on any track. Sometimes we talk in circles. But the fellows are at least getting at some of the vital problems of life and I am learning something from them. Disciplinary problems have disappeared. The only one left is the fellow who is always trying to say something foolish or smart in the discussion.

1920

I went to the funeral of Mrs. T. at St. Cecilia's church. It must be a grateful task to deal as a priest with the definite symbols which the Catholic church uses and to dispense the absolute certainties with which she assures the faithful. Of course the requiem mass contains nothing that would be of obvious comfort to the sorrowing heart. But the implication of the whole transaction is that the soul is now taken up in another world in which the heartaches of this life are overcome.

I don't think the mass is so satisfying as a well conducted Protestant funeral service in which some cognizance is taken of the peculiar circumstances of a great sorrow and of the unique characteristics of the deceased. But it is certainly immeasurably superior to the average Protestant service with its banalities and sentimentalities. Religion is poetry. The truth in the poetry is vivified by adequate poetic symbols and is therefore more convincing than the poor prose with which the average preacher must attempt to grasp the ineffable.

Yet one must not forget that the truth is not only vivified but also corrupted by the poetic symbol, for it is only one step from a vivid symbol to the touch of magic. The priest does, after all, deal with magic. When religion renounces magic it finds itself in the poor workaday world trying to discover the glimpses of the eternal in the common scene. That is not an easy task, but it is not an impossible one. Wherefore let us envy the priest, but pity him too, meanwhile. He has been betrayed by his magic. He has gained too easy a victory over life's difficulties and he helps his people to find a premature peace. The rivers of life in Protestant religion are easily lost in the sand, but if they really run they carry more life than holy water.

1921

I spoke to the —— club today and was introduced by the chairman as a pastor who had recently built a new church at "the impressive cost of $170,000." While the figure was not quite correct it gave me somewhat of a start to find how much emphasis was placed upon what was regarded as a great business achievement. Here was a group of business men, and the chairman knew of no way to recommend me to them but by suggesting that I was myself a business man of no mean ability. That would have given the good men of my church council a laugh. Knowing how little I had to do with the raising of the money for the new church and how I have always failed to put on the kind of "pressure" they desired when we were raising money, they would certainly have smiled wryly at this eulogy.

But it is all natural enough. America worships success and so does the world in general. And the only kind of success the average man can understand is obvious success. There must be

"Things done that took the eye, that had the price;
O'er which from level stand,
The low world laid its hand,
Found straightway to its mind, could value in a trice."

After all the real work of a minister is not easily gauged and the world may not be entirely wrong in using external progress as an outward sign of an inward grace. Even those who value the real work of the ministry sometimes express their appreciation in rather superficial phrases. I remember when dear old —— celebrated his twenty-fifth anniversary the good toastmaster pathetically described his pastor's successful ministry by explaining that under his leadership the congregation had "doubled its membership, installed a new organ, built a parsonage, decorated the church and wiped out its debt." Not a word about the words of comfort the good pastor had spoken or the inspiration he had given to thirsting souls.

Perhaps it is foolish to be too sensitive about these inevitable secularizations of religious values. Let us be thankful that there is no quarterly meeting in our denomination and no need of giving a district superintendent a bunch of statistics to prove that our ministry is successful.

1921

I visited Mrs. S. today. She is suffering from cancer and will not live long. Her young grandson E. came home from high school just as I was leaving. He had a question for me. The Jewish boys at school told him Jesus was a bastard and Joseph was not his father. He also reported that they accused him of having two Gods instead of one. That dissolution of the Trinity into a dualism by high school boys interested me. Even boys seem to sense that if orthodox trinitarianism makes for polytheism it really suggests two gods rather than three. I chided E. for remembering so poorly what he had learned in the preparatory class and for being so irregular in church school where these problems are discussed. I went over some of the ideas on the humanity and the uniqueness of Jesus which we had discussed in the class.

Meanwhile I wished that I could talk to him alone without interference from grandma, who naïvely added her own theological mustard to the dish. It is no easy task to build up the faith of one generation and not destroy the supports of the religion of the other. But fortunately the old lady didn't get what I was driving at and so didn't interfere very seriously. She was thankful to me for straightening the young man out on his theology and seemed to think that I had settled all his difficulties by my few words. "Ich habe ihm gesagt, wart bis der Pastor kommt. Der wird dir alles erklaeren." It isn't a bad idea to find someone who has such confidence in you.

1922

When I sit in my study and meditate upon men and events I am critical and circumspect. Why is it that when I arise in the pulpit I try to be imaginative and am sometimes possessed by a kind of madness which makes my utterances extravagant and dogmatic? Perhaps this change of technique is due to my desire to move the audience. Audiences are not easily moved from their lethargy by cool and critical analyses. An appeal to the emotions is necessary and emotions are not aroused by a critical analysis of facts but by a presentation of ideal values. I do not mean that I disavow the critical method entirely in the pulpit. Indeed many of my friendly critics think I am too critical to be a good preacher. Nor am I ever very emotional. Nevertheless there is a distinct difference between my temper in the study and my spirit in the pulpit.

Perhaps this is as it should be. Let the study serve to reveal the relativity of all things so that pulpit utterances do not become too extravagant, and let the pulpit save the student from sinking in the sea of relativities. However qualified every truth may be there is nevertheless a portion in every truth and value which is essentially absolute and which is therefore worth proclaiming. "All oratory," declares a Greek scholar, "is based on half truths." That is why one ought naturally to distrust and to discount the orator. On the other hand, oratory may be the result of the kind of poetic gift which sees a truth dissociated, for a moment at least, from all relativities of time and circumstance and lifted into the light of the absolute.

I notice that the tendency of extravagance in the pulpit and on the platform increases with the size of the crowd. As my congregation increases in size I become more unguarded in my statements. Wherefore may the good Lord deliver me from ever being a popular preacher. "Why is it," asked one of my elders the other day, "that your Sunday evening sermons are more pessimistic than your morning sermons?" I think what he really meant is that they were more critical in analyzing life's problems. I told him that I tried to give inspiration in the morning and education in the evening.

But the fact is that circumstance probably affects the quality of the message as much as purpose. A full church gives me the sense of fighting with a victorious host in the battles of the Lord. A half empty church immediately symbolizes the fact that Christianity is very much of a minority movement in a pagan world and that it can be victorious only by snatching victory out of defeat.

1922

Just received a pitiful letter from a young pastor who is losing his church because he has been "too liberal." I suppose there are churches which will crucify a leader who tries to lead them into the modern world of thought and life. Yet here I have been all these years in a conservative communion and have never had a squabble about theology. I suppose that is partly due to the fact that there were so few people here when I came that no one had to listen to me if he didn't like my approach. Those who have come have associated themselves with us because they were in general agreement with "our gospel." They have come, however, from conservative communions and churches. But of course they have been mostly young people.

If preachers get into trouble in pursuance of their task of reinterpreting religious affirmations in the light of modern knowledge I think it must be partly because they beat their drums too loudly when they make their retreats from untenable positions of ancient orthodoxy. The correct strategy is to advance at the center with beating drums and let your retreats at the wings follow as a matter of course and in the interest of the central strategy. You must be honest, of course, but you might just as well straighten and shorten your lines without mock heroics and a fanfare of trumpets.

The beauty of this strategy is that there is enough power at the center for a real advance and enough opposition for a real conflict. If you set the message of a gospel of love against a society enmeshed in hatreds and bigotries and engulfed in greed, you have a real but not necessarily a futile conflict on your hands. There is enough natural grace in the human heart to respond to the challenge of the real message in the gospel—and enough original sin in human nature to create opposition to it. The sorriest preachers are those who preach a conventional morality while they try to be intellectually and theologically radical.

Men will not make great intellectual readjustments for a gospel which does not greatly matter. If there is real adventure at the center of the line the reserves are drawn from the wings almost unconsciously.

1923

Gradually the whole horrible truth about the war is being revealed. Every new book destroys some further illusion. How can we ever again believe anything when we compare the solemn pretensions of statesmen with the cynically conceived secret treaties? Here was simply a tremendous contest for power between two great alliances of states in which the caprice of statesmen combined with basic economic conflicts to dictate the peculiar form of the alliances. Next time the cards will be shuffled in a different way and the "fellowship in arms" will consist of different fellows.

As the truth becomes known there are however some compensations for the disillusionment. If the moral pretensions of the heroes were bogus, the iniquity of the villains was not as malicious as it once appeared. The Kaiser was evidently a boob who was puerile enough to permit the German navalists to force him into policies which he did not understand. Von Tirpitz and his crowd may have been the real villains but they probably did not want the war so much as they wanted to glorify the navy and themselves through it. If Poincaré was the villain, it was the limitations of a narrow and bigoted nationalism rather than the malice of an evil heart which prompted his policies. The poor little Czar was the victim of a neurotic wife, and she in turn the tool of religious fanatics and fear-tormented bureaucrats.

There doesn't seem to be very much malice in the world. There is simply not enough intelligence to conduct the intricate affairs of a complex civilization. All the chief actors in the war appear now in the light of children who played with dangerous toys. If they were criminal it was in the sense that the weal of millions was involved in their dangerous games and they didn't let that fact dissuade them from their play. All human sin seems so much worse in its consequences than in its intentions.

But that is not a fact which justifies moral nihilism. The consequences are obvious and inevitable enough to deter a sensitive soul from the course which leads to destruction. Not merely ignorance but callousness to human welfare is an ingredient in the compound of social and personal evil.

In one sense modern civilization substitutes unconscious sins of more destructive consequences for conscious sins of less destructive consequences. Men try consciously to eliminate the atrocities of society, but meanwhile they unheedingly build a civilization which is more destructive of moral and personal values than anything intended in a more primitive society.

1923

I met a wonderful parson in the little village of ———. I went there to speak at a high school commencement. His church seemed to be an ordinary village church, but he was undeniably the real leader of the community. Broad sympathies had made it possible for him to transcend the usual denominational divisions which reduce most ministers to impotence in small communities, at least as far as wider community leadership is concerned. There were a few other churches in town, but he had developed so many types of cooperation between them that they were almost a unit in their enterprise.

He had built a small church house which was a hive of activity throughout the week. He conducted his own week-day school of religion, spending three afternoons at the job. His influence upon the young people was evidently a fruit of this close contact with them. He was so happy in his work that he did not look upon big city churches as the natural goal of his ambition. His wife and he and two little kiddies live very modestly in a little parsonage, and the mistress of the manse seems to find time to mother the neighborhood as well as her children.

Perhaps I am inclined to romanticize about village life. Sometimes it is very petty and mean, I know. But the absence of great class distinctions makes for a higher type of fellowship in church and community than is achieved in the metropolis, and the preacher is not tempted to placate the powerful. The modest stipend which the small church can afford makes for simple living and the absence of social pride. If more young fellows would be willing to go into churches like that and not suffer from inferiority complexes because they had not landed one of the "big pulpits," we might put new power into the church.

Fortunately, this young fellow has an astute intelligence

without being an orator. If he were a more gifted speaker he would probably have been "promoted"—and spoiled—long ago. I have often observed that privilege and power tend to corrupt the simple Christian heart. I am now convinced that to these two must be added the kind of obvious success which the world knows how to measure. The simplicity which is preserved because it does not meet the temptation of success is innocence rather than virtue; but if we can't have virtue, innocence is preferable to moral failure.

There are successful men who have maintained a virtuous humility and sincerity in the day of success, but the achievement is very difficult.

1923

In Europe

I have been spending a few days with S—— and P—— in the Ruhr district. Flew back to London from Cologne by aeroplane. The Ruhr cities are the closest thing to hell I have ever seen. I never knew that you could see hatred with the naked eye, but in the Ruhr one is under the illusion that this is possible. The atmosphere is charged with it. The streets are filled with French soldiers in their grey-blue uniforms. Schools have been turned into barracks. Germans turn anxious and furtive glances upon every stranger. French officers race their automobiles wildly through the streets with sirens blowing shrilly. If you can gain the confidence of Germans so that they will talk they will tell you horrible tales of atrocities, deportations, sex crimes, etc. Imagination fired by fear and hatred undoubtedly tends to elaborate upon the sober facts. But the facts are bad enough.

When we arrived at Cologne after spending days in the French zone of occupation we felt as if we had come into a different world. The obvious reluctance of the British to make common cause with the French in the Ruhr adventure has accentuated the good will between the British troops and the native population. But a day in Cologne cannot erase the memory of Essen and Duesseldorf. It rests upon the mind like a horrible nightmare. One would like to send every sentimental spellbinder of war days into the Ruhr. This, then, is the glorious issue for which the war was fought! I didn't know Europe in 1914, but I can't imagine that the hatred between peoples could have been worse than it is now.

This is as good a time as any to make up my mind that I am done with the war business. Of course, I wasn't really in the last war. Would that I had been! Every soldier, fighting for his country in simplicity of heart without asking many questions, was superior to those of us who served no better purpose than to increase or perpetuate the moral obfuscation of nations. Of course, we really couldn't know everything we know now. But now we know. The times of man's ignorance God may wink at, but now he calls us all to repent. I am done with this business. I hope I can make that resolution stick.

Talking about the possibility of the church renouncing war, as we came over on the boat, one of the cynics suggested that the present temper of the church against war was prompted by nausea rather than idealism. He insisted that the church would not be able to prove for some time that it is really sincere in this matter. I suppose he is right; though I do not know that one ought to be contemptuous of any experience which leads to the truth. A pain in the stomach may sometimes serve an ultimate purpose quite as well as an idea in the head. Yet it is probably true that nausea finally wears off and the question will then be whether there is a more fundamental force which will maintain a conviction in defiance of popular hysteria.

For my own part I am not going to let my decision in regard to war stand alone. I am going to try to be a disciple of Christ, rather than a mere Christian, in all human relations and experiment with the potency of trust and love much more than I have in the past.

1923

This has been a wonderful Christmas season. The people have been splendid. It is fun to go into the homes and see the laughter and joy of the children. It is rewarding to see how the people respond to our call for Christmas giving among the poor. The church was piled high yesterday with groceries and toys of every description. There is so much that is good in human nature.

Of course the cynics will say that it is easier to be charitable than to be just, and the astute social observers will note that what we give for the needy is but a small fraction of what we spend on ourselves. After all, the spirit of love is still pretty well isolated in the family life. If I had a family maybe that thought would never occur to me. The old Methodist preacher who told me some time ago that I was so cantankerous in my spirit of criticism about modern society because I am not married may be right. If I had about four children to love I might not care so much about insisting that the spirit of love shall dominate all human affairs. And there might be more value in loving the four children than in paying lip service to the spirit of love as I do.

1924

A revival meeting seems never to get under my skin. Perhaps I am too fish-blooded to enjoy them. But I object not so much to the emotionalism as to the lack of intellectual honesty of the average revival preacher. I do not mean to imply that the evangelists are necessarily consciously dishonest. They just don't know enough about life and history to present the problem of the Christian life in its full meaning. They are always assuming that nothing but an emotional commitment to Christ is needed to save the soul from its sin and chaos. They seem never to realize how many of the miseries of mankind are due not to malice but to misdirected zeal and unbalanced virtue. They never help the people who corrupt family love by making the family a selfish unit in society or those who brutalize industry by excessive devotion to the prudential virtues.

Of course that is all inevitable enough. If you don't simplify issues you can't arouse emotional crises. It's the melodrama that captivates the crowd. Sober history is seldom melodramatic. God and the devil may be in conflict on the scene of life and history, but a victory follows every defeat and some kind of defeat every victory. The representatives of God are seldom divine and the minions of Satan are never quite diabolical.

I wonder whether there is any way of being potent oratorically without over-simplifying truth. Or must power always be bought at the expense of truth? Perhaps some simplification of life is justified. Every artist does, after all, obscure some details in order to present others in bolder relief. The religious rhetorician has a right to count himself among, and take his standards from, the artists rather than the scientists. The trouble is that he is usually no better than a cartoonist.

1924

After preaching tonight at a union service in —— the pastor loci took me about to show me his "plant" (industrialism has invaded even ecclesiastical terminology) and with obvious pride told me of all the progress that the church had made since his advent. One of the most disillusioning experiences which I have had with ministers is their invariable tendency to belittle or to be unappreciative of the work of their predecessors. If one were to take the implications of their remarks about their churches without a grain of salt one would imagine that every church was in an obvious state of spiritual and organic decay before the present generation of prophets took hold of the desperate situation. There are, of course, marked exceptions to this rule. But there is too much of this petty jealousy of former laborers in the vineyard of the Lord. Some of the men are probably victims of fawning parishioners and others are just naturally petty.

I am not surprised that most prophets are itinerants. Critics of the church think we preachers are afraid to tell the truth because we are economically dependent upon the people of our church. There is something in that, but it does not quite get to the root of the matter. I certainly could easily enough get more money than I am securing now, and yet I catch myself weighing my words and gauging their possible effect upon this and that person. I think the real clue to the tameness of a preacher is the difficulty one finds in telling unpleasant truths to people whom one has learned to love.

To speak the truth in love is a difficult, and sometimes an almost impossible, achievement. If you speak the truth unqualifiedly, that is usually because your ire has been aroused or because you have no personal attachment to the object of your strictures. Once personal contact is established you are very prone to temper your wind to the shorn sheep. It is certainly difficult to be human and honest at the same time. I'm not surprised that most budding prophets are tamed in time to become harmless parish priests.

At that, I do not know what business I have carping at the good people who are doing the world's work and who are inevitably enmeshed to a greater or less degree in the iniquities of society. Conscience, Goethe has observed, belongs to the observer rather than the doer, and it would be well for every preacher to realize that he is morally sensitive partly because he is observing and not acting. What is satisfying about the ministry is to note how far you can go in unfolding the full meaning of the Christian gospel provided you don't present it with the implication that you have attained and are now laying it as an obligation upon others.

If the Christian adventure is made a mutual search for

truth in which the preacher is merely a leader among many searchers and is conscious of the same difficulties in his own experience which he notes in others, I do not see why he cannot be a prophet without being forced into itinerancy.

1924

In Europe

We began the day with a visit to the York minister and ended it with a dinner at the Rountree cocoa works. Some of the men thought there was more spirituality in the discussion of the ethical problems of modern industry in which we engaged at Rountree's than in the communion service we heard so atrociously read in the minster. Of course the dinner discussion was richer in ethical content, but there are nevertheless religious values in the cathedral which one cannot find in a discussion of ethical problems however vital.

Religion is a reaction to life's mysteries and a reverence before the infinitudes of the universe. Without ethical experience the infinite is never defined in ethical terms, but the soul which is reverent and morally vital at the same time learns how to apprehend the infinite in terms of holiness and worships a God who transcends both our knowledge and our conscience. The cathedral with its dim religious light, its vaulted ceiling, its altar screen, and its hushed whispers is symbolic of the element of mystery in religion.

Without an adequate sermon no clue is given to the moral purpose at the heart of the mystery, and reverence remains without ethical content. But a religion which never goes beyond a sense of awe is no more complete (though perhaps less serviceable) than one which has reduced life's ultimate and ineffable truth to a pat little formula which a proud little man expounds before a comfortable and complacent congregation. I am sorry that there is no more ethically vital preaching in the cathedral, though that wretched communion service this morning, which could help no one if he did not believe in magic, is hardly typical of everything which happens in a cathedral. But I am equally sorry that the sense of awe and reverence has departed from so many of our churches.

The very appearance of many of our churches betrays the loss of one necessary element in religion. Everything suggests the secular rather than the religious, from the red hat of the rather too sensuously pretty soprano soloist and the frock coat of the rather too self-conscious parson to the comfortable pew cushions and the splendiferous pew holders. The morning sun shines brightly into the "auditorium" and the sun of worldly wisdom illumines the discourse of the preacher.

Of course I know that the devotional attitude frequently destroys clear thinking, and we need clear thinking for ethical living in a complex civilization. But it ought not be impossible to preserve the poetic with the scientific attitude, the mystical with the analytical, to have both worship and instruction. I think that is what Heywood Broun was driving at some time ago when he expressed a preference for an "Episcopal church with an heretical sermon." Unfortunately the heretical, i.e., the morally vital and contemporaneous religious instruction, does not seem to flourish in the liturgical church.

But there are men here in England who preach prophetic sermons in cathedrals. There might be more. In America they are certainly not numerous. But that is no reason why we should dismiss religious awe and reverence as morally dangerous. After all, the prophetic preaching which we hear in our "church auditoriums" is not so vigorous as to give us any certainty that a secularized church is superior in its moral potency.

1924

While visiting at the home of Mr. and Mrs. ——— today little Ralph felt it incumbent upon himself to entertain me by putting the family dog through his tricks. I have already forgotten the breed of the dog, but his shaggy locks covered his eyes so completely that he seemed to be without eyesight. Ralph told me with great eagerness that the dog would go blind if his locks were cut to improve his eyesight. Thus nature adjusts herself to her own inadequacies, and women of the future may run the peril of deafness if they uncover their ears.

Ralph's dog gave me the clue to much of our irreligion. The eyes of so many people have been covered by superstitions and illusions that they are not strong enough to preserve their sight in the daylight of knowledge. Freed from their superstitions, they are blinded in the very moment that they are given an unhindered view. They could see beauty while they lived in twilight, but a brilliant light obscures life's beauty and meaning.

Of course the eye may ultimately adjust itself to the brilliance of the light, and as men grow accustomed to the concrete and specific objects which distract them on first sight, they will learn again to view the whole scene and to regard all things in their relationships.

It is in relationships and in totalities that life's meaning is revealed.

1924

Since spending the summer in Europe I have been devoting the entire fall to a development of our worship service. The various types of ritualistic services in non-conformist churches I heard over there appealed to me so much that I decided to imitate them. Of course the Anglican services have their own appeal, but the technique which makes them possible is beyond us. For some years I have been having a few prayer responses, but now I am developing a program with litanies, confessions, acts of praise and every other bit of liturgical beauty and meaning by which the service can be enriched.

It's a shame we have permitted our services to become so barren. My only regret is that I did not wake up in time to build our church properly for liturgical purposes. There could be much pleasure in conducting a richly elaborated liturgical service without the restraint of the rubrics to which the Anglicans must submit. I do not know whether the people like the added beauty in the service as much as I do, but many have expressed appreciation. It seems to me to make a great deal of difference in the spiritual value of a service to have some unison prayer with an authentic religious emotion expressed in a well turned phrase, to have choir responses for the prayers and moments of silence for quiet prayer.

The idea that a formless service is more spontaneous and therefore more religious than a formal one is disproved in my own experience. Only a very few men have ever really put me in a mood of prayer by their "pastoral prayers." On the other hand, a really beautiful worship service actually gives me a mystic sense of the divine.

1924

Arrived in —— today and spoke this noon to a group of liberal people. The meeting was arranged by the secretary of the Y.W.C.A. I poked fun at them a little for enjoying their theological liberalism so much in this part of the country, while they were afraid of even the mildest economic and political heresy. Of course that didn't quite apply to the people at the table, but it does apply to this whole section. There is no one quite so ridiculous as a preacher who prides himself upon his theological radicalism in a city where the theological battle was won a generation ago, while he meanwhile speaks his convictions on matters of economics only in anxious whispers.

I was asked to visit —— (leading preacher) and see whether I could not interest him in our organization. He was an interesting study. He told me of his important connections in the city, of his tremendous church program, of the way he had increased the budget of his church, of his building plans, of the necessity "of fighting on one front at a time," of his theological battles; and he ended by declining to join the liberal group which sought his aid.

He thought it would not be advisable, considering his heavy responsibilities, to imperil the many great "causes" to which he was devoting his life by identifying himself with a radical movement. I didn't mind his cowardice so much, though he tried to hide it, as his vanity, which he took no pains to hide. I could just see him cavorting weekly before his crowd of doting admirers.

Obviously one of his chief difficulties is that he is good looking. A minister has enough temptations to vanity without bearing the moral hazard of a handsome face. If this young fellow had only been half as homely as old Dr. Gordon he might have a chance of acquiring a portion of his grace. But I don't want to drive that generalization too far. I know one or two saintly preachers who could pose for a collar ad.

1924

Had a letter today informing me that the First —— church in —— has called a new pastor. After trying futilely to find the right man, who was to have as much scholarship as his predecessor and more "punch," they decided to raise the salary to $15,000. I don't know whether that was the factor which finally solved their problem, but at any rate they have the man they want. I suppose it is not easy to get a combination of Aristotle and Demosthenes, and on the current market, that ought to be worth $15,000. Nevertheless there must be some limit to this matter of oversized salaries.

There ought to be some questioning, too, about the growing tendency of churches to build their congregations around pulpit eloquence. What kind of fundamental ethical question can a man be eloquent about when he draws that much cash, particularly since a Croesus or two usually has to supply an undue proportion of it? I don't know anything about the prophet of the Lord who accepted this call, but I venture to prophesy that no sinner in that pagan city will quake in his boots in anticipation of his coming.

The idea of a professional good man is difficult enough for all of us who are professionally engaged as teachers of the moral ideal. Of course, "a man must live," and it is promised that if we seek first the kingdom and its righteousness "all these things shall be added unto us." But I doubt whether Jesus had a $15,000 salary in mind. If the things that are added become too numerous they distract your attention terribly. To try to keep your eye on the main purpose may only result in making you squint-eyed. I hope the new prophet won't begin his pastorate with a sermon on the text, "I count all things but loss."

1924

I was a little ashamed of what I wrote recently about ministers' salaries, but today I was strangely justified in my criticism. Walking into a store to buy a hat I met an old friend who told me about his new preacher. His church had tried for a long while to secure the right man, and then by dint of a special campaign they raised the salary from $6,000 to $10,000. That is obviously more than most of the people in the congregation make. He said to me with considerable pride, "You ought to hear our new preacher. My, but he is a great talker!" Then he came close and whispered to me out of hearing of the other customers: "He ought to be. We are paying him ten thousand dollars." The cynicism was quite unconscious.

1924

I begin to realize how little religious faith depends upon dialectical support. When called upon to bury some one whose life revealed spiritual charm and moral force I can preach the hope of immortality with conviction and power. But funerals of religious and moral nondescripts leave me enervated. I think I could bury a brazen sinner with more satisfaction. There is always a note of real tragedy in the life of an obvious reprobate that gives point to a sermon. But these Tomlinsons are a trial.

Of course, there is a good deal of pride in such an attitude, and it is partly due to ignorance. As soon as I know the person whose death is mourned I can enter into the occasion sympathetically. There is hardly a soul so poor and flaccid but does not reveal some glimpse of the eternal in its life. If I happen to lack contact with the deceased I might well remind myself that his death is sincerely mourned by those who are near. It is after all a glorious tribute to the qualities of human nature that those who know us best love us most. Perhaps their love is occasionally no more than a natural attachment which men conceive for familiar objects.

Funerals are a terrible trial to me, but I must admit that the stolid courage and quiet grief of most mourners is a real source of inspiration. Only occasionally does one meet with hysterical grief and theatrical and insincere sorrow. How desperately people brush up their little faith in times of sorrow! It is quite easy to see that religious faith prospers because of, and not in spite of, the tribulations of this world. It is because this mortal life is felt as an irrelevancy to the main purpose in life that men achieve the courage to hope for immortality.

1924

We had a union Thanksgiving service today. It would have been a nice service but for the fact that the leader could not get over the fact that four denominations had been able to achieve unity to undertake such a service. This was supposed to be a great advance. As a matter of fact the people in the church were long since united in dozens of community enterprises. The men, whatever church they belonged to, attended the same Rotary and Kiwanis clubs and the women were members of the same literary and review clubs.

The church has lost the chance of becoming the unifying element in our American society. It is not anticipating any facts. It is merely catching up very slowly to the new social facts created by economic and other forces. The American melting pot is doing its work. The churches merely represent various European cultures, lost in the amalgam of American life and maintaining a separate existence only in religion.

What we accomplish in the way of church unity ought to be accepted with humility and not hailed with pride. We are not creating. We are merely catching up with creation.

1924

Going to St. Louis today a portly and garrulous gentleman sat back of me and became very much interested in two nuns who were reading their prayerbooks. The man, who seemed the perfect type of successful drummer, felt very superior to the nuns. How can anyone "fall for that stuff" in this day and age, he wanted to know in a loud whisper. "They remind me of ghosts," he said.

I had to admit that there was something almost unearthly about these black figures with their white-rimmed hoods. But their faces were kindly and human, and the face of the drummer was sensuous and florid. Perhaps the difference between him and the nuns illustrates the quality of our "modernity," though I don't want to maintain that he is the perfect type of a modern man. But we do have a great many moderns who are emancipated from every kind of religious discipline without achieving any new loyalty which might qualify the brutal factors in human life.

It is better that life incarnate some ideal value, even if mixed with illusion, (though anything which has the spirit of love in it is not wholly illusion) than that it should express nothing but the will to live. My drummer thinks of himself as a modern in comparison with those nuns. I looked at him squatting there and glanced again at the homely but beautiful faces of the nuns and said to myself: What is modern and what is ancient? Were there not toads before there were ghosts and fairies?

1924

Bishop Williams is dead. I sit and stare at the floor while I say that to myself and try to believe it. How strangely a vital personality defies the facts of death. Nowhere have I seen a personality more luminous with the Christ spirit than in this bishop who was also a prophet. Here was a man who knew how to interpret the Christian religion so that it meant something in terms of an industrial civilization. His fearless protagonism of the cause of democracy in industry won him the respect and love of the workers of the city as no other churchman possessed it.

Yet I am afraid that it must be admitted that he didn't change the prevailing attitude of Detroit industry by a hair's breadth. He even had to offer his resignation in the face of increasing hostility to his social views. That letter of resignation was incidentally a gem of humble self-analysis and courageous insistence on the truth of his doctrine.

He did not change Detroit industry but he left many of us holding our heads more upright because of his intelligent and courageous analysis of contemporary civilization from the perspective of a Christian conscience. If a bishop with all his prestige could make no bigger dent upon the prevailing mood of the city, what chance is there for the rest of us? Perhaps the best that any of us can do is to say:

> Charge once more then and be dumb,
> Let the victors when they come,
> When the forts of folly fall,
> Find thy body by the wall.

Rejoice, said Jesus, not that the devils are subject unto you but that your names are written in heaven. One ought to strive for the reformation of society rather than one's own perfection. But society resists every effort to bring its processes under ethical restraint so stubbornly that one must finally be satisfied with preserving one's moral integrity in a necessary and yet futile struggle. Of course the struggle is never as futile as it seems from an immediate perspective. The bishop did not change Detroit industry, but if the church ever becomes a real agency of the kingdom of God in an industrial civilization, his voice, though he is dead, will be in its counsels.

1925

When I sit through a church conference I begin to see a little more clearly why religion is on the whole so impotent ethically, why the achievements of the church are so meager compared to its moral pretensions. Sermon after sermon, speech after speech is based upon the assumption that the people of the church are committed to the ethical ideals of Jesus and that they are the sole or at least chief agents of redemptive energy in society.

It is very difficult to persuade people who are committed to a general ideal to consider the meaning of that ideal in specific situations. It is even more difficult to prompt them to consider specific ends of social and individual conduct and to evaluate them in the light of experience.

The church conference begins and ends by attempting to arouse an emotion of the ideal, usually in terms of personal loyalty to the person of Jesus, but very little is done to attach the emotion to specific tasks and projects. Is the industrial life of our day unethical? Are nations imperialistic? Is the family disintegrating? Are young people losing their sense of values? If so, we are told over and over again that nothing will help but "a new baptism of the spirit," a "new revival of religion," a "great awakening of the religious consciousness."

But why not be specific? Why doesn't the church offer specific suggestions for the application of a Christian ethic to the difficulties of our day? If that suggestion is made, the answer is that such a policy would breed contention. It certainly would. No moral project can be presented and no adventure made without resistance from the traditionalist and debate among experimentalists. But besides being more effective, such a course would be more interesting than this constant bathing in sentimentalities. If the church could only achieve schisms on ethical issues! They would represent life and reality. Its present schisms are not immoral as such. They are immoral only in the sense that they perpetuate issues which have no relevancy in our day.

1925

The reactions of a group of ministers to an address on the relation of religion to modern life are always interesting. Invariably there is one group of men who are pathetically eager to "do something about it," to save civilization from its perils. I think the church will compare favorably with the university in the number of men who are not blinded to the defects of modern life and who are not enervated by a sense of futility. The university has plenty of men whose eyes are open, but they despair much more easily of finding a way out than the preachers. The ministers have not lost some of that saving grace, "the foolishness of faith."

Of course there is always a group of those who sit sullenly while you harangue them. I had my eye fixed on one portly and prosperous priest today who was obviously out of accord with what I was saying. Of course I have no right to judge him because he did not agree with me. But he seemed to me to be one of those satisfied and complacent chaplains who has fed so long at the flesh-pots of Egypt that he resents anything which disturbs his ease. A man like that reminds me of the eunuchs of old who were robbed of their virility that they might adorn without endangering their masters' luxurious establishments.

The old gentleman was there too who wanted to know whether I believed in the deity of Jesus. He is in every town. He seemed to be a nice sort, but he wanted to know how I could speak for an hour on the Christian church without once mentioning the atonement. Nothing, said he, but the blood of Jesus would save America from its perils. He made quite an impassioned speech. At first I was going to answer him but it seemed too useless. I finally told him I believed in blood atonement too, but since I hadn't shed any of the blood of sacrifice which it demanded I felt unworthy to enlarge upon the idea.

1925

We went through one of the big automobile factories today. So artificial is life that these factories are like a strange world to me though I have lived close to them for many years. The foundry interested me particularly. The heat was terrific. The men seemed weary. Here manual labor is a drudgery and toil is slavery. The men cannot possibly find any satisfaction in their work. They simply work to make a living. Their sweat and their dull pain are part of the price paid for the fine cars we all run. And most of us run the cars without knowing what price is being paid for them.

Looking at these men the words of Markham's "The Man with the Hoe" came to me. A man with a hoe is a happy creature beside these suffering souls.

"The emptiness of ages in his face"

. . . .

"Who made him dead to rapture and despair,
A thing that grieves not and that never hopes,
Stolid and stunned, a brother to the ox?"

We are all responsible. We all want the things which the factory produces and none of us is sensitive enough to care how much in human values the efficiency of the modern factory costs. Beside the brutal facts of modern industrial life, how futile are all our homiletical spoutings! The church is undoubtedly cultivating graces and preserving spiritual amenities in the more protected areas of society. But it isn't changing the essential facts of modern industrial civilization by a hair's breadth. It isn't even thinking about them.

The morality of the church is anachronistic. Will it ever develop a moral insight and courage sufficient to cope with the real problems of modern society? If it does it will require generations of effort and not a few martyrdoms. We ministers maintain our pride and self-respect and our sense of importance only through a vast and inclusive ignorance. If we knew the world in which we live a little better we would perish in shame or be overcome by a sense of futility.

1925

The new parish organization seems to be working splendidly. The congregation is divided into nine sections, each with a man and woman as parish leaders. Each section meets twice a year in cottage meetings, and meanwhile the leaders and their assistants visit the various families, particularly the new members and those who are sick. Some splendid new leaders have already been developed by this plan. Since I must be absent from the city so much, the plan is all the more valuable.

Last Sunday we discussed in the class whether a church ought to develop fellowship for its own sake or whether fellowship ought to be the inevitable by-product of unifying convictions. I suppose a small church in a hostile environment would not have to worry about fellowship. If people fight shoulder to shoulder they will be brothers. But even the most heroic church is not so definitely in conflict with the society in which it lives that you can really count on that kind of fellowship. A local congregation is, after all, a social organism in which heroic idealism is expressed in an occasional adventure, if at all, rather than in a constant tension between its principles and the moral mediocrities of the world.

Meanwhile, it seems to me to be worth while to cultivate the graces of neighborliness merely for their own sake. This is particularly true in the large city where life is so impersonal and where the church has a fine opportunity to personalize it a little. What surprises me is the readiness with which people give themselves to various forms of mutual aid once they are prompted to engage in them.

Most people lack imagination much more than they lack good will. If someone points out what can be done and what ought to be done there is usually someone to do it.

1925
On a Western Trip

Out here on the Pacific coast, particularly in Los Angeles, one is forcibly impressed with the influence of environment upon religion. Every kind of cult seems to flourish in Los Angeles, and most of them are pantheistic. Every sorry oriental religious nostrum is borrowed in the vain effort to give meaning to pointless lives and to impart a thrill to vacuous existences. The pantheism is partly due, no doubt, to the salubrious nature of the southern California climate. Wherever nature is unusually benignant, men tend to identify God and the natural world and to lose all moral vigor in the process.

But that is hardly the whole explanation. There are too many retired people in Los Angeles. They left the communities where their personalities had some social significance in order to vegetate on these pleasant shores. In this sorry and monotonous existence they try to save their self-respect by grasping for some religious faith which will not disturb their ease by any too rigorous ethical demands. Of course Aimee Semple McPherson is more successful than the pantheistic cults. She fights the devil and gives the people a good show. She storms against the vices which flourish in this paradise without touching their roots. Furthermore she has the art of casting the glow of religious imagination over sensuality without changing its essential nature. In that art she seems to be typical rather than unique for this whole civilization. If she is unique it is only in her success.

They are always telling me that Detroit is the most typically American of our cities. Perhaps Detroit is typical of the America which works feverishly to get what it wants, while Los Angeles is typical of the America which has secured what it wants. On the whole I prefer the former to the latter. An honest enthusiasm even for inadequate ends is better than a vacuous existence from which even the charm of an imperfect ambition has departed. Of course the paganism of power is more dangerous than the paganism of pleasure, but from the perspective of a mere observer it is more interesting. Who would not prefer Napoleon to his imbecile brothers who merely luxuriated in the prosperity created by his ambition?

Only in the case of complete innocency, as that of a child's, is life more beautiful in repose than in activity. Character is created by a balance of tensions, and is more lovely even when the balance is imperfect than in a state of complete relaxation.

Of course Los Angeles has more culture than our midwestern cities. Culture flourishes in leisure and sometimes redeems it. But it will be a long time before this kind of leisure will produce more than dilettantism.

1925

We had a communion service tonight (Good Friday) and I preached on the text "We preach Christ crucified, to the Jews a stumbling block and to the Gentiles foolishness, but to them that are called the power of God and the wisdom of God." I don't think I ever felt greater joy in preaching a sermon. How experience and life change our perspectives! It was only a few years ago that I did not know what to make of the cross; at least I made no more of it than to recognize it as a historic fact which proved the necessity of paying a high price for our ideals. Now I see it as a symbol of ultimate reality.

It seems pathetic to me that liberalism has too little appreciation of the tragedy of life to understand the cross and orthodoxy insists too much upon the absolute uniqueness of the sacrifice of Christ to make the preaching of the cross effective. How can anything be uniquely potent if it is absolutely unique? It is because the cross of Christ symbolizes something in the very heart of reality, something in universal experience that it has its central place in history. Life is tragic and the most perfect type of moral beauty inevitably has at least a touch of the tragic in it. Why? That is not so easy to explain. But love pays such a high price for its objectives and sets its objectives so high that they can never be attained. There is therefore always a foolish and a futile aspect to love's quest which give it the note of tragedy.

What makes this tragedy redemptive is that the foolishness of love is revealed as wisdom in the end and its futility becomes the occasion for new moral striving. About heroes, saints, and saviors it must always remain true "that they, without us should not be made perfect."

1925

I wonder if the strong sense of frustration which comes over me so frequently on Sunday evening and to which many other parsons have confessed, is merely due to physical lassitude or whether it arises from the fact that every preacher is trying to do a bigger thing than he is equal to—and fails. I have an uneasy feeling that it may be native honesty of the soul asserting itself. Aren't we preachers talking altogether too much about what can be proved and justified only in experience?

1925

Mr. —— spoke at a luncheon meeting today. He made everyone writhe as he pictured the injustices and immoralities of our present industrial system. The tremendous effect of his powerful address was partially offset by the bitterness with which he spoke and by the ill-concealed assumption that his hearers would not care enough about what he said to change their attitudes. I suppose it is difficult to escape bitterness when you have the eyes to see and the heart to feel what others are too blind and too callous to notice. The mordant note in the discourse of the prophet may not only be inevitable but pedagogically effective.

Perhaps there is no other way to arouse a people who are so oblivious to the real issues of modern civilization. Yet I am compelled to doubt the pedagogical benefits of this approach. While I use it myself, sometimes I don't like to have it used on me. It freezes my soul. And there is usually some injustice, some insupportable generalization, involved in this method which obsesses my mind and makes it difficult for me to see the general truth with which the speaker wants to impress me.

If I had to choose between this bitterness and the blandness of many pulpiteers I would, of course, choose the former. Better a warrior's grimness than the childish sentimentalities of people who are too ignorant or too selfish to bear the burdens of the world. There are too many men in the pulpit who look and act for all the world like cute little altar boys who have no idea that the mass in which they are participating is a dramatization of tragedy.

Yet there seems to be no reason why a warrior ought not maintain his effectiveness and yet overcome his bitterness, particularly if he is a warrior who is fighting "not against flesh and blood but against spiritual wickedness in high places." The one certain cure for a bitter spirit seems to me

72

a realization that the critic is himself involved in the sins which he castigates. Man is imperialistic and even parasitic in his nature. He lives his life at the expense of other lives. By both outer compulsion and inner restraint, his expansive desires are brought under sufficient discipline to make social life possible.

But there is no social life, not even in the family, which does not illustrate this native imperialism in life. Look at all these professional people, preachers, professors and doctors! Even in the moment in which they declare their superiority over the commercial world, where life is more frankly selfish and more obviously brutal, they illustrate the common human frailty by some petty jockeying for position, or some jealous depreciation of the success of others, or some childish ego-assertion.

The pessimist might draw the conclusion from this fact that we can make progress only by a reorganization of society and never by a reformation of human nature. But that conclusion does not seem to me to follow from the facts. We do need a constant reorganization of social processes and systems, so that society will not aggravate but mitigate the native imperialistic impulses of man. The greed of modern civilization is partly an expression of a universal human tendency and partly a vice peculiar to a civilization with our kind of productive process.

But meanwhile we can not afford to leave the capacities of man out of the picture. There seems to me no reason why we can not cure people of greed by making them conscious of both the nature and the consequences of their expansive tendencies. Only we ought to realize, while we are doing it, that our own life reveals some refined form of the sin which we abhor. That will make it possible to undertake the task of world regeneration with a spirit of patience and humility.

The modern pulpit does not face this problem because it is not really preaching repentance. Its estimate of human nature is too romantic to give people any appreciation of the brutalities of life which are frequently most real where they are most covert—in the lives of the respectable classes. But whenever a prophet is born, either inside or outside of the church, he does face the problem of preaching repentance without bitterness and of criticising without spiritual pride.

It is a real problem. Mr. —— is effective, after a fashion, because he is an itinerant. We only have to hear him once in so many years. But think of sitting Sunday after Sunday under some professional holy man who is constantly asserting his egotism by criticising yours. I would rebel if I were a layman. A spiritual leader who has too many illusions is useless. One who has lost his illusions about mankind and retains his illusions about himself is insufferable. Let the process of disillusionment continue until the self is included. At that point, of course, only religion can save from the enervation of despair. But it is at that point that true religion is born.

1926

Preachers who are in danger of degenerating into common scolds might learn a great deal from H——'s preaching style. I am not thinking now of the wealth of scholarship which enriches his utterances but of his technique in uniting religious emotion with aspiration rather than with duty. If he wants to convict Detroit of her sins he preaches a sermon on "the City of God," and lets all the limitations of this get-rich-quick metropolis emerge by implication. If he wants to flay the denominationalism of the churches he speaks on some topic which gives him the chance to delineate the ideal and inclusive church.

On the whole, people do not achieve great moral heights out of a sense of duty. You may be able to compel them to maintain certain minimum standards by stressing duty, but the highest moral and spiritual achievements depend not upon a push but upon a pull. People must be charmed into righteousness. The language of aspiration rather than that of criticism and command is the proper pulpit language. Of course it has its limitations. In every congregation there are a few perverse sinners who can go into emotional ecstasies about the "City of God" and yet not see how they are helping to make their city a hell-hole.

It is not a good thing to convict sin only by implication. Sometimes the cruel word of censure must be uttered. "Woe unto you Scribes and Pharisees, hypocrites" was spoken by one who incarnated tenderness. The language of aspiration is always in danger of becoming soft; but it is possible to avoid that pitfall and yet not sink into a habit of cheap scolding. I like the way H—— does it.

1926

Cynics sometimes insinuate that you can love people only if you don't know them too well; that a too intimate contact with the foibles and idiosyncrasies of men will tempt one to be a misanthrope. I have not found it so. I save myself from cynicism by knowing individuals, and knowing them intimately. If I viewed humanity only from some distant and high perspective I could not save myself from misanthropy. I think the reason is simply that people are not as decent in their larger relationship as in their more intimate contacts.

Look at the industrial enterprise anywhere and you find criminal indifference on the part of the strong to the fate of the weak. The lust for power and the greed for gain are the dominant note in business. An industrial overlord will not share his power with his workers until he is forced to do so by tremendous pressure. The middle classes, with the exception of a small minority of intelligentsia, do not aid the worker in exerting this pressure. He must fight alone.

The middle classes are in fact quite incapable of any high degree of social imagination. Their experience is too limited to give them a clear picture of the real issues in modern industrial life. Nonunion mines may organize in West Virginia and reduce miners to a starvation wage without challenging the conscience of a great middle class nation. If the children of strikers are starving it is more difficult to find support for them than to win contributors for the missions of the church. America may arouse the resentment of the world by its greed and all the good people of the American prairie will feel nothing but injured innocence from these European and Asiatic reactions to our greed.

Men are clearly not very lovely in the mass. One can maintain confidence in them only by viewing them at close range. Then one may see the moral nobility of unselfish parenthood, the pathetic eagerness of father and mother to give their children more of life than they enjoyed; the faithfulness of wives to their erring husbands; the grateful respect of mature children for their old parents; the effort of this and that courageous soul to maintain personal integrity in a world which continually tempts to dishonesty, and the noble aspirations of hearts that must seem quite unheroic to the unheeding world.

The same middle classes which seem so blind to the larger moral problems of society have, after all, the most wholesome family life of any group in society.

1926

Here is a preacher whom I have suspected of cowardice for years because he never deviated by a hair's breadth from the economic prejudices of his wealthy congregation. I thought he knew better but was simply afraid to speak out and seek to qualify the arch-conservatism of his complacent crowd with a little Christian idealism. But I was mistaken. I have just heard that he recently included in his sermon a tirade against women who smoke cigarettes and lost almost a hundred of his fashionable parishioners. He is evidently not lacking courage in matters upon which he has deep convictions. Nobody, for that matter, lacks courage when convictions are strong. Courage is simply the rigorous devotion to one set of values against other values and interests.

Protestantism's present impotence in qualifying the economic and social life of the nation is due not so much to the pusillanimity of the clerical leaders as to its individualistic traditions. The church honestly regards it of greater moment to prevent women from smoking cigarettes than to establish more Christian standards in industrial enterprise. A minister who tries to prevent fashionable women from smoking cigarettes is simply trying to enforce a code of personal habit established in the middle classes of the nineteenth century upon the plutocratic classes of the twentieth century. The effort is not only vain but has little to do with essential Christianity.

I would not deny that some real values may be at stake in such questions of personal habits. But they affect the dominant motives which determine the spirituality or sensuality of character but slightly. The church does not seem to realize how unethical a conventionally respectable life may be.

1926

Some of these young business men in the congregation would compare favorably with any leaders who grace the pulpits of our churches. Their family relations seem to be almost ideal. They are trying honestly to live a Christian life in their business relations. Lack of power sometimes means that they cannot go as far in experimenting with Christian values as they would like. But they are not complacent. They are eager to learn, and are fair and careful in their judgments. Their virtues are acquired with less self-conscious effort than those of more studious people. They think and plan, but they do not stop the adventure of life to meditate upon its difficulties and inadequacies.

Extravert people are on the whole happier and more wholesome than the introverts. If they do not act too unreflectively, they are able to define their goals fairly accurately and they certainly pursue them with more robust energy than do the moody intellectuals.

It is surprising, too, how considerate and generous they are in their relations with one another and with me. They take my impetuosities for granted and exhibit little pettiness in their dealings with one another. The women do not get along quite so well together. They are too new at playing the game of life with others. But I will not belabor that point. I may be exhibiting bachelor prejudices in making it. At any rate I am willing to compare this group of young men who bear the burdens of our church with any faculty group in the country. They can teach you nothing about philosophy, but they do teach you much about life and they reënforce your confidence in human nature.

1926

After Attending a Jewish-Christian Conference

Fellowship with peoples of other religious groups always results in the grateful experience of discovering unsuspected treasuries of common sentiment and conviction. More contact between enlightened Jews and Christians would change the emphasis in many a Christian homily. This conference was rewarding in many ways. But at one point I fail absolutely to understand my Jewish friends. All of them, high and low, intelligent and those who are less so, insist that the story of the crucifixion is the real root of all or of most antisemitism, and they seem to have some vain hope that broadminded Christians will be able and willing to erase the story of the cross from the gospel record. The least they expect is that the odium of the cross be placed upon the Romans rather than the Jews.

I can see that there would be some advantage in ascribing a historic sin to a people who live only in history and who can therefore not be victimized by belated vindictive prejudices. But would that be history? The record is pretty plain and the fact that the Jewish elders rather than Roman soldiers were the real crucifiers is supported not only by evidence but by logic. The prophets of religion are always martyred by the religious rather than by the irreligious. The Romans, being irreligious, were not sufficiently fanatical to initiate the crucifixion.

It must be admitted that the phraseology of the Fourth Gospel may easily incite the prejudices of the ignorant. But the enlightened will find a better method to allay any antisemitic feeling which may result from the record than to ascribe the crucifixion to the Romans. They need only ascribe it to the general limitations of human nature and society. Jews are not the only people who martyr and who have martyred their prophets. The history of every nation and every people makes the crucifixion a perennial and a universal historical fact.

That is the very reason why Christians can no more afford to eliminate the cross than they can ascribe it to the fortunately extinct Romans. Anyone who incarnates the strategy of love as Jesus did meets the resistance and incites the passions of human society. The respectabilities of any human society are based upon moral compromises and every community is as anxious to defend these compromises against the prophet who presents some higher moral logic as against the criminal who imperils the structure from below.

The cross is central in the Christian religion, moreover, because it symbolizes a cosmic as well as an historic truth. Love conquers the world, but its victory is not an easy one. The price of all creativity and redemption is pain. Most modern religionists who understand the God of creation and not the God of redemption fail in understanding the latter precisely because they do not see how closely related creation and redemption are. Which simply means that they don't understand that creation is a painful process in which the old does not give way to the new without trying to overcome it.

The cross of Jesus is truly the most adequate symbol of both the strategy and the destiny of love not only in history but in the universe. We may grant our Jewish brethren that it is not the only possible symbol of eternal verities, but it is a true one, and it cannot therefore be sacrificed.

Incidentally, I believe that Jewish people have a tendency to overestimate the religious bases of antisemitism. Racial rather than religious prejudice is the dominant factor in this social disease. All ignorant people hate or fear those who deviate from their type. Religious divergences may be as important as cultural and physical differences, but they are not dominant. The Jews could accept our religion and if they maintained their racial integrity they would still suffer from various types of social ostracism. After all the Negroes are Christian, but that hasn't helped them much. Some Jews dislike this comparison very much. They do not like to be put upon the same basis with the Negroes. But that reveals unrealistic social analysis. The majority group is intolerant of minorities whether their culture is inferior, superior or equal.

1926

One is hardly tempted to lose confidence in the future after listening to a group of young people discussing the important problems of life. Of course the number who approach the future reflectively and with real appreciation for the issues involved in the readjustment of traditions to new situations is not large. There are not many such groups and even in these the number who really take part in the discussion is small.

Nevertheless their wholesomeness is impressive. I can't always withhold a sense of pity for them. With traditions crumbling and accepted standards inundated by a sea of moral relativity, they have a desperate task on their hands to construct new standards adequate for their happiness. There is always the temptation to be too rebellious or too traditional, to be scornful of the old standard even when it preserves obvious virtues, or to flee to it for fear of being lost in the confusion of new standards. Yet the best way of avoiding these dangers is to subject them to the scrutiny of a thoughtful group which knows how to discern the limitations of any position, old or new.

On the whole the discussions of our young people at the church seem to be more wholesome than those in which I participate in the colleges. Most of these young folks have assumed responsibilities and are therefore not as inclined to be morbidly critical and sceptical as the college group. The cases cited from their own experience help to give vitality to their discussion, and they are not enervated by that extreme sophistication which imperils the college youth and tempts him to end every discussion and discount every discovery with the reflection, "This also is vanity."

I really wonder how we are going to build a civilization sufficiently intelligent to overcome dangerous prejudices and to emancipate itself from the inadequacies of conventional morality without creating the kind of sophistication which destroys all values by its scepticism and dampens every enthusiasm by its cynicism. In America that possibility is particularly dangerous because our intellectualism is of the sophomoric type. There is no generation, or only one generation, between the pioneers who conquered the prairies and these youngsters who are trying to absorb the whole of modern culture in four years. The traditions against which they react are less adequate, less modified by experience and culture, than those which inform the peoples of Europe.

And the teachers who guide them into the world of new knowledge are frequently themselves so recently emancipated that they try to obscure their cultural, religious and moral heritages by extreme iconoclasm. It is difficult to be patient with one of these smart-aleck Ph.D.s on a western campus who imagines that he can impress the world with his learning by being scornful of everything that was thought or done before this century.

1926

A letter from Hyde brings the sad news that C——
has lost his pastorate. I am not surprised. He is courageous
but tactless. Undoubtedly he will regard himself as one of
the Lord's martyrs. Perhaps he is. Perhaps loyalty to principle will always appear as tactlessness from the perspective
of those who don't agree with you. But I agree with C——
and still think him wanting in common sense. At least he is
pedagogically very awkward.

You can't rush into a congregation which has been fed
from its very infancy on the individualistic ethic of Protestantism and which is immersed in a civilization where ethical individualism runs riot, and expect to develop a social
conscience among the people in two weeks. Nor have you a
right to insinuate that they are all hypocrites just because
they don't see what you see.

Of course it is not easy to speak the truth in love without
losing a part of the truth, and therefore one ought not be
too critical of those who put their emphasis on the truth
rather than on love. But if a man is not willing to try, at
least, to be pedagogical, and if in addition he suffers from a
martyr complex, he has no place in the ministry. Undoubtedly there are more ministers who violate their conscience
than such as suffer for conscience sake. But that is no reason why those who have a robust conscience should not try
to master the pedagogical art. Perhaps if they would learn
nothing else but to be less emotional and challenging in the
pulpit and more informative and educational not only in
the pulpit but in their work with smaller groups, they could
really begin to change the viewpoints and perspectives of
their people.

1926

Spoke tonight to the Churchmen's Club of ——. The good Bishop who introduced me was careful to disavow all my opinions before I uttered them. He assured the brethren, however, that I would make them think. I am getting tired of these introductions which are intended to impress the speaker with the Christian virtue of the audience and its willingness to listen to other than conventional opinions. The chairman declares in effect, "Here is a harebrained fellow who talks nonsense. But we are Christian gentlemen who can listen with patience and sympathy to even the most impossible opinions." It is just a device to destroy the force of a message and to protect the sensitive souls who might be rudely shocked by a religious message which came in conflict with their interests and prejudices.

There is something pathetic about the timidity of the religious leader who is always afraid of what an honest message on controversial issues might do to his organization. I often wonder when I read the eleventh chapter of Hebrews in which faith and courage are practically identified whether it is psychologically correct to assume that the one flows from the other. Courage is a rare human achievement. If it seems to me that preachers are more cowardly than other groups; that may be because I know myself. But I must confess that I haven't discovered much courage in the ministry. The average parson is characterized by suavity and circumspection rather than by any robust fortitude. I do not intend to be mean in my criticism because I am a coward myself and find it tremendously difficult to run counter to general opinion. Yet religion has always produced some martyrs and heroes.

I suppose religion in its most vital form does make men indifferent to popular approval. The apostle Paul averred that it was a small thing to be judged of men because he was seeking the approval of God. In a genuinely religious soul faith does seem to operate in that way. Issues are regarded *sub specie aeternitatis* and the judgment of contemporaries becomes insignificant. But the average man fashions his standards in the light of prevailing customs and opinions. It could hardly be expected that every religious leader would be filled with prophetic ardor and heedless courage. Many good men are naturally cautious. But it does seem that the unique resource of religion ought to give at least a touch of daring to the religious community and the religious leader.

1926

The excitement about the Federation of Labor convention in Detroit has subsided, but there are echoes of the event in various magazines. Several ministers have been commended for "courage" because they permitted labor leaders to speak in their churches who represented pretty much their own convictions and said pretty much what they had been saying for years.

It does seem pretty bad to have the churches lined up so solidly against labor and for the open shop policy of the town. The ministers are hardly to blame, except if they are to be condemned for not bringing out the meaning of Christianity for industrial relations more clearly in their ministry previous to the moment of crisis. As it was, few of the churches were sufficiently liberal to be able to risk an heretical voice in their pulpits. The idea that these A. F. of L. leaders are dangerous heretics is itself a rather illuminating clue to the mind of Detroit. I attended several sessions of the convention and the men impressed me as having about the same amount of daring and imagination as a group of village bankers.

The ministers of the country are by various methods dissociating themselves from the Detroit churches and are implying that they would have acted more generously in a like situation. Perhaps so. There are few cities in which wealth, suddenly acquired and proud of the mechanical efficiency which produced it, is so little mellowed by social intelligence. Detroit produces automobiles and is not yet willing to admit that the poor automata who are geared in on the production lines have any human problems.

Yet we differ only in degree from the rest of the country. The churches of America are on the whole thoroughly committed to the interests and prejudices of the middle classes. I think it is a bit of unwarranted optimism to expect them to make any serious contribution to the reorganization of society. I still have hopes that they will become sufficiently intelligent and heroic to develop some qualifying considerations in the great industrial struggle, but I can no longer envisage them as really determining factors in the struggle. Neither am I able for this reason to regard them as totally useless, as some of the critics do.

The ethical reconstruction of modern industrial society is, to be sure, a very important problem, but it is not the only concern of mankind. The spiritual amenities and moral decencies which the churches help to develop and preserve in the private lives of individuals are worth something for their own sake. Yet it must be obvious that if anyone is chosen by talent and destiny to put his life into the industrial struggle, the church is hardly his best vehicle.

The church is like the Red Cross service in war time. It keeps life from degenerating into a consistent inhumanity, but it does not materially alter the fact of the struggle itself. The Red Cross neither wins the war nor abolishes it. Since the struggle between those who have and those who have not is a never-ending one, society will always be, in a sense, a battleground. It is therefore of some importance that human loveliness be preserved outside of the battle lines. But those who are engaged in this task ought to realize that the brutalities of the conflict may easily negate the most painstaking humanizing efforts behind the lines, and that these efforts may become a method for evading the dangers and risks of the battlefield.

If religion is to contribute anything to the solution of the industrial problem, a more heroic type of religion than flourishes in the average church must be set to the task. I don't believe that the men who are driven by that kind of religion need to dissociate themselves from the churches, but they must bind themselves together in more effective association than they now possess.

1926

After preaching at —— University this morning I stopped off at —— and dropped in at the Presbyterian church for the evening service. The service was well attended and the music was very good. The minister had a sermon which might best be described as a fulsome eulogy of Jesus Christ. I wonder whether sermons like that mean anything. He just piled up adjectives. Every hero of ancient and modern times was briefly described in order that he might be made to bow before the superior virtue of the Lord. But the whole thing left me completely cold. The superiority of Jesus was simply dogmatically asserted and never adequately analyzed. There was not a thing in the sermon that would give the people a clue to the distinctive genius of Jesus or that would help them to use the resources of his life for the solution of their own problems.

Through the whole discourse there ran the erroneous assumption that Christians are real followers of Jesus and no effort was made to describe the wide chasm which yawns between the uncompromising idealism of the Galilean and the current morality. I wonder how many sermons of that type are still being preached. If that sermon is typical it would explain much of the conventional tameness of the church.

How much easier it is to adore an ideal character than to emulate it.

1926

That resolution we passed in our pastors' meeting, calling upon the police to be more rigorous in the enforcement of law, is a nice admission of defeat upon the part of the church. Every one of our cities has a crime problem, not so much because the police are not vigilant as because great masses of men in an urban community are undisciplined and chaotic souls, emancipated from the traditions which guided their fathers and incapable of forming new and equally potent cultural and moral restraints. The children of the puritans are in this respect no better than the children of the immigrants. Both have reacted against traditions which do not fit their new circumstances and both are unable to escape license by new and better standards.

Perhaps the real reason that we live such chaotic lives in urban communities is because a city is not a society at all, and moral standards are formed only in societies and through the sense of mutual obligation which neighbors feel for one another. A big city is not a society held together by human bonds. It is a mass of individuals, held together by a productive process. Its people are spiritually isolated even though they are mechanically dependent upon one another. In such a situation it is difficult to create and preserve the moral and cultural traditions which each individual needs to save his life from anarchy.

All of us do not live in moral chaos. But in so far as we escape it, it is due to our loyalty to religious, moral and cultural traditions which have come out of other ages and other circumstances. That is why churches, Protestant, Catholic and Jewish, however irrelevant their ethical idealism may be to the main facts of an industrial civilization, are nevertheless indispensable. It is enough that our society should be morally chaotic without also losing the kind of moral restraint which still determines the life of many individuals.

There is something very pathetic about the efforts of almost every one of our large cities to restore by police coercion what has been lost by the decay of moral and cultural traditions. But of course we do have to save ourselves from anarchy, even if it must be done by force. Only I think the church would do well to leave the police problem alone. If violence must be used temporarily, let the state do so without undue encouragement from the church. The church must work in another field and if it has failed in that field, it cannot recoup its failures by giving advice to the police department. The priest as a sublimated policeman is a sorry spectacle.

1926

We were discussing the first commandment in the preparatory class today. The boys were trying to see whether "Thou shalt have no other Gods before me" meant anything in modern life. It is a constant source of surprise and delight to see with what profundity these boys and girls deal with the problems of life. They decided that anything that we loved more than God was in effect another god. But how do we love God, I asked. There were the usual answers which show how some children still identify religion with religious practices and customs, particularly Sunday observance. But one of the boys came through with this answer, "We love God by loving the best we know." That seemed to me not bad at all.

Now we put on the blackboard all those interests which threatened to become gods to us: money, clothes (volunteered by a girl, of course), automobiles, eating, playing. We took up each one of these interests and tried to determine when they were in danger of becoming too central in life. On automobiles the boys didn't have much conscience except that they thought one ought not to clean them on Sunday. They take the cult of the automobile for granted as everyone else. The girls had quite a time defining the place where clothes cease to be a legitimate interest and become an obsession. I was probably a poor one to lead them in that discussion.

On the matter of eating there was considerable difficulty. "We have to eat to grow," said one of the boys. Correct answer. When then, is eating a form of idolatry? "When we eat all the time," suggested another boy. That left Junior in a corner. "I like to eat most all the time," he confessed ruefully. How can a hungry boy be anything but a sceptic about a philosophy of values which does not have eating at the center of it? Thus do the necessities of a robust organism defy the value schemes prompted by tradition or arrived at by reflection.

Junior just about stopped our discussion of comparative values by that confession, "I like to eat most all the time," and I couldn't help but think that my pedagogical impotence before this demand of natural life was closely akin to the impotence of the church before a youthful and vigorous national life, immersed in physical values and intent upon physical satisfactions. Our youthful nation is also declaring, "I love to eat most all the time"; and the error in its judgment is not easily overcome by preachment and precept until time and experience will show it the limits of animal satisfactions and teach it that man does not live by bread alone.

1926

I had a letter from a young preacher today who told me how he was suffering for truth's sake. He had merely been telling his congregation that Jesus was a great spiritual teacher, as was Confucius and Laotsze, and that the Christ idea was the product of Greek legend and ancient mythology. His good people were so ignorant, he thought, that they failed to show proper appreciation of his learning and resented his iconoclasm.

I find myself reacting violently to the sophomoric cocksureness of this young fellow. I suppose I am getting old and have made those compromises with the devil of superstition against which the editor of the Christian Register warns so hysterically. But for the life of me I can no more reduce Jesus to the status of a mere Galilean dreamer and teacher than I can accept the orthodox Christologies. The person who can make no distinction between a necessary symbolism and mythology seems to me no better than the wooden-headed conservative who insists that every bit of religious symbolism and poetry must be accepted literally and metaphysically.

It is not easy to define the God idea. Scientifically I suppose God is "the element of spirituality which is integral to reality," but for all practical and religious purposes I find it both helpful and justified to define him by saying that "God is like Jesus." The ultimate nature of reality cannot be grasped by science alone; poetic imagination is as necessary as scientific precision. Some of the supposedly ignorant peasants against whom my youthful friend is drawing his heroic sword may have more truth on their side than any fresh young theologue could possibly realize.

1926

In the young men's class this morning we continued our discussion of the Sermon on the Mount. The boys have been making some interesting contributions. On the whole they are sceptical of the practicability of the demands which Jesus makes in the matter of trust and love and forgiveness. It is rather interesting to have this revelation of the basic cynicism of even the adolescent mind. They think that to follow Jesus "would put a business man out of business in no time," as one expressed it today. Of course, it is better to see the difficulties than to engage in some kind of sentimental avowal of Christian faith without realizing how stubbornly life resists the ideal.

After all, those boys are up against what St. Anthony saw when he was tempted by the vision of the young woman and the old woman. The one meant life but also lust, and the other meant faith but also death. At least that is the way Flaubert has it. It is certainly not easy to separate life from lust without destroying life. Yet Jesus came to give us a more abundant life.

"Maybe it would work if we tried it hard enough," thought one of the boys today when we discussed the practicability of trusting people. That may be the answer to the whole question.

1926

Bishop —— and I shared the platform tonight. Fortunately, I spoke first so that I did not have to compete with his powerful eloquence. His sermon warmed the heart, but it was based upon the uncritical assumption that modern Christianity is an exact replica of primitive Christianity and is characterized by the same qualities of heroism and faith. There was a disquieting tendency to patronize in the good man's demeanor. I should think it would be a very difficult achievement for a bishop to be a real Christian. The position is bound to aggravate the inclination to pride which all of us possess. I do not know many bishops intimately. The few that I have known well have been singularly free of arrogance; but they were unusual, for they were saved by a sense of humor which is not frequently found in the pulpit and certainly hardly ever in the episcopacy.

"Be not ye called rabbi," said Jesus, "and call no man father upon earth, for one is your father which is in heaven." I am not interested in applying the words of Jesus literally, but it seems to me that the principle involved in these words would wipe out the episcopacy. It wouldn't leave much justification either for "The Reverend Doctor." Of course the Christian community cannot do without leaders. But it might learn to save them from pride and arrogance.

The highest type of leadership maintains itself by its intrinsic worth, sans panoply, pomp and power. Of course, there are never enough real leaders to go around. Wherefore it becomes necessary to dress some men up and by other artificial means to give them a prestige and a power which they could not win by their own resources. But it would be well if the church realized how dangerous power and prestige are, and how easily they corrupt a man's spiritual integrity.

It is certainly not to the credit of the church that it is less eager than the democratic state to circumscribe the authority and socialize the power of the leader. The Methodists try to preserve the proper spirit of humility among the bishops by relegating them to parliamentary impotence once every four years. But who wouldn't be willing to suffer for that brief period for the sake of the power and authority which the bishop exercises for the rest of the quadrennium?

Somewhere I read the observation of an anthropologist that naked savages could never have evolved a priesthood or an hereditary monarchy. No one is so much superior to his fellows that he deserves the positions of authority which a complex society finally evolves. That is why the leader must be put over with the proper clothes and paraphernalia. The throne and the crown make the king. Even the President of the United States has impressive naval and military aids to offset the unimposing frock which the democratic tradition prescribes. As for the bishop, who could be more awe-inspiring than a hierarch sitting upon his "throne" in his full regalia? That does not apply to Methodist bishops. But they have so much power that they don't need the panoply.

Think how insufferable bishops might be if they had to be both worshiped and feared. I am afraid that is true of Catholic bishops. Perhaps that is why the Catholic saints are not frequently found in the hierarchy.

1927

An impertinent youngster at the forum (midwestern college) accused me today of being an authoritarian because I quoted several modern philosophers and scientists in my address in support of my theistic belief. I made a deep bow before him and congratulated him upon being so proficient in laboratory experiments in every science and so profound in his philosophical meditations that he could arrive at his conclusions without the help of anyone else, scientist or philosopher.

His question did set me thinking on the problem of freedom. Why do we believe what we believe, and why do we do what we do? If the religion of my home had been harsh and unlovely I would probably be today where that young man is, in a position of rebellion against all religion. If I had not had the aid of this helpful professor and that illuminating book when my religious convictions were undergoing adjustment I might not have made the necessary adjustments but would have thrown religious convictions into the discard.

If I were not in a position where human nature reveals itself in its more lovely characteristics would I be able to maintain confidence in the integrity of man, upon which so much of the confidence in God depends? Has the class-conscious worker not a right to dismiss both my political and my religious convictions as bourgeois prejudices? And could I not with equal justice condemn his as myopic views which his resentments against society explain but do not prove true?

What we know as truth is determined by peculiar and individual perspectives. Pressures of environment, influences of heredity, and excellencies and deficiencies of teachers help to determine our life philosophies. We ought therefore to hold them with decent humility and a measure of scepticism. But if we permit ourselves to be tempted into a complete subjectivism and scepticism by these facts, we put an end to all philosophy and ultimately to civilization itself. For civilization depends upon the vigorous pursuit of the highest values by people who are intelligent enough to know that their values are qualified by their interests and corrupted by their prejudices.

1927

Perhaps there is no better illustration of the ethical impotence of the modern church than its failure to deal with the evils and the ethical problems of stock manipulation. Millions in property values are created by pure legerdemain. Stock dividends, watered stock and excessive rise in stock values, due to the productivity of the modern machine, are accepted by the church without a murmur if only a slight return is made by the beneficiaries through church philanthropies.

Here is C—— recapitalizing his business and adding six million dollars in stock. At least five of these millions will not be invested in physical expansion but pocketed by the owner. They simply represent capitalization of expected profits. Once this added burden has been placed upon the industry any demands of the workers for a larger share in the profits will be met by conclusive proof that the stock is earning only a small dividend and that further increase in wages would be "suicidal" to the business.

Meanwhile C—— has become quite philanthropic. He gives fifty thousand dollars here and a hundred thousand there. Since the good man is a "Christian," religious organizations profit most by his benefactions. Every new donation is received with pæans of praise from church and press.

What I wonder is whether the gentleman is deceiving himself and really imagines himself a Christian or whether he is really quite hard-boiled and harbors a secret contempt for the little men who buzz about his throne, singing their hallelujahs. One can never be sure how much we mortals are fooled by our own inadequate virtues and sanctified vices and how much we accept the world's convenient tribute without being convinced by it. Nor do I know which interpretation of the facts is to be preferred, not as a matter of truth, but as a matter of charity. What is worse—to be honest with yourself while you are dishonest with the world, or to be dishonest with the world because you have deceived yourself?

1927

Dropped in on the First —— Church of —— on my way back from —— University. Went into the young people's meeting before the evening service and found a typical Endeavor meeting in progress. Some ninety wholesome youngsters were in attendance. All the various tricks of a good Endeavor meeting were used. Several little poems clipped from the Endeavor World were recited at the appropriate time and some of the members contributed quotations from Scripture and from well-known authors. The leader gave a good but platitudinous talk. There was no discussion. My impression was that this type of meeting, if still held, would be very poorly attended. But here the facts belied my theories. So much the worse for the young people of the church. Only a very inert type of youngster could be satisfied with such a meeting, and only a very uncritical mind would accept the pious platitudes which filled it, without uttering a protest or challenging a dozen assumptions.

However much such meetings may cultivate habits of loyalty to the church among young people and preserve among them the traditional religious attitudes and customs, they do nothing to fit young people to live a Christian life amid the complexities of the modern world or to hold to the Christian faith in the perplexities of a scientific world view. What worries me particularly in regard to these meetings is the assumption which underlies them that nothing but moral good will is necessary to solve the problems of life. Almost every other meeting is a consecration meeting. No one seems to introduce the young people to the idea that an ethical life requires honest and searching intelligence. Nothing is done to discover to their eyes the tremendous chasm between the ideals of their faith and the social realities in which they live.

Under such circumstances we can expect no new vitality

103

in the Christian life as the new generation takes hold. Old virtues and respectabilities will be maintained, but the areas of life which are still unchristian will remain as they are. I see the danger in our own discussion groups that the young people may satisfy all their idealism in incessant talk. But the talk has at least the merit of exploring all sides of a problem and of revealing the limitations of traditional attitudes and the need of new ventures in faith.

1927

Whenever I exchange thoughts with H——, as I do with greater frequency and with increasing profit to myself, I have the uneasy feeling that I belong to the forces which are destroying religion in the effort to refine it. He is as critical as I am—well, perhaps not quite so critical; but in all his critical evaluations of religious forms he preserves a robust religious vitality which I seem to lack. His scholarship is of course much more extensive than mine, but it has not robbed him of religious naïveté, to use Schweitzer's phrase. He has preserved a confidence in the goodness of men and the ultimate triumph of righteousness which I do not lack, but to which I do not hold so unwaveringly. While we understand each other, we really belong to different schools of thought.

I have been profoundly impressed by the Spenglerian thesis that culture is destroyed by the spirit of sophistication and I am beginning to suspect that I belong to the forces of decadence in which this sophistication is at work. I have my eye too much upon the limitations of contemporary religious life and institutions; I always see the absurdities and irrationalities in which narrow types of religion issue. That wouldn't be so bad if I did not use the instruments of intellectualism rather than those of a higher spirituality for the critical task.

Nevertheless I hate a thoroughgoing cynic. I don't want anyone to be more cynical than I am. If I am saved from cynicism at all it is by some sense of personal loyalty to the spirit and the genius of Jesus; that and physical health. If I were physically anæmic I never would be able to escape pessimism. This very type of morbid introspection is one of the symptoms of the disease. I can't justify myself in my perilous position except by the observation that the business of being sophisticated and naïve, critical and religious, at one and the same time is as difficult as it is necessary, and only a few are able to achieve the balance. H——— says I lack a proper appreciation of the mystical values in religion. That is probably the root of the matter. Yet I can't resist another word in self-defense. The modern world is so full of bunkum that it is difficult to attempt honesty in it without an undue emphasis upon the critical faculty.

If in this civilization we cannot enter the kingdom of God because we cannot be as little children, the fault, dear Brutus, is in our stars and not in ourselves.

1927

I fell in with a gentleman on the Pullman smoker to-day (Pullman smokers are perfect institutes for plumbing the depths and shallows of the American mind) who had made a killing on the stock exchange. His luck appeared like success from his perspective, and he was full of the confidence with which success endows mortals. He spoke oracularly on any and all subjects. He knew why the farmers were not making any money and why the Europeans were not as prosperous as we. Isn't it strange how gambler's luck gives men the assurance of wisdom for which philosophers search in vain? I pity this man's wife. But she probably regards a new fur coat as adequate compensation for the task of appearing convinced by his obiter dicta.

1927

Seven clergymen sat down today with the national defense committee of the board of commerce. They invited us to talk over our stand against compulsory military education in the schools. It was an interesting experience, particularly as it came but shortly after our conflict with the same group on the matter of labor speakers in our pulpits. The contrast in the attitude of the business men in these two controversies is very illuminating.

In the labor controversy they were hard-boiled realists who simply wanted to prevent labor from getting its side before the public. At that time they did not invite us to a round table discussion. They had nothing to discuss. They simply used their power in the city to prevent any discussion of the character of their power and the method of its preservation. In this case they were aggrieved and bewildered romanticists and idealists. They want military training in the schools because they have been told by the army officers that such training makes for patriotism. And patriotism is the only religion they know.

They invited us to a luncheon precisely because they felt themselves in a morally, not to say spiritually, impregnable position. I think they were quite sure that a little argument would convince us of the error of our ways. Our resistance was obviously very disconcerting to them. Perhaps they had a right to be disconcerted; for it is only a little while since there was a perfect alliance between the religion of patriotism and organized Christianity. Since most of the men do not attend church they had not heard of the qualms of conscience in the pulpit that had, at least for the time being, dissolved that alliance. We stood our ground and the meeting dissolved without any results.

I wonder if it isn't a little bit wicked to challenge the validity of the only kind of altruism which men know. But no—narrow loyalties may become more dangerous than selfishness.

I wonder why it is that so many of the churches which go in for vaudeville programs and the hip-hip-hooray type of religious services should belong to the Methodist and Baptist denominations. The vulgarities of the stunt preacher are hardly compatible with either the robust spiritual vitality or the puritan traditions of the more evangelistic churches. Perhaps the phenomenon of which I speak is due merely to the size of the two denominations. They may have more showmen simply because they are big enough to have more leaders of all varieties. Certainly no church surpasses the Methodist in the number of men who possess real social passion and imagination. Nor are the old emotionally warm and naïvely orthodox preachers wanting in either church.

Nevertheless there is a growing tendency toward stunt services in both denominations. Perhaps it represents the strategy of denominational and congregational organisms which are too much alive to accept the fate of innocuous desuetude, which has befallen some other churches. Finding the masses, which they once attracted by genuine religious emotion, less inclined to seek satisfaction in religion, they maintain themselves by offering such goods in entertainment and social life as the people seem to desire.

When the naïve enthusiasms of those generations, among whom religion is an emotional experience and not a social tradition, begin to cool, the churches which serve the new generations must either express religious feeling through devotion to moral and aesthetic values or they must substitute a baser emotionalism for the lost religious feeling. Perhaps the prevalence of cheap theatricality among the churches of our great democracy is a sign of the fact that the masses in America have lost the capacity for unreflective and exuberant religious feeling before they could acquire the kind of religion which is closely integrated with the values of culture and art.

There is something pathetic about the effort of the churches to capture these spiritually vacuous multitudes by resort to any device which may intrigue their vagrant fancies. But it may not represent a total loss. The entertainment they offer may be vulgar, but it is not vicious, and without them the people might find satisfaction in something even cheaper.

1927

At the Lenten service today the dynamic speaker dilated upon the heroic character of the Christian faith. "Someone said to me recently," he reported, " 'Do you realize that it is dangerous to be a Christian?' 'Certainly,' I answered, 'It always has been and always will be.' "

Isn't it strange how we preachers insist on emphasizing the heroic aspect of the Christian faith? That pose today was exactly like the one struck by the minister in —— who loved to say dramatically, "The church needs a new casualty list," while it was generally known that he carefully evaded every issue which might create dissension or contention.

I think we ministers strike these heroic poses because we are dimly aware of the fact that the gospel commits us to positions which require heroic devotion before they will ever be realized in life. But we are astute rather than heroic and cautious rather than courageous. Thus we are in the dangerous position of being committed to the cross in principle but escaping it in practice. We are honest enough to be uneasy about that fact, but insincere enough to quiet our uneasiness by heroic poses.

Let any group of ministers gather and you will find someone declaring fervently, "No one ever tells me what to say. My congregation gives me perfect liberty." That is just another way of quieting an uneasy conscience; for we all know that if we explore the full meaning of a gospel of love its principles will be found to run counter to cherished prejudices. It is of course not impossible to retain freedom of the pulpit, but if anyone is doing so without the peril of defections from his ranks and opposition to his message, he is deceiving himself about the quality of his message. Either his message is too innocuous to deserve opposition or too conventional to arouse it.

An astute pedagogy and a desire to speak the truth in love may greatly decrease opposition to a minister's message and persuade a difficult minority to entertain at least, and perhaps to profit by, his message; but if a gospel is preached without opposition it is simply not the gospel which resulted in the cross. It is not, in short, the gospel of love.

1927

Talked today at the open forum which meets every Sunday afternoon in the high school. The "lunatic fringe" of the city congregates there, in addition to many sensible people. The question period in such meetings is unfortunately monopolized to a great extent by the foolish ones, though not always. Today one old gentleman wanted to know when I thought the Lord would come again, while a young fellow spoke volubly on communism and ended by challenging me to admit that all religion is fantasy. Between those two you have the story of the tragic state of religion in modern life. One half of the world seems to believe that every poetic symbol with which religion must deal is an exact definition of a concrete or an historical fact; the other half, having learned that this is not the case, can come to no other conclusion but that all religion is based upon fantasy.

Fundamentalists have at least one characteristic in common with most scientists. Neither can understand that poetic and religious imagination has a way of arriving at truth by giving a clue to the total meaning of things without being in any sense an analytic description of detailed facts. The fundamentalists insist that religion is science, and thus they prompt those who know that this is not true to declare that all religious truth is contrary to scientific fact.

How can an age which is so devoid of poetic imagination as ours be truly religious?

1927

Our city race commission has finally made its report after months of investigation and further months of deliberation on our findings. It has been a rare experience to meet with these white and colored leaders and talk over our race problems. The situation which the colored people of the city face is really a desperate one, and no one who does not spend real time in gathering the facts can have any idea of the misery and pain which exists among these people, recently migrated from the south and unadjusted to our industrial civilization. Hampered both by their own inadequacies and the hostility of a white world they have a desperate fight to keep body and soul together, to say nothing of developing those amenities which raise life above the brute level.

I wish that some of our romanticists and sentimentalists could sit through a series of meetings where the real social problems of a city are discussed. They would be cured of their optimism. A city which is built around a productive process and which gives only casual thought and incidental attention to its human problems is really a kind of hell. Thousands in this town are really living in torment while the rest of us eat, drink and make merry. What a civilization!

Incidentally I wish the good church people who hate our mayor so much because he doesn't conform to their rules and standards could appreciate how superior his attitudes and viewpoints on race relations are to those held by most church people. It seems to me rather unfortunate that we must depend upon the "publicans" for our social conscience to so great a degree while the "saints" develop their private virtues and let the city as such fry in its iniquities.

1927

I think I have solved the Sunday night service problem for good. I give a short address or sermon upon a more or less controversial moral issue, or upon a perplexing religious question, and after closing the service we have a half-hour to forty-five minutes of discussion. The group attracted by this kind of program is not large. It is not the usual forum crowd. But it is a group of unusually thoughtful people, and the way they explore the fundamental themes and problems of life is worth more than many sermons.

I am absolutely convinced that such discussions come to grips with life's real problems much more thoroughly than any ex cathedra utterance from the pulpit. For one thing the people themselves make the application of general principles to specific experiences. Then, too, they inevitably explore the qualifications which life seems to make upon every seemingly absolute principle. The real principles of Christian living seem so much more real and also so much more practicable when a group of thoughtful people make an honest effort to fit them into the complexities of modern life.

Perhaps the most interesting point about such a discussion is the way every type of experience can be used to illustrate a certain general truth. Last Sunday night an advertising man made a most interesting contribution to the question of marriage and divorce out of his experience as advertising counsel. He said that he had learnt in business that it is always well to regard relationships as permanent even when they are not so absolutely in a legal sense. If the parties to a contract assume that it can be broken easily they will not extend themselves as they ought to make those adjustments which a permanent relationship requires.—Thus we make the experience gained in one field of activity serve the problem of another field. Again and again thoughtful mothers have thrown light upon the problems of democracy, the place of coercion in life and the efficacy of trust out of experience gained in their work with their children.

If there were only more thoughtful people it would be worth while to change every service into something like this evening discussion. But discussion requires time and it doesn't mean much to people who are looking for "inspiration" rather than guidance. I suppose there is still a place for inspirational addresses. But in a world in which so many traditional moral ideas are in solution and so many others are generally accepted and never applied, this kind of honest searching with others, rather than for them, is particularly rewarding.

1927

I wonder if it is really possible to have an honest Thanksgiving celebration in an industrial civilization. Harvest festivals were natural enough in peasant communities. The agrarian feels himself dependent upon nature's beneficence and anxious about nature's caprices. When the autumnal harvest is finally safe in the barns there arise, with the sigh of relief, natural emotions of gratitude that must express themselves religiously, since the bounty is actually created by the mysterious forces of nature which man may guide but never quite control.

All that is different in an industrial civilization in which so much wealth is piled up by the ingenuity of the machine, and, at least seemingly, by the diligence of man. Thanksgiving becomes increasingly the business of congratulating the Almighty upon his most excellent co-workers, ourselves. I have had that feeling about the Thanksgiving proclamations of our Presidents for some years. An individual living in an industrial community might still celebrate a Thanksgiving day uncorrupted by pride, because he does benefit from processes and forces which he does not create or even guide. But a national Thanksgiving, particularly if it is meant to express gratitude for material bounty, becomes increasingly a pharisaic rite.

The union Thanksgiving service we attended this morning was full of the kind of self-righteous bunk which made it quite impossible for me to worship. There was indeed a faint odor of contrition in one of the prayers and in an aside of the sermon, but it did not spring from the heart. The Lord who was worshiped was not the Lord of Hosts, but the spirit of Uncle Sam, given a cosmic eminence for the moment which the dear old gentleman does not deserve.

It is a bad thing when religion is used as a vehicle of pride. It would be better to strut unashamedly down the boardwalk of nations than to go through the business of bowing humbly before God while we say, "We thank thee Lord that we are not as other men."

1927

Mother and I visited at the home of —— today where the husband is sick and was out of employment before he became sick. The folks have few connections in the city. They belong to no church. What a miserable existence it is to be friendless in a large city. And to be dependent upon a heartless industry. The man is about 55 or 57 I should judge, and he is going to have a desperate time securing employment after he gets well. These modern factories are not meant for old men. They want young men and they use them up pretty quickly. Your modern worker, with no skill but what is in the machine, is a sorry individual. After he loses the stamina of youth, he has nothing to sell.

I promised —— I would try to find him a job. I did it to relieve the despair of that family, but I will have a hard time making good on my promise. According to the ethics of our modern industrialism men over fifty, without special training, are so much junk. It is a pleasure to see how such an ethic is qualified as soon as the industrial unit is smaller and the owner has a personal interest in his men. I could mention quite a few such instances. But unfortunately the units are getting larger and larger and more inhuman.

I think I had better get in contact with more of these victims of our modern industrialism and not leave that end of our work to mother alone. A little such personal experience will help much to save you from sentimentality.

1927

Have just returned from the student conference at ——. A smart young professor told the students that all social customs are based upon irrational taboos. Our generation is the first with the opportunity to build a rational social order. The way to build a rational society, according to this savant, is to regard every relationship, custom, convention and law as irrational until it has proved itself rational by experience.

A sample of the kind of society he would build by his reason was given in his discussion of sex relations. He thinks the highest kind of family life would result from the love of one woman for one man while both indulged in promiscuous relations. Thus would the values of both freedom and love be maintained. The smart young man seems never to have heard that you cannot have your cake and eat it too.

If you want love and cooperation in any kind of society, and most of all in the family, it is necessary to sacrifice some freedom for its sake. What strange fanatics these moderns are! Imagining themselves dispassionate in their evaluation of all values, they are really bigoted protagonists of the one value of freedom. Every other value must be subordinated to it.

It is true that every convention, custom, law and usage contains an irrational element. Some were unreasonable from the beginning and others have become so by shifting circumstance. It is necessary, therefore, that we approach the facts of life experimentally and scientifically, rather than traditionally. However, it seems to me quite unreasonable to proceed upon the assumption that all traditions are wholly unreasonable. Most of the moderns who think so are significantly defective in the knowledge of history.

There is at the heart of almost every tradition an element

of reasonableness and around its circumference a whole series of irrationalities. Our business must be to destroy the
latter and restore the former by fitting it to contemporaneous circumstances and conditions.

I doubt whether it is wise for every person to be extremely
critical of all traditions in every field of thought and life. I
imagine we ought to specialize a little in this matter and let
various people experiment in various areas. This seems to
me a wise policy for the simple reason that it does not make
for happiness for one person to do the experimenting in every field. At any rate most of the intellectuals I know who try
to do it are miserable souls. I am always glad to escape their
company and consort with folks who take some things for
granted. There is an unnatural strain in their lives and, having made a virtue of the critical temper, they usually discount virtue and achievement even where it is indubitable.

Since there are many more traditionalists than experimentalists, all this may be bad advice. But I doubt whether
the lethargy of the many justifies the few in spoiling their
tempers and their judgment. Let every reformer find at least
one field of interest and life where he can be happily conventional. If he is trying to remake the economic order, let
him accept family life and be happy in it without too many
scruples about its alleged imperfections. On second thought
I don't like this advice. At any rate it is inconsistent with
my scorn for the liberal theologians who are so preoccupied
with the task of reforming religion that they have no interest in the iniquities of society which ought to challenge
their conscience.

Let us have reformers, then, who try to reform everything at the same time! But I am going to keep my distance
from them.

1927

The new Ford car is out. The town is full of talk about it. Newspaper reports reveal that it is the topic of the day in all world centers. Crowds storm every exhibit to get the first glimpse of this new creation. Mr. Ford has given out an interview saying that the car has cost him about a hundred million dollars and that after finishing it he still has about a quarter of a billion dollars in the bank.

I have been doing a little arithmetic and have come to the conclusion that the car cost Ford workers at least fifty million in lost wages during the past year. No one knows how many hundreds lost their homes in the period of unemployment, and how many children were taken out of school to help fill the depleted family exchequer, and how many more children lived on short rations during this period. Mr. Ford refuses to concede that he made a mistake in bringing the car out so late. He has a way of impressing the public even with his mistakes. We are now asked to believe that the whole idea of waiting a year after the old car stopped selling before bringing out a new one was a great advertising scheme which reveals the perspicacity of this industrial genius. But no one asks about the toll in human lives.

What a civilization this is! Naïve gentlemen with a genius for mechanics suddenly become the arbiters over the lives and fortunes of hundreds of thousands. Their moral pretensions are credulously accepted at full value. No one bothers to ask whether an industry which can maintain a cash reserve of a quarter of a billion ought not make some provision for its unemployed. It is enough that the new car is a good one. Here is a work of art in the only realm of art which we can understand. We will therefore refrain from making undue ethical demands upon the artist. Artists of all the ages have been notoriously unamenable to moral discipline. The cry of the hungry is drowned in the song, "Henry has made a lady out of Lizzy."

1927

This prayer book controversy in the Church of England ought to give us liberals who make so much of tolerance a pause. What are the limits of tolerance? Does not tolerance of a theological position which one knows or believes to be untrue become a betrayal of the truth? How can one be tolerant of medievalism without playing traitor to the best in the modern day?

Here is the Episcopal church which many of us have counted blessed because it was the one bridge over the chasm which separates Catholicism and Protestantism. But the chasm is now revealed as too wide for any bridge. Co-operation with the Catholic demands connivance with religious practices which reduce religion to magic. No wonder the Protestant laymen in Parliament threw the revised prayer book out. How can anyone in the year of our Lord 1927 be seriously exercised over the problem of the "real presence" in the Eucharist? Think of the spiritual leaders of a torn and bleeding world debating learnedly on whether and how God can be magically localized and salvation be confined in a capsule. To read the arguments of the sacerdotalists is enough to drive one into the arms of the unrepentent rationalists who regard all religion as dangerous.

The weaknesses of Catholicism ought not prompt one to disregard all the finer spiritual and moral values which still live in this ancient church. But there can be no final unity between an institution which reduces religion to magic and a fellowship of the spirit which tries to subdue the chaos of life under the ideal of faith.

Magic is an enemy of all morality. It offers a short cut to all prizes of the spirit which can be won only by heroic effort.

1927

After speaking at —— University today Professor —— said he objected to my assumption that the family is the root of human societies. He said he believed that most forms of human cooperation were formed by men who had to resist the special interests of the family, as typified particularly by the narrow loyalty of the mother to her own offspring, before they could establish wider fellowships. That was a new idea to me and one that seems to be not without merit. Of course it does not invalidate the thesis that the family is the first unit of society; for the first fighting unit was probably composed of a group of fathers and sons and sons' sons. That is, not the family in the narrowest but in the widest sense, the family as it develops into the clan is the first real society.

The idea that the family is frequently opposed to ventures in wider fellowship is justified by more than one present fact. The family is still essentially selfish, and many a man is beguiled from ideal ventures by a false sense of obligation to his family. Think of the number of men who sell their souls merely that their wives and children may enjoy higher standards of living than other families. Think of the number of mothers whose interest in life never goes beyond the ambition to secure special advantages for their children. The mother of the sons of Zebedee is a good example. In her you have motherhood in its tragic limitations as well as in its sublime beauty.

The family is not inevitably selfish or invariably opposed to larger ventures in fellowship, but it may easily become so. Jesus' ruthless words, "He who loveth father or mother more than me is not worthy of me, he who loveth son and daughter more than me is not worthy of me," have more meaning than most Christians have realized. Celibacy may be wrong because it escapes rather than solves this problem. But the invariable tendency of religious movements of great moral sensitiveness to experiment with celibacy is significant. Thus speaks a bachelor. Let the cynic make the most of the private prejudice which colors this judgment.

1928

This conference on religious education seems to your humble servant the last word in absurdity. We are told by a delightful "expert" that we ought not really teach our children about God lest we rob them of the opportunity of making their own discovery of God, and lest we corrupt their young minds by our own superstitions. If we continue along these lines the day will come when some expert will advise us not to teach our children the English language, since we rob them thereby of the possibility of choosing the German, French or Japanese languages as possible alternatives. Don't these good people realize that they are reducing the principle of freedom to an absurdity?

Religion, like language, is a social product. The potentialities for both are in the child, but their highest articulations are the result of ages of cultural and spiritual experience, and in the right kind of religious education the experience of the race is joined with the inclinations of the individual. We do not get a higher type of religious idealism from children merely by withholding our own religious ideas from them (however they may be filled with error), any more than we would get a higher type of civilization by letting some group of youngsters shift for themselves upon a desert island.

A wise architect observed that you could break the laws of architectural art provided you had mastered them first. That would apply to religion as well as to art. Ignorance of the past does not guarantee freedom from its imperfections. More probably it assures the repetition of past errors. We ought of course to cultivate a wholesome scepticism in our young people so that they will not accept the ideas of the past too slavishly. But appreciation must come before criticism.

We do not teach a child the limitations of Beethoven before we have helped it to appreciate him; nor do we withhold any appreciation of the classics in order that the child might be free to prefer Stravinsky to Beethoven. What some of these moderns are doing is simply to destroy the organs of religious insight and the atmosphere in which religious attitudes may flourish, ostensibly for the sake of freedom, but really at its expense.

I have a dark suspicion that some of these modern religious educators do not really know what religion is about. They want a completely rational faith and do not realize that they are killing religion by a complete rationalization. With all their pious phraseology and supposedly modern pedagogy they really are decadent forces.

Life is a battle between faith and reason in which each feeds upon the other, drawing sustenance from it and destroying it. Nature has wisely ordained that faith shall have an early advantage in the life of the child to compensate for its later difficulties. If we imagine that we help the progress of the race by inoculating children with a premature sophistication we are of all men most miserable. Reason, without the balance of faith, destroys a civilization soon enough, without giving it this advantage among the young. I wonder if any of these modern religious pedagogues have ever read Unamuno's "The Tragic Sense of Life"?

Here I am talking like a fundamentalist. But why not? If we must choose between types of fanaticism is there any particular reason why we should prefer the fanatics who destroy a vital culture in the name of freedom and reason to those who try to strangle a new culture at birth in the name of authority and dogma? The latter type of fanaticism is bound to end in futility. The growth of reason cannot be stopped by dogma. But the former type is dangerous because it easily enervates a rational culture with ennui and despair.

1928

This Federal Council meeting is an interesting study in the geography of morals. The race commission presented a report today in which it tried to place the council on record as favoring the enforcement of the fifteenth amendment as well as the eighteenth. It was obviously an effort to exploit the strong prohibition sentiment of the churches for the sake of committing them to the espousal of the interests of the disfranchised Negroes in the south. That is not a bad political strategy. But it did not quite work.

A good brother from the southern Presbyterian church warned that to interfere with this "political issue" would "soil the garments of the bride of Christ." To him the eighteenth amendment represented a "moral" issue but the fifteenth was a "political" one. I have a sneaking suspicion that the fifteenth amendment expresses more of the genius of the gospel than the eighteenth, but that is neither here nor there. What was interesting was the way in which various church leaders tried to rescue us from the embarrassment into which the council was brought by this proposal.

A good brother who was raised in the south and now lives in the north tried to act as mediator. He introduced his remarks with the usual nice story about how much he loved his negro mammy. Some day he ought to have a lesson in ethics and learn how much easier it is to love those who acknowledge their inferiority than those who challenge our superiority. It is indeed a virtuous woman who can love her social competitor as sincerely as she loves her faithful maid.

Another mediator was a southern bishop who has many northern connections. He made much of the fact that the south disregards only the spirit and not the letter of the enfranchising amendments to the constitution. The bishop is really a man of some courage who has spoken out bravely on the industrial conditions in the south. But he was evidently afraid in this instance either to accept or to reject a Christian view of race relations. So he stuck to casuistry about the letter of the law. He has probably preached many a sermon on the text about the letter killing and the spirit making alive. At any rate everyone who spoke revealed how geographic and historical circumstance had qualified Christian conviction.

That was as true of those of us who took an uncompromising position as the southern equivocators and the semi-southern mediators. To the southerners we are not Christian idealists but merely "Yankee" meddlers. And perhaps we are. At any rate it was easy to see from the debate that the north cannot help the south much in solving its race problem. If it is solved the solution must come out of the conscience and heart of the south.

After all, the problem, as every moral problem, is not merely conditioned by geography but by mathematics. Contact between races when the one race is almost as numerous as the other is quite a different story from a relationship in which the subject race is numerically very much weaker than the dominant group. Therefore let us not judge, lest we be judged. It is so easy to repent of other people's sins.

Nevertheless it does not make one feel very comfortable to have a great church body seek some politic solution for a problem in which the ideal of Christian brotherhood leaves little room for equivocation.

1928

There is a discouraging pettiness about human nature which makes me hate myself each time I make an analysis of my inner motives and springs of action. Here I am prodding and criticizing people continually because they have made too many compromises with the necessities of life and adjusted the Christian ideal until it has completely lost its original meaning. Yet I make my own compromises all the time.

It is Christian to trust people, and my trust is carefully qualified by mistrust and caution.

It is Christian to love, and to trust in the potency of love rather than in physical coercion. Logically that means nonresistance. Yet I believe that a minimum of coercion is necessary in all social tasks, or in most of them.

It is Christian to forgive rather than to punish; yet I do little by way of experimenting in the redemptive power of forgiveness.

I am not really a Christian. In me, as in many others, "the native hue of resolution is sicklied o'er by a pale cast of thought." I am too cautious to be a Christian. I can justify my caution, but so can the other fellow who is more cautious than I am.

The whole Christian adventure is frustrated continually not so much by malice as by cowardice and reasonableness. Of course everyone must decide for himself just where he is going to put his peg; where he is going to arrive at some stable equilibrium between moral adventure and necessary caution. And perhaps everyone is justified if he tries to prove that there is a particular reasonableness about the type of compromise which he has reached. But he might well learn, better than I have learned, to be charitable with those who have made their adjustments to the right and to the left of his position. If I do not watch myself I will regard all who make their adjustments to my right as fanatics and all who make them to the left as cowards. There is a silly egotism about such an attitude. But it is difficult to be pedagogically effective if you do not hold pretty resolutely to some position.

A reasonable person adjusts his moral goal somewhere between Christ and Aristotle, between an ethic of love and an ethic of moderation. I hope there is more of Christ than of Aristotle in my position. But I would not be too sure of it.

1928

Jack Hyde came up today for a chat. These newspaper men are always interesting company. As religious editor of the Daily ———, he has been following the preachers of the town pretty closely. Of course he is a cynic, though a gentle one. He tells many an interesting story on how the preachers try to get free publicity.

I think there ought to be a club in which preachers and journalists could come together and have the sentimentalism of the one matched with the cynicism of the other. That ought to bring them pretty close to the truth. The interesting part of the contrast is that the newspaper is officially as optimistic about contemporary life as the pulpit. The difference between the two is that the preacher is ensnared by his own sentimentality and optimism while the newspaper man has two views, one for official and one for private consumption.

1928

My good friend —— has sent me his church calendar. Among other things he reports "Last Sunday almost as many strangers as members were present. The weather was a bit cold. Was your loyalty chilly too? You cannot fight battles with half the soldiers in their tents. Lent is here. Give your church the right of way. Do your duty next Sunday."

Here we see how easily even the Protestant minister gravitates to the viewpoint of the priest. He thinks people ought to regard it as a duty to hear him preach. What is still worse is that he identifies church attendance with moral heroism. Does he not realize that faithful church attendance develops and reveals the virtue of patience much more than the virtue of courage?

I must admit that I have urged people to come to church myself as a matter of duty. But I can do so no longer. The church service is not an end in itself. Not even religion is an end in itself. If the church service does not attract people by the comfort and challenge it brings to them, we only postpone the evil day if we compel attendance by appealing to their sense of duty. It may not be wrong to appeal to their sense of loyalty to the institution and tell them that if they have identified themselves with the institution as members they owe it to the strangers to be there. But even that is dangerous. The church is already too much an end in itself.

These appeals make it appear that we regard religious devotion as a service to God, a very dangerous idea. Of course a modern preacher doesn't really believe that. What is really in his mind, consciously or unconsciously, is that the people owe him the duty to hear him preach. That is perhaps a natural glorification of his own function but it cannot be denied that there is something pathetic about it.

I can see, of course, that all good things depend in part upon right habits. Customs, attitudes and actions which are desirable cannot always depend upon impulse and will. It may be a good thing that people attend church as a matter of habit and because of a general sense of obligation to the institution. If churches depended only upon people who must make up their minds each Sunday whether or no they will attend church, our attendance would be even smaller than it is.

Yet habitual actions easily become meaningless, and institutions which depend upon them lose their vitality. If habitual actions are not continually revitalized by the compulsion of ideals and the attraction of the values involved in them, they may easily become useless.

1928

Detroit observed Good Friday today as never before. Sixteen theatres and many churches besides were filled to capacity during the three-hour period. I wonder how one is to understand this tremendous devotion of this pagan city. How little place the real spirit of Christ has in the industrial drive of this city. And yet men and women flock by the thousands to meditate upon the cross. Perhaps we are all like the centurion who helped to crucify Jesus and then was so impressed by the whole drama of the cross that the confession was forced from his lips "Surely this was the son of God."

Before going to the theatre service I passed a Methodist church with a message on its bulletin board that explains many chapters in American church history. It was: "Good Friday service this afternoon. Snappy song service." So we combine the somber notes of religion with the jazz of the age.

I wonder if anyone who needs a snappy song service can really appreciate the meaning of the cross. But perhaps that is just a Lutheran prejudice of mine.

A very sophisticated young man assured me in our discussion today (student discussion at a middle western university) that no intelligent person would enter the ministry today. He was sure that the ministry was impossible as a vocation not only because too many irrationalities were still enmeshed with religion but also because there was no real opportunity for usefulness in the church. I tried to enlighten this sophomoric wise man.

Granted all the weaknesses of the church and the limitations of the ministry as a profession, where can one invest one's life where it can be made more effective in as many directions?

You can deal with children and young people and help them to set their life goals and organize their personalities around just and reasonable values.

You can help the imperiled family shape the standards and the values by which the institution of family life may be saved and adjusted to the new conditions of an industrial civilization.

You can awaken a complacent civilization to the injustices which modern industrialism is developing. While ministers fail most at this point there is nothing to prevent a courageous man from making a real contribution to his society in this field.

You can soften the asperities of racial conflict and aid the various groups of a polyglot city to understand one another and themselves.

You can direct the thoughts and the hopes of men to those facts and those truths which mitigate the cruelty of the natural world and give men the opportunity to assert the dignity of human life in the face of the contempt of nature.

You can help them to shape and to direct their hopes and aspirations until their lives are determined and molded by the ideal objects of their devotion. While it is true that magic and superstition are still entwined, seemingly inextricably intertwined, with the highest hopes and assurances of mankind, you may find real joy as a skillful craftsman in separating hopes from illusions so that the one need not perish with the other.

Here is a task which requires the knowledge of a social scientist and the insight and imagination of a poet, the executive talents of a business man and the mental discipline of a philosopher. Of course none of us meets all the demands made upon us. It is not easy to be all things to all men. Perhaps that is why people are so critical of us. Our task is not specific enough to make a high degree of skill possible or to result in tangible and easily measured results. People can find fault with us easily enough and we have no statistics to overawe them and to negate their criticisms.

1928

I spoke today at the "Victory dinner" of one of our civic organizations which had been conducting a financial campaign in the interest of its worthy objects. Not being well prepared I animadverted disconnectedly upon the lack of culture in Detroit and expressed the hope that the dawn of a new day was breaking.

Mr. —— who sat close to me was so angry about what I said that he confessed that he had been tempted to interrupt me in the middle of my address. He cited a large benefaction of his in the interest of a religious organization as proof of Detroit's culture and insisted that the "old families," to which he belonged, had real culture, whatever might be said about the newer crowd. I told him his contribution was in the interest of righteousness rather than culture. Inasmuch as it is generally known that he made a fortune by rigging the stock market, he was a little nonplussed by my answer. We finally came to an amicable agreement upon the proposition that the streets of Detroit are cleaner than those of Chicago.

1928

I believe every preacher ought to take several radical journals, preferably the ones which are extremely inimical to religion. The ethical ideals of Christianity are so high and the compromises which the average church and the average minister has made between these ideals and the economic necessities of society are so great, and self-deception is so easy, that we need the corrective of a critical and perhaps cynical evaluation of religion in modern life.

I should like to recommend this kind of reading particularly to successful ministers who are so easily obsessed by a messianic complex because of the compliments they receive. Let them remind themselves that there are astute observers who think that all their preaching is superficial and never touches the fundamental defects of modern society, and that these critics are at least as near the truth as their too generous devotees.

1928

I think I ought to repent of the many unkind things I have said about various ministers. We liberal preachers (I am thinking of social liberalism now) are too ready to attribute conventional opinions to cowardice. What we don't realize is that the great majority of parsons simply don't share our radical convictions. If they get along very handsomely in the kind of a civilization in which we live, that is simply because they are in sincere general agreement with the prevailing ideas of our day. Of course I think we have a right to wonder a little how one can claim discipleship to one who disturbed history so much and yet be such a thorough conformist. Yet it is usually not cowardice but mental inertia which creates the conformity; and sometimes the conformity is the honest fruit of a finely poised rather than a daring mind. After all most of us are conformists in some sense, and it is rather presumptuous on our part to condemn every type of conformity except our own.

I am moved to this reflection by the insistence of such men as the editor of the Christian Register that every liberal who remains in an evangelical communion and does not immediately join the Unitarian church must be prompted by cowardice. When it is theological rather than social liberalism that is made the test of conformity or radicalism, it is my ox that is gored, and I begin to recant my previous harsh opinions. If the editor of the Register can go so far wrong in gauging the motives of evangelical liberals we social radicals may be wrong in explaining why parsons fail to be thoroughgoing pacifists. Great achievement! I learn how to be tolerant when I become the victim of somebody else's spiritual pride.

1928

Had a profitable talk with a Jewish friend in the east. He said the only Christian church that he could ever join would be that of the Quakers. Of course he would not join the Quakers in the kind of a world in which we are living, where Christians practice social ostracism against Jews and thereby force every Jew to regard such a transfer of religious loyalty in the light of treason to his racial community. He felt that if he were free to choose his religious group he would choose the Quakers because they have no professional ministry. He dabbles in psychiatry and thinks he has looked through the professional minister.

I would like to have him talk to a group of preachers sometime. Like all realists he barely escapes the kind of cynicism which destroys wholesome human relations. But he does escape it and is not at all bitter in his analysis of human nature. That is why his reaction to the ministry disquiets me. He has his hands on considerable truth.

There is something very artificial about the professional ministry. When religion deals with magic the professional priests can dispense the magic and be quite happy. But when religion becomes a search for all of life's highest values there is something incongruous about making your living in the business of helping people to discover and develop these values. I don't think this consideration invalidates the ministry as a profession. In a day of specialists and experts there ought to be room for a specialist in moral and spiritual values. But think of commanding a large salary because you are a better preacher than someone else! Isn't that putting a market value on the ability of a man to help people find God? Fortunately it is the rhetorical rather than the spiritual gift that usually creates the different prices in the preacher market.

142

1928

Passing one of our big churches today I ran across this significant slogan, calculated to impress the passing wayfarer: "We Will Go Out of Business. When? When Every Man in Detroit Has Been Won to Christ." Of course it is just a slogan and not to be taken too seriously, but the whole weakness of Protestantism is in it. Here we are living in a complex world in which thousands who have been "won to Christ" haven't the slightest notion how to live a happy life or how to live together with other people without making each other miserable.

Yet the church goes about the business of winning people to Christ—that is, pulling them through some kind of emotional or social experience in which they are made to commit themselves, or in which they really do commit themselves, to the good life as it is symbolized in Christ, and imagining that this is the end of the task. I do not say that such commitments do not have their value. But surely one must be very blind to live under the illusion that the desire or even the will to live a Christ-life is automatically fulfilled in present-day society or in any society.

The church which conceived that slogan is really better than the silly advertisement might lead one to suppose. I think people receive some light and leading there. Nevertheless, most of its energies go into the business of "winning others."

The saddest part about these highly evangelistic churches who put everything into the recruiting task is that they generally tempt those who are already "won" to imagine themselves perfect, or at least "saved." I know one lawyer in that church, and not a bad man either, who needs to be "won" to several ideas in the gospel of Christ about which he hasn't the faintest glimmer of light. But he is too sure of himself to get a new idea.

143

1928

Here is a minister making a confession in his weekly paper: "Last Sunday night," he writes, "I was at my worst and unfortunately there were many strangers in the audience. I tried, but I could not get the ball over the plate. I had taught a Sunday-school class, preached over the radio, gone out to dinner, entertained a guest at supper, met the —— committee and failed to get rest after Easter. I will try to do better next Sunday, so come then."

It is all very nice and humble, but there is an implication of professionalism in the whole thing that is appalling. The idea is that he didn't put on a good performance, "didn't get the ball over the plate." There you have the whole weakness of a professional ministry, striving each Sunday to make an interesting speech. It simply can't be denied that the business of furnishing inspiration twice each week, on a regular schedule, by a person who is paid to do just that and whose success is judged by the amount of "pep" he can concentrate in his homilies, is full of moral and spiritual dangers. To follow such a program without running into spiritual bankruptcy requires the resources of a saint.

1928

Arriving at —— today, I was put up at the luxurious home of a very charming potentate of the local pulpit. I was driven to my meeting in a big Packard car (a gift of the congregation, my host informed me) with a liveried chauffeur at the wheel. I don't think I would have reacted so strongly against this kind of life if I hadn't been reading Savotorelli's Life of St. Francis on the way down and was inclined to look at the world through the little brother's rather than my own eyes.

To object to this kind of luxury for ministers, and not voice the same objection in regard to the standards of living among laymen, may seem to involve us in a moral dualism. But I am no longer afraid of dualism. We might well have more of it. It will be long while before we can convince laymen of the spiritual implications in standards of living in a civilization which knows of no other way to give a man a sense of achievement than to let him advertise it by outward show. But ministers ought to know better.

Furthermore there is a moral peril in accepting the largess of men to whom you are trying to minister. It is not that they try to take conscious advantage of your sense of gratitude, but that such dependence upon their generosity creates a psychological hazard against honest presentation of the truth. Of course it is probably true that men who receive these excessive benefactions are usually too tame to need taming. Innocuous virtue is always more charming and more liable to prompt a generous affection than the kind which raises disquieting questions.

Then too, ministers who can preach the gospel of Jesus in our kind of civilization without making anyone uncomfortable deserve an automobile for the difficult feat. And they need one to compensate them for that lack of spiritual vitality which makes the performance of the feat possible. Most of these modern appurtenances are toys which appeal to childlike people. When we sacrifice the adventure of trying to maintain an inner moral integrity, we are bound to seek for compensating thrills and to find them in our mechanical toys.

But all this may be the voice of jealousy. I love nothing so much in the realm of physical pleasure as the sense of power which comes from "stepping on the gas" when ensconced in a big car.

1928

Spoke today at the Jewish temple in ——. The more I make contact with the Jews the more I am impressed with the superior sensitiveness of the Jewish conscience in social problems. I have yet to find a Christian men's group that can surpass and few to equal the intelligent interest of a Hebrew group in the economic and social issues of the day. I do not say that there is not in privileged Jewish groups more moral complacency than is compatible with their avowed devotion to the Hebrew prophets, but there is at least a considerable appreciation of the genius of prophetic religion and some honest effort to apply the prophetic ideal to life.

I am afraid that the individualistic traditions of Protestantism, and perhaps also the strong Pauline strain in Protestant theology, have obscured the social implications of Jesus' gospel much more than is the case in Jewish religion. I am not sure that the religious life in the Jewish temple is always as obviously vital as it is in many Christian churches, but what there is of it seems to me to be directed much more astutely, at least from the social viewpoint, than in our groups.

The Jews are after all a messianic people, and they have never escaped the influence of their messianic, or if you will, their utopian dreams. The glory of their religion is that they are really not thinking so much of "salvation" as of a saved society.

1928

The way Mrs. —— bears her pains and awaits her ultimate and certain dissolution with childlike faith and inner serenity is an achievement which philosophers might well envy. I declare that there is a quality in the lives of unschooled people, if they have made good use of the school of life and pain, which wins my admiration much more than anything you can find in effete circles. There is less of that whining rebellion against life's fortunes, less morbid introspection and more faith in the goodness of God. And that faith is, whatever the little cynics may say, really ultimate wisdom.

Mrs. —— has had a hard life, raised a large family under great difficulties, is revered by her children, respected by her friends, and she has learned to view the difficult future with quiet courage as she surveys the painful and yet happy past with sincere gratitude. She thanks me for praying with her and imagines that I am doing her a favor to come to see her. But I really come for selfish reasons—because I leave that home with a more radiant faith of my own. My confidence in both man and God is strengthened.

It is the quality in that woman's life that seems to me to be dissipated in the modern day, for all our progress. Perhaps we will work out something comparable to it some day in a highly disciplined culture. But as we lose the moral fibre of the generation of pioneers and wait for the discipline of a generation of moral aristocracy, it is ordained that we should wander through this present world where life is too comfortable to have the tragic nobility which our fathers had and too chaotic to disclose the charms which come from a great cultural and moral tradition.

1928

Here is a pastor singing himself to sleep. He writes: "Business men who attend church have sense enough to go out and run their business as Christians without the minister interfering with the technique. Many of the most spiritual and influential ministers I know never deal directly with politics, industry or reform." It is true of course that a minister can't offer expert advice on the detailed application of Christian principles to specific fields. But neither can he assume that principles get themselves automatically applied in the world's complexities.

One of the most fruitful sources of self-deception in the ministry is the proclamation of great ideals and principles without any clue to their relation to the controversial issues of the day. The minister feels very heroic in uttering the ideals because he knows that some rather dangerous immediate consequences are involved in their application. But he doesn't make the application clear, and those who hear his words are either unable to see the immediate issue involved or they are unconsciously grateful to the preacher for not belaboring a contemporaneous issue which they know to be involved but would rather not face.

I have myself too frequently avoided the specific application of general principles to controversial situations to be able to deny what really goes on in the mind of the preacher when he is doing this. I don't think I have always avoided it, and when I haven't I have invariably gotten into some difficulty. Nobody challenges principles.

Like the diplomats, the average man always accepts the gospel "in principle," and then proceeds to emasculate it by a thousand reservations. I know we can't be expert on every technical problem involved in modern industrial and national civilization. But the ministers who make a virtue of their pious generalities are either self-deceived or conscious deceivers.

1928

I am glad to hear of the new honors which have come to Bishop M——. He seems to me to be the most glorious figure in American church life. To have a philosopher, prophet and statesman all rolled into one, and to have that one achieve a peculiar eminence in our religious life is a clear illustration of how the richest character is achieved when various, seemingly incompatible, tendencies and functions are fused in one personality.

Philosophers are not usually prophets. They are too reasonable and circumspect to create or preserve the prophetic vision. The wise man is too capable of balancing the truth, to which he ought to be loyal, with some other truth with which it is in conflict. Thus he involves himself in the endless antinomies of intellectualism.

This philosopher is enough of a Christian to escape this fate. But he has another hazard to overcome; for he is a statesman. For years he has carried heavy responsibilities as a church leader; and it is always more difficult for a responsible leader, tied to an organization, to speak bravely than an irresponsible prophet. Yet he has accomplished it. Here is a vindication of the power of the Christian life. Here is a Thomas Aquinas and an Innocent III and something of a Francis all under one hat. He is not as much of an absolutist as Francis, of course; and his power is not as great as that of Innocent. But his learning would compare favorably with that of Aquinas, and like the great medieval philosopher, he has combined the study of metaphysics with that of social economy.

Strange that while I am so critical of bishops my greatest hero should be a bishop and that, while I call myself an anti-puritan, that hero should be a Methodist bishop. So life defies our prejudices and generalizations.

1928

I always thought I was a fairly brutal realist, but I am beginning to suspect that the whole thing is a pose to hide the sentimental preacher. At any rate now that the time has come to sever my connections with the church I find it almost impossible to take the step. There is nothing quite like the pastoral relationship. I would almost be willing to sacrifice the future for the sake of staying here and watching the lovely little kiddies grow up, and see the young boys and girls that I have confirmed blossoming into manhood and womanhood. There must be something bogus about me. Here I have been preaching the gospel for thirteen years and crying, "Woe unto you if all men speak well of you," and yet I leave without a serious controversy in the whole thirteen years.

It is almost impossible to be sane and Christian at the same time, and on the whole I have been more sane than Christian. I have said what I believe, but in my creed the divine madness of a gospel of love is qualified by considerations of moderation which I have called Aristotelian, but which an unfriendly critic might call opportunistic. I have made these qualifications because it seems to me that without them the Christian ethic degenerates into asceticism and becomes useless for any direction of the affairs of a larger society.

I do not say that some one ought not to undertake an ascetic revolt against civilization. Certainly there would be a peace in it which no one can find who tries to adapt the principles of love to a civilization built upon the drive of power and greed. Those of us who make adjustments between the absolute ideal of our devotion and the necessities of the immediate situation lack peace, because we can never be sure that we have our adjustment at the right place.

Every moral position which has left the absolute basis is in danger of becoming a rationalization of some selfish purpose. I am not unconscious of the fact that my tendency to criticise

151

others so severely for their alleged rationalizations and hypocrisies springs from my own sense of insecurity.

I persevere in the effort to combine the ethic of Jesus with what might be called Greek caution because I see no great gain in ascetic experiments. I might claim for such a strategy the full authority of the gospel except that it seems to me more likely to avoid dishonesty if one admits that the principle of love is not qualified in the gospel and that it must be qualified in other than the most intimate human associations. When one deals with the affairs of a civilization, one is trying to make the principle of love effective as far as possible, but one cannot escape the conclusion that society as such is brutal, and that the Christian principle may never be more than a leaven in it.

There has never been a time when I have not been really happy in the relationships of the parish ministry. The church can really be a community of love and can give one new confidence in the efficacy of the principles of brotherhood outside of the family relation. The questions and qualms of conscience arise when one measures the church in its relationships to society, particularly to the facts of modern industry. It is at this point where it seems to me that we had better admit failure than to claim any victory. The admission of failure may yet lead to some kind of triumph, while any premature confidence in the victory of a Christian ethic will merely obfuscate the conscience.

Modern industry, particularly American industry, is not Christian. The economic forces which move it are hardly qualified at a single point by really ethical considerations. If, while it is in the flush of its early triumphs, it may seem impossible to bring it under the restraint of moral law, it may strengthen faith to know that life without law destroys itself. If the church can do nothing else, it can bear witness to the truth until such a day as bitter experience will force a recalcitrant civilization to a humility which it does not now possess.

LaVergne, TN USA
13 January 2010
169849LV00001B/1/A

BEACON STREET GIRLS

This book belongs to:

VERITAS AMICITIA GAUDIUM
truth friendship fun!

Be sure to read all of our books:

BOOK 1 - worst enemies/best friends

BOOK 2 - bad news/good news

BOOK 3 - letters from the heart

BOOK 4 - out of bounds

BOOK 5 - promises, promises

BOOK 6 - lake rescue

BOOK 7 - freaked out

BOOK 8 - lucky charm

BOOK 9 - fashion frenzy

BOOK 10 - just kidding

BOOK 11 - ghost town

BOOK 12 - time's up

BOOK 13 - green algae and bubble gum wars

BOOK 14 - crush alert

BSG Special Adventure Books:

charlotte in paris

maeve on the red carpet

freestyle with avery

katani's jamaican holiday

isabel's texas two-step

Coming Soon:

BOOK 15 - the great scavenger hunt

SPECIAL ADVENTURE - ready! set! hawaii!

Maeve on the Red Carpet

BY
ANNIE BRYANT

mix
aladdin

ALADDIN MIX

NEW YORK   LONDON   TORONTO   SYDNEY

We'd like to thank the New York Film Academy team for their invaluable information about the world of acting and filmmaking, and for helping to make *Maeve on the Red Carpet* a reality. A special thank-you to Chris, David, Eylem, and Jerry for their input on what it's like to go to film and acting camp, and their feedback on the book. Thanks also to the NYFA students who let us sit in on their classes.

ALADDIN MIX

Simon & Schuster Children's Publishing Division

1230 Avenue of the Americas, New York, NY 10020

Designed by Dina Barsky

The text of this book was set in Palatino Linotype.

Photos courtesy: The New York Film Academy Tween Workshops

Manufactured in the United States of America

First Aladdin MIX edition October 2009

2 4 6 8 10 9 7 5 3 1

Library of Congress Control Number 2008942851

ISBN: 978-1-4169-6432-2

Who's Who

BSG

Katani Summers
a.k.a. Kgirl . . . Katani has a strong fashion sense and business savvy. She is stylish, loyal & cool.

Avery Madden
Avery is passionate about all sports and animal rights. She is energetic, optimistic & outspoken.

Charlotte Ramsey
A self-acknowledged "klutz" and an aspiring writer, Charlotte is all too familiar with being the new kid in town. She is intelligent, worldly & curious.

Isabel Martinez
Her ambition is to be an artist. She was the last to join the Beacon Street Girls. She is artistic, sensitive & kind.

Maeve Kaplan-Taylor
Maeve wants to be a movie star. Bubbly and upbeat, she wears her heart on her sleeve. She is entertaining, friendly & fun.

Ms. Razzberry Pink
The stylishly pink proprietor of the "Think Pink" boutique is chic, gracious & charming.

Marty
The adopted best dog friend of the Beacon Street Girls is feisty, cuddly & suave.

Happy Lucky Thingy and alter ego Mad Nasty Thingy
Marty's favorite chew toy, it is known to reveal its alter ego when shaken too roughly. He is most often happy.

more on beaconstreetgirls.com

Lights . . . camera . . . action!

Part One
Movie Wishes and
Hollywood Dreams

1

Fortune Cookie Fabulous

*M*y personal stretch limo, very pink of course, and decked out in plushy velvet seats, is pulling up to the crowd of fans and photographers outside the theater. Lights, camera, action! The red carpet is rolled out before me . . . little moi! Be still my heart! A white-gloved hand taps on my window—it's my cue. Someone very handsome opens the door. I step out to the "click, click, click" of cameras. The fans are screaming. They hope for a smile, a wave, or an autograph. Naturally, I oblige. Are you kidding? I LIVE for this moment! "Maeve, who are you wearing?" "Are the rumors true? Is Maevonardo finally tying the knot?" "Maeve, are you really selling your mansion in Malibu?" "Smile, Maeve!" "Maeve, is it true you've been asked to play the role of Eliza Doolittle in the remake of My Fair Lady?"*

"Maeve, why are you drawing a gigantic pink marshmallow?" asked my brainiac little brother, Sam. I was sitting at the kitchen table, right in the middle of my all-time fave movie star fantasy . . . until Sam's rude question popped it.

I threw my arms over my notebook. "It's NOT a marshmallow, Sam. I'm *trying* to design the perfect dress for my future movie premiere. If I'm going to be a famous star, I have to totally look the part . . . *helloooo*?"

Sam leaned in again. "Well you sorta look more like a pink s'more than a famous star. Sorry." He smiled sweetly. How could someone so adorable be so annoying?

Obviously, the picture was supposed to be me. I mean, the girl in it had long red curls like me. I thought my dress looked just faaaaabulous. It was a flapper dress, vintage style. (The flappers were the "it girls" of the 1920s who wore lots of pearls with short, loose dresses — awesome for dancing in!) *Classic vintage is so timeless!* I sighed dreamily.

But when I looked down, I saw the terrible, terrible truth — Sam was right. My design was definitely coming out more like a pink s'more than a red carpet–worthy outfit. I chewed the end of my pen. "Okay, Sam, I know. How about when I'm famous, I'll just make Katani my personal stylist!" I clapped my hands together. "Voilà. Problem solved." Katani is the fashionista of the BSG. The BSG stands for the Beacon Street Girls. It's kind of like a best friends club. There are five of us in all — Avery, Charlotte, Isabel, Katani, and *moi* — Maeve Kaplan-Taylor.

"I told you it looked funny." Sam pretended to start walking away and then dropped to the floor. "Stealth mission!" he shouted and slithered toward me on his elbows.

He reminded me of a pygmy copperhead snake. (I saw a picture of one in my science book once.)

"Eeew! Sam!" I shrieked. "Get *off* the kitchen floor! That's so gross."

Sam's life goal—so far—was to be an Army dude. In fact, he was pretty much obsessed. I thought it was kind of weird for a seven-year-old, but it seemed like adults thought it was cute or something. Whenever Sam wore his Army camouflage and crawled behind the furniture, my mom would say, "Don't you just love that little cutie?" Of course I loved that little cutie, but seriously, I'd had about all the Army stuff I could handle.

Just then, I heard a "bonk" from underneath the table. A tiny hand shot up and snatched my notebook. "Mission accomplished!" Sam cried. "Headquarters, alert! Headquarters, alert! The eagle has landed! Repeat, the eagle has landed!"

"Sam! That's mine! Give it *back*!" My little brother was really good at school and pretending to be an Army guy, but his best talent was definitely being a major tease. I grabbed my notebook and pulled it as hard as I could. Sam pulled too. "I *said* give it back . . ." We were both yanking with all our might, when suddenly the front door burst open.

"Mom!" Sam exclaimed, letting go of the notebook.

"Saaaaam!" I went flying backward and landed flat on the kitchen floor, hugging the notebook to my chest. "Ooof. Thanks for that."

"Maeve, Sam, what is going on here?" Mom's hood

was over her head and her tan coat was soaked with slushy snow. She was holding a huge brown bag with a tinier plastic bag of dressings and soy sauce stapled to the top. That could only mean one thing.

"Chinese food!" I cried. "Wow, Mom, thanks!"

"Whoa, Mom. You rock." Sam beamed at Mom and she beamed right back. Takeout Chinese was an instant hit, as everyone in the Kaplan-Taylor household *loved* Chinese food. Mom was a chicken lo mein person, the scallion pancakes were my personal fave, and Sam liked the moo shu pork. It was perfect. I just loved it when everyone agreed!

Mom plopped the bag down and pulled down her hood. I blinked. For a split second, I barely recognized her. "Oh my gosh! Mom, your hair!" I gasped.

Mom had gotten her shoulder-length brown hair cut into a wispy chin-length bob. And . . . it had blond streaks in it! Mom looked at me with worried eyes and glanced at her reflection in the hallway mirror.

"I know. I went a little crazy today at the salon. I just needed a change. Does it look terrible?"

I almost laughed out loud. I'd never seen my mom nervous about her hair before. In fact, as the redheaded, curly-haired drama queen of the family, I was always the one asking for hair feedback. (Believe me, one wrong move and it was frizz city.) But now that Mom's new look was sinking in, I had to admit—I really did like it.

"Terrible? Are you kidding me? It's totally *stunning*! *Très* retro, Mom!" I wasn't sure what "*très* retro" meant exactly, but I knew it was a compliment. I think. I picked it up from a fashion article in my latest *Teen Beat* magazine.

Mom laughed and ruffled her new short 'do as she primped in the mirror.

"I think you look beautiful *all the time*, Mom," Sam added, probably trying to out-compliment me. Typical! I opened my mouth to say something not-so-nice to Sam, but then I decided it was a much better idea to fill it with something delish instead.

"Scallion pancakes, please!" I reached into the bag, grabbed the carton, took a deep breath, and then—a giant bite. *Mmm, mmm.* Crispy on the outside, soft in the middle, and crunchy all around. *Perfecto!*

"Ah, ah, ah, young lady. Plate, please . . . and chopsticks?" Mom pointed at me and Sam.

"Mom . . . there's no time for chopsticks. Please pass the forks!" Sam declared between bites. He was totally right. Both of us were already munching away. We were waaaay past the point of chopsticks.

"Yikes," Mom shook her head *and* her newly cropped hair. "You'd think you two were raised in a barn."

"Actually, I was raised right above a very famous theater. Hello? Does the Movie House ring a bell? And I happen to have fabulous manners, thank *you*. I mean, I'll need them for the Oscars some day."

"Oh, is that a fact?" Mom hurried us along to the table. "Well then, when you're at the Oscars I suggest you chew with your mouth closed. And will you say hi to George Clooney for me?"

I giggled. "Okay." George Clooney was my mom's favorite actor.

As much as I loved the scallion pancakes and everything, the part of Chinese takeout I *really* looked forward to was dessert. It was the most exciting, because dessert meant fortune cookies, and fortune cookies meant reading FORTUNES. I saved my favorite fortune ever in my jewelry box. I *had* to. It said, *"You are destined to see your name in lights."* Then—you won't believe this—the next day I got the lead role in the school play! Totally weird, right?

I grabbed a cookie and squeezed my eyes shut. "Dear goddess of fabulousness, please let my fortune be fabulous," I whispered to myself. Maybe it would have to do with romance . . . or something about becoming a huge movie star. Either one was fine by me. I cracked the cookie in two and pulled out the strip of paper inside.

"AHEM," I coughed. I loved reading out loud and performing, but I had to make sure I got all the words right first. I have this thing called dyslexia—it's a learning disability—oops, I mean learning challenge—and can be a little annoying. Even though I know I'm pretty smart, reading, writing, and spelling can be hard for me. It especially doesn't help that Sam is a like a mini-genius in school. I concentrated very hard on the fortune, hoping that I'd get the words perfect on the first try.

I took a deep breath. *"New and exciting things will be happening in your future."* I groaned. "Oh *no*. That could mean anything. I wanted to hear *real news*, like: 'You are most definitely going to be a major star.'"

"Now, Maeve, new and exciting things . . . that's a fun one!" Mom was trying to be supportive, but I still felt tragically disappointed.

"Mom, puhleeease. What do I have to look forward to—a long school vacation stuck at home doing *nothing*. I have one word for you: BORING." I was still feeling sorry for myself because I was the only one of the BSG *not* doing something fun over winter break. In two weeks, all my friends would be off on their special vacations. Avery was going snowboarding in Colorado, Katani was staying with her cousin in New York City and taking fashion design classes, Charlotte was going on a trip to Montreal with her dad, and Isabel was visiting her father in Detroit. I would officially be the only BSG left here in boring, old Boston. Not exactly the life of a future movie star.

Even my little brother had cool plans . . . at least, cool for *him*. Grandpa was taking Sam on a tour of Gettysburg, Pennsylvania, where this big Civil War battle was fought. Sam was beyond excited. All week he'd been running around the house yelling, "Four score and seven years ago . . . CHARGE!" Whatever *that* was supposed to mean.

My fortune probably *should've* said "Danger, Maeve Kaplan-Taylor! Outlook B-O-R-I-N-G, *boring*!" Why, *oh why*, was life so unfair?

I turned to Sam. "What does *your* fortune say?"

Sam rubbed his tummy. "Don't know. I think I ate the paper." I made a face at him. "Just kidding!" He grinned. Sam opened his mouth—full of half-eaten cookie. Ugh. Boys were soooo rude. "My fortune said I will be famous beyond my wildest dreams. Score!" Sam pumped his fist in the air and ran out of the room.

"*Soooo* unfair," I moaned, burying my head on the kitchen table.

Just then, a gust of wind blasted into the kitchen. Who was standing like an icicle in the doorway but . . . Dad, with a huge grin on his face.

"Ross!" Mom leapt up from the table immediately. "What are you doing here?" She twirled her new short, blond hair. My parents separated a few months ago and they still acted kind of funny when they were around each other. Right now, Mom was trying to look annoyed that Dad had dropped in unexpectedly but I could tell she secretly was happy about it. She was using her *fake*-angry voice—the same one she used on me when I sang show tunes too loudly in my room.

"Carol, I have the most exciting news." My dad threw his arms in the air. "You're going to have to sit down. You too, Maeve."

I laughed. "But I'm already sitting!" Dad could be way over-dramatic about good news . . . just like me.

"Okay. I have two words for you," Dad paused for dramatic effect. "*Film camp*."

"Film camp?" Mom and I repeated at the same time.

Dad nodded, looking even more goofy and excited. "A film camp! At the Movie House!"

"Oh!" I cried and sprang out of my chair to give Dad a hug. "It's brilliant!" I didn't know what film camp meant exactly, but I knew it had to do with making movies. And if it had to do with making movies, I would definitely *love it*.

But Mom didn't look as excited. "Ross . . ." She shook her head and said in a quiet voice, "We can't afford—I mean, you can't afford—I mean . . . *film camp?*"

"Carol, you are absolutely right." Dad smiled. *"We* can't afford to run a film camp. But the New York Film Academy can!"

"A film camp! At the Movie House!
It's brilliant!"

For a second my heart nearly stopped in my chest. What was going on? Why was Dad still smiling?

Then his smile got *even wider*. "And . . . there's more. Carol, have you ever heard of Walter Von Krupcake? As in Krupcake's Pies and Cakes Incorporated? As in . . . the Krupcake King himself?"

"Wait a minute, Ross. *You know* the Krupcake King?" Mom gasped.

"Mom! *Everybody* knows the Krupcake King!" I exclaimed. "He's on TV, like, all the time." I cleared my throat, pretended to put on a giant whipped cream crown—like the Krupcake King wore in his commercials —and recited in a proper voice, "It's the krup that makes a cake for a king."

Dad grinned and his eyes widened. "Exactly! Wow, Maeve, very good."

"Thanks." I shrugged. I had to admit, I was pretty famous for my impressions.

Dad went on, "Carol, I don't just *know* the Krupcake King . . . you're looking at his new business partner! The New York Film Academy wanted to run a film camp here in Boston, but they needed a top-notch facility. Walter Von Krupcake—who has Hollywood connections and still lives in Boston—has offered to make the Movie House a little . . . you know . . ."

"Cooler?" Sam piped.

Dad patted Sam on the head. "Thanks for that, son. The theater just needs a little sprucing up to accommodate a real film camp. And Mr. Von Krupcake is going to make the facility more accessible for people with disabilities . . . something I've been saving to do for the Movie House for a while now."

Mom looked suspicious. She was always very careful not to get her hopes up. She liked to get all the facts straight first. "Spruce up the Movie House? In two weeks? Ross, don't you think that's a little . . . unrealistic?"

Dad shrugged. "That's what I thought too. But Walter Von Krupcake assured me that it could be done. He's bringing in his crew tomorrow to get started." Dad's eyes were wide. "You know, sometimes you just get lucky."

"But that's . . . that's . . . *huge* . . ." I could see Mom's mouth start to turn into a smile, then stop. "Wait. How are you going to get the equipment, Ross?"

"All provided courtesy of the New York Film Academy." Dad grinned.

"And who's going to sign up for this film camp on such short notice?"

"Ah-ha, Carol, I'm glad you asked. Mr. Von Krupcake says he already has a list of kids from all over Massachusetts. Apparently our wonderful city of Brookline has been crying out for a film camp for a long time!" Dad's voice was full of excitement.

Sam and I giggled. My drama genes definitely came from my dad.

"Ross, that's just wonderful!" Mom said, sounding a little surprised to hear the words coming out of her mouth.

"It's absolutely *fantabulous*!" I agreed. "Wait, this *does* mean I get to go to film camp . . . right?"

Dad glanced at Mom. "Well, I don't know . . . you already have so much on your plate, Maeve. Carol, what do you think?"

Before Mom had a chance to answer, the words started spilling out of my mouth. "Dad, are you kidding me? Movies are my life—my DREAM! And now there's going to be a film camp downstairs in our very own Movie House and you're—"

"Relax, Maeve, I *was* kidding. Of course you can go."

I breathed a sigh of relief. "Hey, no kidding about movies, remember?"

Dad laughed. "I'm sorry. How could I forget?"

I gave Mom and Dad a hug. "Listen, Dad, do you think I can be the star of the film? No, don't tell me. I know I have to audition like everybody else. But maybe if you could put in a good word for me . . ."

Dad made a stressed-out face.

"Completely kidding! Oops!" I covered my mouth, realizing that I just broke my own rule.

"Well, kidding aside, the Film Academy is going to be in charge of casting decisions," Dad said. "Which is a good thing." He looked at Mom. "Turns out, the Krupcake King has a princess."

"Ross . . ." Mom began.

"Hey! I know who you mean!" I exclaimed. "That's that little blond girl who plays Princess Maddiecake in the commercial with the Krupcake King! She's sooooo cute. At the end of the commercial she always says, 'Remember Maddiecakes are chock full of Vitamin L . . . for Love!' Oh, I *adore* her!"

"Well that Pastry Princess is coming to camp. She's your age, Maeve, and apparently she wants to break into the world of film now."

"Ross, I hope this doesn't mean what I think it does . . ." Mom warned. "No special treatment . . ."

I looked back and forth between Mom and Dad.

Dad laughed, getting rid of any nervousness I was starting to feel. "No, Carol. I told you . . . the New York Film Academy is completely in charge of the camp, and they're probably going to have an *ensemble* cast." I knew what ensemble was—a group of stars instead of one big lead. Dad continued, "Maeve, you're a very talented actress. I'm sure you'll have nothing to worry about."

"I'm sure too." I laughed. It was very important to have confidence if you were going to be an actress. *Dream big* was what I always reminded myself.

"We're going to have a lot of work to do these next few weeks, kiddo," Dad told me. I kinda sorta had a feeling I was going to be his number-one helper. "I hope you're not afraid to get your hands dirty," he added.

I looked at my hands and faked a terrified face. Last night I painted my nails and they looked truly smashing. It was called "Sparkly Seashell Pink." (I know—redheads are supposed to avoid pink like the plague, but I was born loving pink. I mean, it's just what happened to me.) Plus, I had just bought some new pink bracelets from Think Pink—my main pink shopping headquarters—last weekend. I bit my lip and glanced at Dad. "Do I *have to* get my hands dirty?"

Dad and Mom looked at each other and at the same time answered, "YES."

"Look at it this way," Mom said. "Maybe your fortune

cookie was right . . . there are new and exciting things happening in your future."

"Starting with cleaning the Movie House bright and early tomorrow," Dad chimed in. "The camp will be bringing in their equipment and I'd like the place to look spic and span."

I smiled. There was simply no use pretending. I knew I wouldn't mind the cleaning one bit if it meant FILM CAMP! Besides, with Sam off visiting Grandpa, I didn't have to worry about any little brother annoyingness getting between me and the stage! Plus, the thought of having the camp at our very own Movie House, was, well . . . "UNBELIEVABLE!" I shouted out loud.

Dad winked at Mom. "I told you so."

Mom shook her head but even she couldn't keep a wide grin off her face.

"Hey, Carol . . ." Dad said, giving Mom a funny look. "Did you do something to your hair?"

Lights, Camera, Action!

New York Film Academy Camp
is here!

WHERE: THE MOVIE HOUSE IN BROOKLINE
WHEN: SCHOOL VACATION WEEK

Learn to tell a story with moving images.

Campers will learn:
Directing
Writing
Editing
Cinematography
Production
Acting for film

Special Bonus: Artemia Aaron—famous Hollywood Director of *Kung Fu Crazy*— will be directing the camp.

CHAPTER

2

Close Encounter
with the Rich and Famous

G ee, Maeve, we always knew we'd see your *name* in lights . . . but this is *craazzy*! What's going on?"

"Huh?" I popped up from the nest of wires I was untangling in the back corner of the Movie House and tripped right away. "Oof," I moaned, rubbing my knee. I looked up to see Avery gazing over at me with a puzzled look on her face. Behind her were my three other very best friends in the world—Katani, Isabel, and Charlotte. I felt my face break into a huge smile—I couldn't help it! Even though tomorrow all my friends would be leaving for their winter vacations and I'd be left here in Boston, totally and utterly BSG-less . . . I had film camp. If I didn't have Princess Maddiecake and film camp to look forward to, it would be the worst week of my life. . . . or one of the worst. Well, maybe not that bad, but staying at home with no friends would have been really depressing. Now my entire life had changed into a wonderful dream. I was going to be good friends with Princess Maddiecake . . . and be a star.

"Thanks for stopping by, guys!" I cried and reached out for a huge group hug. Isabel and Avery leaned in right away. Since Avery was a soccer superstar and Izzy loved her art, both of them were usually wearing something with grass stains or paint smears. Katani and Charlotte hung back though.

"Uh, Maeve, no offense, but this white jacket is sort of making its runway debut today and you're kind of . . . well . . ." Katani smiled apologetically.

Charlotte—who was wearing a light blue coat and looked particularly cute—put her hand over her mouth and giggled. "Absolutely filthy!" she said, turning pink. "Sorry, but I've never seen you quite so un-Maeve-like."

I blew a curl out of my eyes because my hands were way too dirty to touch my face (Mom always says not to if I want beautiful skin). I waved my arm in the air and did a half-spin. "Well you've never seen me totally inspired to clean! Can you believe this place?"

The girls took a long look around. The Movie House was nearing the end of its major sprucing-up project . . . but it definitely had a long way to go. Everything was covered with dust, and the new decorations were still in boxes. The New York Film Academy people were marching in with tons of equipment and leaving it around in random places. Personally, I wasn't sure how we were going to get everything in shape for camp on Monday, but Dad assured me that Mr. Von Krupcake knew exactly what he was doing.

"I'm excited to see what it looks like when we get back," Iz said sweetly.

"Me too!" added Katani. "I just love a good make-over." Her eyes sparkled.

"Same here!" I sighed. I was so exhausted I collapsed into one of the chairs in the auditorium. It was pretty dirty, but I was too, so I didn't even care.

At that moment the doors to the theater burst open, and in walked my dad followed by a round man in a pin-striped suit and a fedora hat with a dark red feather. I gasped and covered my mouth. Crown or no crown, I recognized him right away—it was Mr. Von Krupcake, the Krupcake King himself. I jabbed Avery to whisper this information quickly, but there was no time. Dad was so excited he was practically sprinting down the aisle, and chubby Mr. Von Krupcake was huffing and puffing to keep up.

"What do you think?" Dad asked.

"Amazing! This is a vast improvement from before," the Krupcake King declared, dabbing his sweaty brow with a hanky. "Ross, I am pleased as punch. The Movie House is turning out splendidly. And I feel like I had something to do with it."

"Uh . . . well, you did."

The man began laughing in a way that reminded me of jolly Old King Cole. He grabbed his belly, and the tip of his nose and both cheeks turned bright red. "I know. Supporting a great cause like the arts is so rewarding."

"He looks like he's a big fan of his own Krupcakes," murmured Avery. I gave her a nudge. No matter how funny he looked, Mr. Von Krupcake had done a lot for the Movie House. It wouldn't be nice to upset him.

"I still can't thank you enough." Dad ran a hand nervously through his curly, dark hair, then noticed us standing in the front corner of the theater. "Oh, and here are some very special VIPs I'd like you to meet." Dad led Mr. Von Krupcake down the aisle.

"Hello!" I said with a cheerful wave. I couldn't believe that we were actually getting to meet the Krupcake King. He looked a lot sillier on TV with his gigantic crown than in person.

"You are a dear!" Mr. Von Krupcake said and turned quickly back to Dad. "Wherever did you find such spirited youths to volunteer on such short notice?"

"Mr. Von Krupcake, I'd like you to meet my daughter, Maeve, and her best friends, Katani, Isabel, Charlotte, and Avery."

"Oh my . . . so which of you is Maeve, the aspiring ack-*tour*?" he asked, pronouncing "actor" with a dramatic theatrical accent. Mr. Von Krupcake searched our faces and then smiled. "Yes, of course. This one. Why I could tell by the way you carry yourself, my dear. I'm a very good judge of character." Mr. Von Krupcake rested a hand on Charlotte's head.

The girls and I exchanged looks that made it hard not

to laugh. Charlotte was the shyest BSG by far. She some-times liked to do magic shows, but when it came to acting, Charlotte was a total shrinking violet.

"I, I don't really act," Charlotte confessed.

The Krupcake King wasn't buying this explanation. "But you look so . . . so . . . like my own little Maddie," he sputtered, then said to Dad, "My Maddie's always ready for her closeup."

Charlotte shook her head. "Nope. I'm only dressed up because I'm on my way to dinner with my dad and Miss Pierce," she explained. "It's a little going away party before our trip to Montreal. And a thank-you to Miss Pierce for watching Marty." Miss Pierce was Charlotte's sweet old landlady, and Marty was the BSG's very-much-loved dog. We found Marty together—the poor little dude was an orphan, but he now lived with Charlotte. When Charlotte and her dad went away, Miss Pierce was more than happy to take care of Marty . . . and she could almost always count on one of the BSG dropping by to say hi. Except this time everyone was going away too. Well, everyone except me.

"I'm the ack-*tour*," I informed Mr. Von Krupcake as I tucked a frizzed-out curl behind my ear.

Mr. Von Krupcake's eyes widened. He looked like he was having a hard time believing that I was the drama queen. Then I caught a glimpse of myself in a prop mir-ror that was resting near the stage. Yikes! No wonder he couldn't believe it . . . I did not look anything like my usual glamorous self at all.

"I think I told you my daughter is going to be attending the camp," Dad added.

"Maeve, a pleasure. Of course you are the ack-*tour*. Your eyes have the gleam of one who has been bitten by the movie bug. And my, aren't you the little worker bee."

I exhaled and smiled, relieved that the universe was finally falling back into place. "I'm just so excited about film camp!"

Mr. Von Krupcake turned to Dad. "Oh, Ross, she's just precious. I can't wait until she meets my Maddie. Why, the two of them are really going to hit it off!"

"I can't wait!" I exclaimed, my face flushing with excitement. Imagine—me being best friends with the famous Krupcake Pastry Princess! I wondered what she'd be like. *Would we get to ride around Boston in the Krupcakes' stretch limo? Would we go to fancy galas? Would we—*

Suddenly my thoughts were interrupted by the sound of Avery coughing. Oh my goodness, I'd been so caught up with my Madeline Von Krupcake daydream that I totally forgot that my BSG BFFs were standing right there. *Make new friends, but keep the old* . . . I think that's how the expression went.

I looked at each of my friends and gave them a warm smile. "I'm really going to miss you guys," I assured them all. Film camp or no film camp, the BSG were my best forever friends.

Dad clapped his hands and switched directions. "Okay, so moving right along. Would you like to see backstage, Mr. . . . Walter?"

"It's just glorious, Walter!" sang a woman's voice. The Beacon Street Girls and I whipped our heads around to see who was speaking.

"There you are, my dear girl!" Mr. Von Krupcake boomed and ran to the stage. "Ross, it is my pleasure to introduce you to the one and only Artemia Aaron—film director extraordinaire."

Dad and I stared at each other. If we were cartoon characters, this would have been the part when our eyeballs bugged out of our heads and our tongues unrolled out of our mouths and hit the floor.

Standing in the center of the stage was none other than Artemia Aaron, the famous film director herself! There were butterflies in my stomach big-time! Avery and I looked at each other and squeezed our hands together. We both had been Artemia Aaron fans ever since we could remember. Her movie *Kung Fu Crazy* came out last fall, and it was the coolest! Seriously, it had everything from hip hop dancing, to amazing costumes, to hardcore kung fu moves . . . the kind where they do kung fu upside down on the ceiling. After *Kung Fu Crazy* stopped playing at the Movie House, Dad gave me the poster to put in my room. I considered it *inspirational*!

"I absolutely adore this theater, Walter!" Artemia announced. "You were right. This is going to be the perfect project for me."

Dad gulped. "Project?"

Artemia folded her arms and nodded. "Project. I'm working for the camp. I've signed on to direct this session!"

Dad gulped again. "Camp director?"

"Yes, Ross. Artemia and I have been dear friends since college. When I heard that she was taking some time off from L.A. and wanted a chance to see Boston, I knew this camp would be the perfect winter *project* for her. You know . . . a break from all that glitter and glamour. Of course the New York Film Academy was thrilled to have the director of *Kung Fu Crazy*. It was destiny!"

"I was the thrilled one, Mr. Taylor," she said to Dad. "This will finally give me the chance to spend some time with my son. He needs a break from Hollywood more than I do!" I glanced at the BSG. Artemia's son was Apollo Aaron, the famous child star. He was only a cute little nine-year-old in his biggest hit, *Home Unsupervised*. Apollo plays a little kid whose family accidentally leaves him in a big mansion alone when they go on vacation to Nepal. It was a really cool movie.

"He's going to love getting a chance to work on a film behind the scenes!" Artemia added, inspecting the theater with sparkling eyes. The picture she saw was something wonderful—I could tell. It was what we creative types called "vision."

Mr. Von Krupcake began chortling. (I love that word! My friend Charlotte, who is a major word nerd, used it once, and I made sure to make a note of it.) "So you've definitely signed on for this session?" he asked.

Artemia nodded enthusiastically. "Oh, yes, Walter, I'm *honored* to direct the camp."

Mr. Von Krupcake winked at Dad. "Well now, I think we're going to have a real success here."

Dad rubbed his temples and looked around the theater at the piles of lights, broken floorboards, and dusty, old props. "I think it's going to be amazing to have Artemia's expertise, but I have to admit, Walter, I'm a little worried about this Movie House. There's still a lot of work to be done."

Mr. Von Krupcake chuckled. "Don't worry about a thing, Ross. I told you, it's my pleasure to help out. Why, I've been coming to this theater since I was just a small boy."

I glanced at Avery, who covered her mouth. We both couldn't imagine Mr. Von Krupcake as ever being small . . .

"It's all very generous of you, Walter. I just feel a little funny accepting such . . . generosity," Dad confessed.

"Pish posh. Not another word." Mr. Von Krupcake put his arm around Dad's shoulder. "Trust me, Ross. This place is going to sparkle . . . Von Krupcake style. And I don't want to hear another word about it. Deal?"

Dad's face broke into a smile. He grabbed Mr. Von Krupcake's hand and shook it. "Deal." He got so excited, he did the same thing to Artemia! Poor Artemia probably wasn't used to this kind of "regular person" behavior (sooo un-Hollywood), because she looked shocked for a second. Then she started to laugh. I loooooved her laugh— it sounded like bells!

"Welcome to Boston, Ms. Aaron," Dad gasped. (I think he was kind of star-struck!) "I'm honored to have you here at the Movie House."

"And me too!" I added.

"Oh, this is my daughter, Maeve."

I stepped forward and held out my hand. But how embarrassing was this? My hand was actually shaking! I meant to tell her that I was going to be in the camp . . . AND that I was going to be an actress . . . but instead all that came out was "I loved *Kung Fu Crazy!*" Oops. Guess I was a little star-struck too.

But Artemia was Hollywood cool—one hundred percent. "Thank you so much. Your support means so much to me," she answered. Wow. For someone so glamorous she sure was nice! I adored her outfit too—from her big designer glasses to her white wool coat to her high-heeled black leather boots. Artemia's hair was dark red (another talented redhead!) and super-sleek in a chin-length bob. Too bad I could never get *mine* to look so chic. I could tell Katani, Ms. Fashionista, was totally impressed.

I opened my mouth to ask her a more mature question. Something that would show her a true future-starlet destined for big things, and not just another fan. But then Mr. Von Krupcake opened *his* mouth first.

"Now, Ross, how about we go somewhere and talk details," Mr. Von Krupcake said, squeezing Dad's shoulder.

Katani leaned over and whispered in my ear, "In the business world, 'details' means moo-lah!" Kgirl was totally the business-savvy BSG. She was going to be CEO of her very own fashion empire one day—we all just knew it.

Mr. Von Krupcake threw one arm over Artemia's shoulder and the other over my dad's. "I'll book my usual table at the Four Seasons," he said in a this-is-final type of voice and steered Dad and Artemia down the aisle.

"Sounds good!" I heard Dad say. As he was being escorted out by the very-round Krupcake King, Dad turned, looked over his shoulder, and gave me a goofy smile with a thumbs-up. "Lunch at the Four Seasons!" he mouthed, looking completely ecstatic.

The BSG and I giggled to each other. My dad could be too funny sometimes, especially when he acted like a kid trapped in an adult's body.

"Wow!" I breathed. "This is *TOO MUCH*! You guys, can you believe we actually met Artemia Aaron?"

"Met her? Girl, you're going to *work with her*!" Katani pointed out.

"Now I wish I wasn't going to Detroit! I'd love to help with set design," Isabel said. "Just think, I could make a flying kung fu bird." Isabel loved drawing birds—it was her passion.

"Yeah, Iz, that would've been so fun . . . but Detroit and your dad—that's too cool to pass up!" I tried to look very serious, but even using my very best acting skills I couldn't keep the smile off my face. "I'M WORKING WITH ARTEMIA AARON!" I shouted.

"I think Maeve is really going to miss us . . ." Avery joked, lightly punching my arm.

"I *will* miss you," I promised. I looked at each one of my best friends very seriously. Then I could feel it coming back—my uncontrollable smiling and laughing. "Just imagine! Hollywood stars . . . right here in Boston!"

Charlotte put her arm around my shoulder. "Maeve, I know stars . . ." she began. (Charlotte *did* know stars. She loved astronomy and telescopes and stuff.) "And you know what? You're already a star."

Katani, Avery, and Isabel nodded. Wow—did I have the most supportive friends ever, or what? Even though I loved that they all believed in me, I knew I wouldn't feel like a *real* star until I was in a *real* movie. And now . . . my dream was so close to coming true I could almost taste it.

CHAPTER
3

A Thinking Tiara

How *kind* of you to let me come," I recited, throwing a pink boa over my shoulders and batting my long eyelashes. I stood in front of the full-length mirror at Think Pink. "How *kind* of you to let me come!" I repeated, sounding so elegantly English! It was a line from the movie *My Fair Lady*, one of my all-time favorites.

"I didn't know Audrey Hepburn was going to be shopping here today!" Razzberry Pink, the proprietor of Think Pink, gushed. Audrey Hepburn was a classic Hollywood actress AND my idol (even though I didn't look anything like her—she had short, straight black hair and mine was red and curly). It was a total compliment that Ms. Pink recognized exactly who I was pretending to be.

"I'm looking for inspiration," I explained, carefully wrapping the soft magenta boa back on one of the pink mannequins. "I'm starting the New York Film Academy Camp tomorrow, and I can't think of any good movie ideas! I thought I'd try to get in touch with the Audrey in me."

"I see," Ms. Pink replied. She stood behind me and admired her own reflection. I admired her reflection too! She was, as usual, a burst of colorful pink rosiness—right to her hair, which was dyed bright pink. What I loved most about Ms. Pink was her motto—*surround yourself with what you love*. Guess what Ms. Pink loved? Obviously . . . *pink*. Oh, and her dog, the beauteous pink poodle and Marty's sweetheart, La Fanny.

"My brother, Sam, left to visit my grandpa this morning, so I thought it would be easy for me to come up with an idea at my house . . . but now that I *finally* have some peace and quiet . . ."

"Let me guess . . . the peace and quiet made it *harder* to think?" It was like Ms. Pink could read my mind.

"*So* much harder," I confessed. "It's so frustrating! I really want to impress Artemia Aaron tomorrow. Oh, this is horrible. I think I have ack-*tour*'s block."

Ms. Pink daintily adjusted her pink wool beret in the mirror and smiled. "I have an idea." She ran into the back room for a second and came back with both hands hidden behind her back.

"What is it?" I asked Razzberry, my voice shaking a little with excitement.

"Think pink!" Ms. Pink exclaimed and held up a sparkling pink tiara. "This is my own little treasure. I've had it forever, but haven't had the heart to sell it. I couldn't imagine *just anyone* taking it home."

"Oh it's beautiful!" I gasped. "I couldn't possibly . . . Thank you!"

Ms. Pink's smile got even wider. "I thought it could be your thinking cap."

I tucked the tiara into my red curls, loving how it made my hair sparkle. If Hollywood wasn't my destiny, maybe royalty was! "I love it," I breathed. "It'll definitely help me think of some good ideas!"

"*Beeeeeep! Beeeeeep!*"

Ms. Pink and I jumped at the sound of the loud horn. "Oh no!" I moaned. My mom was parked outside, and I could see Mom frantically leaning out the window and yelling something to me.

"What?" I shouted.

"You're LATE!" Mom yelled and tapped her watch. I glanced at my cell phone and saw that I'd missed four calls! All from Mom.

"Yikes! Matt!" I forgot about my math and science tutor. Total disaster city. I promised Mom I would remember this time. I snatched my backpack from the floor and threw on my coat. "Thanks for the, um, *thinking cap*, Ms. Pink!" I cried as I sprinted out of the store.

"You're welcome!" she called after me. "Let me know how it works out."

The icy air bit my nose the moment I stepped outside. Thank goodness Mom was parked right in front. "Brrrr!" I said as I snuggled into the front seat of the car.

"Maeve Kaplan-Taylor . . ." (I knew it was bad when Mom used my first AND last name.) "You have a lesson in . . . well . . . five MINUTES AGO. Where have you been? You were supposed to come straight home after school."

"I'm sorry! I'm sorry! I sorta kinda accidentally forgot."

Mom shook her head as we sped down Beacon Street. "Forgot? How could you forget? I've been calling you for the past twenty minutes! Why didn't you pick up your cell phone?"

"I sorta kinda accidentally put it on silent . . ."

"Silent?" Mom rolled her eyes. "Honestly, what's the point of getting your daughter a cell phone if she doesn't pick it up?"

I reached into my pocket, pulled out my little pink cell phone, and waved it in the air. "Because . . . it matches perfectly with my *new pink tiara*!" I shook my ringlets at Mom so she'd notice my newest accessory.

"Pink tiara . . ." Mom's frown slowly turned into a half-smile. "Maeve, I hate to break it to you, but you're not really a princess!"

"Then why do I *feel* like a princess?" I asked as I twirled my hair and stared out the car window at the stores whizzing by.

"You feel like a princess?" Mom glanced over at me like I'd absolutely lost my mind. "You're on your way to meet with your math tutor. How do you feel like a princess?"

I wedged my tiara snugly into my curls. "Well, first of all, I do have a totally dreamy math tutor . . . who *could* be my Prince Charming . . . maybe . . ." I giggled. My math tutor, Matt, went to Boston College. Because of the whole dyslexia thing, I had to work really hard in school, and having a tutor was pretty important. Even though I hated doing so much extra work, the fact that Matt was completely adorable and nice was definitely a bonus.

"Oh boy, here we go . . ." Mom said, shaking her head. "I don't know where your fascination with everything romantic comes from!"

"Mom, you know that it comes from the movies. And everybody knows that being a princess means having to keep annoying appointments even though all you want to do is have fun!"

Mom grinned. "Is that a fact?"

"Of course it is! Haven't you ever seen *Roman Holiday* with Audrey Hepburn and Gregory Peck? Audrey Hepburn plays Princess Ann—a princess who gets sick of having every minute of her life scheduled, and she runs away to have a holiday in Rome. Then Princess Ann meets an American reporter—that's Gregory Peck—and she doesn't tell him about her secret identity. But he discovers it anyway, and he takes her on a tour of Rome, and they go dancing, and ride around on mopeds, and fall in love, and oh, it's soooo romantic!" I sighed as the car turned onto our street.

"Well then, tell me this. Do princesses have to clean their rooms?" asked Mom.

I shook my head. I knew what this was leading up to.

"Are there any Vespas in Boston?" she asked.

"What's a Vespa?"

Mom looked smug. "That's what you call those 'mopeds' from the movie."

"Ha! So you *have* seen it!" I cried.

"Don't think that you and your dad are the only movie buffs in this family. It just so happens I also know a thing or two about the classics." She looked at me and winked. I forgot that before Mom and Dad separated, they used to watch movies together all the time. Especially when I was younger.

We stopped in front of our apartment building and I noticed there was already a car parked in the driveway. But it wasn't Matt's.

"Hey, speaking of Dad, what's he doing here?" I asked.

"Huh?" Mom said, just as shocked as I was.

There, sitting on the steps, were Dad and Sam, surrounded by two huge suitcases. I felt my stomach flip-flop. This was not good. Not good at all.

"And WHAT'S SAM DOING HERE?" I said louder, slamming the car door. So much for the peace and quiet.

Sam folded his arms. "Hey! You guys locked me out!" he grumbled.

Mom looked totally confused and stroked Sam's hair. "I'm sorry, sweetie. I didn't know you were going to be here." She glanced at Dad. "Ross? What's going on?"

"Slight change of plans," Dad said, ruffling Sam's hair. "We were halfway through Connecticut when my mother called. Grandpa's come down with the flu. Sam's going to have to do the Gettysburg trip another time."

"Nooooo . . . Sam *has* to go!" I blurted out. Suddenly all eyes were on me. "I mean, poor Grandpa . . ."

"Grandpa will be fine in about a week. Not that you were worried about THAT . . ." Dad raised his eyebrows.

"Yeah," Sam agreed. "It's so obvious, Maeve. You just don't want me around."

I suddenly felt bad that I'd been so mean. "No, Sam. It's just . . . this week is New York Film Academy Camp. And film camp is supposed to be my thing."

Mom unlocked the house and hoisted Sam's suitcase inside. "Film camp still IS your thing . . ." she assured me.

"Well, actually . . ." Dad interrupted.

"Ross?" Mom had a panicky look in her eyes.

"Dad?" I was a million times more panicky than Mom.

"I thought Sam might like to be an assistant to me," Dad said sheepishly.

"Yeah! I'm going to be a filmotographer!" Sam shouted.

"There's no such thing as a *filmotographer*," I informed my brother.

"There is now. And it's me. So there. I'm going to be the best filmotographer ever! *Lights, camera, action!*" Sam pretended to tape me as I followed Mom and Dad into the house.

"Daaaaaad! Are you serious?" I could hear the whininess in my voice but I just couldn't help it. Sam plus film camp would surely equal *absolute disaster*.

"I think Sam will be excellent at the technical elements. He's very good with computers. And Maeve, I'd appreciate it if you'd be a little supportive. Remember, Sam was really looking forward to his Gettysburg vacation. I'm sure this is very disappointing for him."

"No, it's not disappointing!" Sam continued to pretend taping me while I grabbed an Oreo from the cookie jar. "I'm going to be a filmotographer!"

"There's no such thing . . ." I mumbled again.

"Film history in the making"

"Maeve," Mom warned. "Be nice to your brother. And get your homework ready for Matt. He's *waiting* for you."

"Ugh! Now I really feel like Princess Ann!" I moaned. "Only I don't get to ride on a Vespa. Oh, and I'm totally *not* on a Roman Holiday."

"No, because you're in Boston," Sam noted. "But you can be on a Boston Holiday!"

"Yeah, and there's no such thing as a Boston Holiday—" I began . . . then suddenly I had a brilliant beyond brilliant idea. "Unless . . ."

"Unless what?" asked Sam.

"Hold on. No time to chat. I have my inspiration!" I cried and bolted out of the kitchen.

"Maeve!" Mom called. "Math. Tutor. Chop-chop. Matt's waiting in the dining room."

I knew that Mom was right, but how was I supposed to think about doing boring old math when I had the best movie idea in the history of the world? Okay, well at least in the history of Boston. Matt would just have to wait a few more minutes. Film history was in the making.

CHAPTER

4

Brides of Frankenstein Caught on Tape!

And then they'd go on the swan boats, and see New-bury Street, and Beacon Hill, and oh, the Wang Center, and the whole time the princess would have to keep her identity a secret! How fabulous does *that* sound?"

There was silence on the other end of the phone.

"Hellooooo?"

Finally, I heard Isabel sigh. "So wait. I don't get it. Does the cute guy *know* she's a princess or not?"

"Yeah, he knows. But she doesn't know he knows," I explained. I was holding the phone with my shoulder as I painted my nails—"Silver Star" was the name of the shade. How perfect for film camp!

"And does *she* know who *he* is?"

"Nope! She thinks he's just a mysterious stranger, but

really he's a kung fu fighting reporter who was sent on a secret mission to protect her! I think it'll be terribly romantic, don't you?"

"Yeah I guess. I'm just still confused about why they're kung fu fighting in Boston."

"Because kung fu is like totally Artemia Aaron's thing. And it's exciting! AND this is a *Boston* Holiday!"

"So does the princess know kung fu too?"

I paused. "Hmm . . . I still need to figure that part out."

"Knock knock," Mom interrupted, tapping on my already open door.

"Ooh, Iz, I gotta go. Miss you . . . have fun!" I closed my cell phone, careful not to smudge my wet nails. "Enter!" I said to Mom, in my royal-est and proper-est voice.

"Maeve, what on Earth are you wearing?"

"Excuse me. Don't you mean, Your Royal Highness Princess Sophia?" I joked. I was trying to get into character—that is, the character I made up. That character was Princess Sophia of Tazmundo. I was totally decked out in a long lavender nightgown with my pink tiara still in my hair. I'd been wearing it all night except for when I sat with Matt and did my absolutely annoying pre-algebra equations. I couldn't have Matt thinking I was babyish.

Mom folded her arms and shook her head. "You need your rest, young lady. Tomorrow's a big day!"

"I know. I know. Film camp in the morning. Destiny awaits!" I stared at my *Kung Fu Crazy* poster and felt shivers down my spine. "Hiiiiii-YAA!" I cried and did a sharp, serious kung fu kick.

"Now, wait a minute. Are you a princess or a kung fu fighter?" Mom asked.

"I'm both!" I replied. "Check it out." I spun around in a double kick and with all my might did a kung fu chop (or maybe it was a karate chop—I still wasn't sure) right in the middle of my dresser. As soon as my pinky hit the wood, I knew that I'd made a gigantic mistake. "OUCH!" I cried. ("Note to self: The desk is definitely stronger than my hand.")

"Okay, kung fu princess. Enough. You don't want start film camp in a cast."

I sucked on my sore pinky and nodded. Sometimes I got sort of carried away with my ideas. I ran over and gave Mom a light kiss the cheek. "Night, Mom."

"Goodnight, sweetie," Mom said. "Lights out in ten minutes, okay?"

I nodded but didn't say anything because my fingers hurt so much. Mom was right—it was really important to be as rested as possible for the first day of film camp. And I had to do my whole beauty regime *before* I could get my beauty sleep.

I grabbed a hair elastic and piled my curls on top of my head. My hair was so thick and crazy that it practically stood straight up. Actually, it was toppling a little. *The Leaning Tower of Hair*, I thought with a giggle. Talk about sight-seeing in Boston! "*And here she is now . . . Boston's own Maeve Kaplan-Taylor . . . and her Leaning Tower* of Hair. Let's have a big round of applause." Just as I bent to do my bow, Sam ran by my door, stuck his tongue out, and blew a huge raspberry. If I wasn't so tired I would have chased him down and sprayed him with perfume. He totally hated the smell of Pink Hearts, my favorite new spray.

But I had to put my hair in a silly 'do so I wouldn't get any goop on it. Well, not goop, really, but my sea algae mud mask. It sure felt like goop though! I took a huge scoop and smeared it aaaaall over my cheeks, nose, chin, and forehead. It looked soooo gross but it smelled absolutely divine! By the time I was done, the only spots that weren't slimy and green were my eyes and lips. Now my reflection was seriously ridiculous. I mean, I looked like a creature from a Dr. Seuss book.

First thing I did was put the music on. I had to get my favorite jam pumping ASAP—"Girl Authority Theme" by Girl Authority. Girl Authority was a group of girls my age from the Boston area, and they totally rocked out. *Talk about living the dream*, I sighed. I got up from my dresser and did a few yoga stretches to warm up. Then I started to practice my kung fu moves. After my little pinky accident, I definitely had some work to do.

My room was the perfect place for movie planning and really practicing anything. (As a true performer, practicing was very important to me.) Everything around me was pink, pink, pink, from my fluffy comforter to my feathery lamp. It is a known fact that pink is the color of inspiration. The first time Avery saw my room, she said it looked like a bottle of Pepto Bismol exploded over everything. But Katani said that even though it was waaaay too pink for her taste, at least it all matched. I didn't care what my friends thought. I *knew* my room was spectacular.

My walls were covered with movie posters—fabulous posters from the greatest movie classics ever. And the best part was they were free! Dad gave me tons of them from the Movie House. I had so many posters that I liked to switch them around depending on my mood. But *Breakfast at Tiffany's* always stayed right above my bed. I didn't have the heart to ever take that one down. Audrey Hepburn would always be at the top of my all-time favorite actresses list.

I stood in the center of my pink rug, took a deep yoga breath, and pronounced out loud, *"You . . . are a princess."* I stared at myself in my full-length mirror and had to try hard not to laugh. "A dazzlingly beautiful, kung fu fighting princess! Hiiiiii-YAAA!" I leaped up and did a double kick with both my hands slicing the air. I was starting to get way pumped up! "You cannot be defeated. No one is more powerful than the dazzlingly beautiful, kung fu fighting princess. Hiiiiii-YAAA!"

My heart was really pounding now. This was all part of my beauty regime. I loved dancing and moving around because it helped me burn off nervous energy. And dancing made me soooo happy. I mean, who wouldn't be happy singing and dancing?

"Hey, Nik and Sam," I called out to my guinea pigs. "Check out these moves! Hiiii-YAAA!" I did a quick spin-kick. I liked to change their names around a lot, depending on my favorite couple of the moment. Of course, Nik and Sam were actually two twin sister country western stars, and my guinea pigs were a boy and a girl, but I didn't think the little guys would mind.

Suddenly I heard a creaking noise . . . and it wasn't coming from the guinea pigs' cage! I turned around and nearly fainted when I saw a little black circle sticking through the crack of my door. It was a camera. And the person holding it was . . . *no way*!

"SAAAAAAM!" I hollered at the top of my lungs. "That thing better not be on!"

"Of course it's on! This stuff is funny." He barged into the room, pointing the camcorder right at me. "Welcome to the bedroom of the green slime monster," he spoke in a cartoon voice.

"Stop it! Get OUT!" I shrieked. "Seriously! Moooooom! Sam's teasing me. That thing better be turned off!" I screamed as I lurched toward him.

"The monster is very mean!" yelled Sam as he leapt backward toward the door.

I heard the sound of angry footsteps outside and in a few seconds Mom appeared in the door. When I saw her I instantly burst out laughing. Mom's face was covered with green slime too! Sam spun around and pointed the camera at her.

"Wow! The big bad mommy monster's here too!"

Mom didn't seem too happy about being taped either. "Turn it off, Sam. That's supposed to be for film camp."

I nodded. "Yeah! You're not supposed to play with that." If Sam broke one of those cameras we'd be in serious trouble.

"I have *permission*," Sam said in a braggy voice. "Dad wants me to tape the whooooole film camp. It's my job, remember? *I'm* the filmotographer."

"Mom!" I gasped.

"Honey, if your dad gave him the camera there really isn't anything I can do. But Sam, you have to respect your sister's privacy."

"That's right. Dad wants me to documentize *everything*." Sam held the camera close to my face, and I suspected he was zooming in on the green goopiness.

I reached my hand out to block the lens, just like I'd seen real celebs do when they were caught with no makeup coming out of the gym or something. "Errrr! I can't believe this! I'm not even famous yet and *already* I have to deal with paparazzi!"

Sam giggled. "The monster's getting angry. Maybe it's feeding time!" Sam spun around, going back and forth between Mom and me. If this was his idea of filming, his audience was going to be very dizzy!

"Sam, turn it off," Mom ordered. "I'd rather not make my film debut looking like Frankenstein's bride."

"Don't worry, Mom. You guys *both* look like Frankenstein's bride," Sam reminded her.

Sam kicked the air in one of his tae kwon do moves, so obviously making fun of me. Just because he had lessons once a week, he thought he was some kind of expert.

"Wait 'til I learn some serious kung fu moves from Artemia," I began. "Then you'll really—"

"—have something good to tape," Mom finished for me. Then she literally lifted Sam (which must have been kind of hard because he was going through a major growth spurt lately), plopped him down in the middle of the hallway, and firmly closed the door behind her.

"Hey!" I heard Sam object. "I'm working here!"

I took a makeup remover towel thingy and wiped the goop off my face. Now I knew how stars felt when their photos ended up on the cover of those tabloid magazines—caught! One thing was for sure—if I wanted to do well at film camp I was going to have to put in an A++ effort the whole time. Especially with Sam snooping around. *Well, if there's one girl who can do it, it has to be yours truly!* I thought with a smile. And plus, when everyone heard about my oh-so-incredible *Boston Holiday* idea, there'd be no question about who was the star of the show.

CHAPTER
5

Drama, Drama, Drama— and a Big Red Ribbon

Maeve, I'm leaving!" Mom hollered from the bottom of the stairs.

I burst out of the bathroom and started feeling a panicky tightness in my throat. "But, Mom, I'm not even *close* to ready!" I protested.

It was actually true. I had a hot curling iron in one hand and my toothbrush in the other. One half of my hair was twisted into banana-curl perfection and the other half looked like I'd just been through some kind of electric shock. There was no way I'd be ready to make a star-quality entrance at film camp . . . not *yet*.

"Pleeeease can I just have ten more minutes?" I begged. "I'll be your servant for life," I added, even though I knew that promise was never going to happen. Even if Mom *wanted* to hire me, I'd be the messiest servant ever.

"Maeve, I don't have ten more minutes to wait. I've got my Monday meeting this morning."

"The train is leaving! All aboard!" Sam announced from the hallway. *Err.* It was so unfair sometimes how boys could just throw on jeans and a shirt and be all set to go. Girls just didn't have it that easy. And for girls with super curly hair . . . well . . . *forget it*!

The plan for the first morning was for Mom to walk us downstairs to camp on her way to work so we could be in front of the Movie House with the rest of the campers. Since camp started at 9 a.m., and Mom had to be at work at 8:30 a.m., I'd end up being way early. That should have been the first clue that this plan was just plain-old not going to work. After all, I was Maeve Kaplan-Taylor . . . how was I supposed to show up at film camp bright and early when it was practically a part of my DNA to be fashionably late?

I grabbed my puff of frizz and gave Mom a look of total desperation. "This might just be the single most important day of my life," I informed her. "Please can I have just a teeny-weeny bit longer?"

Mom sighed. "All right, fine. I'll call your father and see if he wants to walk you in."

"Yessssss!" I breathed. I knew Dad would pull through. He was always a late-bird like me.

"Sam, would you like to wait here with your sister?" Mom asked.

I held my breath. After Sam's paparazzi attack the night before, I certainly did NOT want my little brother snooping around the bathroom with my hair in major rescue-911 mode.

"No way!" Sam exclaimed. "What if something exciting happens at the Movie House and I miss it . . . waiting for Mrs. Frankenstein?" I wanted to chase him, but I was on frizz patrol. (His monster routine was getting really annoying.) "I'd be the worst filmotographer in the world!"

I was going to point out that he was the *only* filmotographer in the world, but I bit my lip and decided not to say anything. Mom had an expression for that—"don't instigate." That meant—in Mom talk—don't give Sam any reason to start teasing me. For now, I was safe, and I wasn't going to push it!

"All right, your dad is on his way," Mom called, snapping her cell phone closed.

"Eek!" I squealed. "Now I really need to get going!"

I heard Sam mutter something but Mom quieted him down with an "Enough."

"Good luck today, sweetheart!" Mom called.

I felt lucky. "Thanks, Mom." The stage was where I felt confident. My hairball—on the other hand—well, that needed all the luck it could get. Thankfully if there was one thing I could count on Dad for it was running late. By the time he finally rang the doorbell I not only had my hair in tip-top form, but I even had time to put on a little blush and lip gloss, giving my face a healthy glow for the big morning.

"Okay, Dad, be honest . . . what do you think?" I

walked slowly down the stairs. I had selected my outfit the night before and I was going for "smashing" . . . the way Artemia looked in the Movie House the other day. I was wearing a new, crisp white blouse with a black velvet blazer. My pants were soft pink corduroy, perfectly matching my pink headband. I hoped my look said "star" and "serious ack-*tour*."

Dad stood in the hallway with a little white bag in one hand and a steaming hot cup of coffee in the other. "You look sharp, Maeve," he said, slurping the coffee.

"Sharp? Or glamorous?"

"Glamorous," Dad gulped.

"Hah! It was a trick question. You were supposed to say sharp *and* glamorous!"

"There, Miss Sharp and Glamorous." Dad placed the bag in my hand. "Your hot chocolate. That's why I was late. You wouldn't believe how long the line was at Montoya's this morning. You aren't the only student from Abigail Adams who is staying home during vacation, kiddo. Now let's get a move on. There are already campers waiting."

Now I was seriously excited. I loved meeting new people. I slung my Think Pink velvet bag over my shoulder and instantly felt like I was being pulled to the ground by a ton of bricks. How had my bag gotten so heavy? I only had packed the essentials—a printed outline of my *Boston Holiday* idea, a makeup bag, a change of shoes for dance, an extra sweatshirt, my cell phone, a few magazines, an umbrella in case it rained, a snack for later, and a water bottle, as I *would* be singing. I mean, a girl has to be prepared.

"Dad, one thing. Why can't I come in through the back of the theater with you like I always do?" I asked, even though I already knew what Dad was going to say. Mom had explained it to me over and over again during dinner. It was just that I didn't want my hair to get ruined. Having a giant bozo frizzball effect the first day of camp was not my idea of a perfect first impression. I wanted everyone to see me as the Princess. A girl's gotta dream.

"Because," Dad reminded me, "since I own the Movie House and the camp is being held *here* . . . I just don't want the kids to get jealous."

"Jealous? Of little old me?"

"Okay, not jealous exactly," Dad tried again to explain. "I just don't want the kids to see you popping backstage all the time and thinking you're getting some kind of special treatment . . . you're talented already, Maeve."

I looked away to cover up my proud smile. "What does being talented have to do with anything?"

"Because, let's just say you were to get a lead part in the film—"

"But you said it was going to be an *ensemble* cast," I pointed out.

"Well, there might be a change of plans," Dad said and I felt my cheeks flush with excitement. *Why the change of heart?* I wondered. But then I was like, *Who CARES? Starring roles and everything!* This film camp was getting better and better by the moment. "Anyway, if you were to get a lead part, you'd want the other students to know that you earned it . . ."

"But I *would* earn it. *Duh* . . . maybe you own the building, but you have nothing to do with who gets to be the star of film camp. Even if you *are* the coolest dad ever."

"Thanks, but rumors spread fast in small theaters, Maeve. Take my word for it. Just walk around to the front with the rest of the kids and wait for me to unlock the front doors."

I started to walk away. "Wait—" Dad shouted. "Come back. We're already five minutes late! If you walk around to the front you're going to be even later . . ."

I sighed, folded my arms, and tapped my foot. "Yes?"

Dad scratched his dark, curly hair and furrowed his brow. "Come with me," he decided.

"Cool," I replied.

"No, wait . . . walk around."

"Daaaaaad!" I was getting seriously exasperated.

"Okay, okay, come with me."

I rolled my eyes and walked next to Dad. *Why is he being so weird?* I wondered. It wasn't 'til I noticed his hand shaking as he unlocked the backdoor that it finally dawned on me. *Oh my gosh, Dad's actually nervous!* I realized. This camp was a huge deal. And Dad was about to make his big introduction in front of all the kids . . . plus Artemia Aaron and Mr. Von Krupcake. I couldn't believe it. Dad loved the spotlight as much as I did.

Dad shakily flipped on the lights in the hall of the theater. A shiver went down my spine as one by one the framed posters of classic movies lit up. I always got that feeling—a mixture of pride and excitement. It was like the great movies were in my blood. "How does it look? Is everything . . . you know . . . spic and span?" he asked.

Spic and span was an understatement. The Krup-cake King's renovations had made a big difference, and the Movie House had gone from classic to fantastic. Mr. Von Krupcake wasn't kidding when he said he'd make the whole place glisten. The wood was freshly glossed and polished, and every seat in the theater was covered with red velvet. Plus we had a brand new plush curtain for the stage. I gave Dad a quick hug. "It's going to be great! *We're* going to be great," I promised him.

Dad patted my back. "Okay then, let's go."

There was a little march in his step as he strolled down the carpeted aisle to unlock the door. Mr. Von Krupcake even had new, sparkling crystal chandeliers installed. It was like something out of a dream. Then it got so dream-like I actually had to pinch myself.

Gathered there, outside the theater, were tons of kids and parents . . . all here for film camp at *our* Movie House. I squeezed Dad's hand for good luck. I felt like I was about to make my very own red carpet entrance!

Dad unlocked the door and I gasped. Sure, the inside of the Movie House was fabulous, but seeing the front of the theater now was really the icing on the cake . . . the Krup-cake, that is. The whole front was blocked off with a huge white ribbon with the words "New York Film

Academy" printed in red letters. All the campers gathered close around it. In front of the theater, passersby had stopped on the street and sidewalk to see what all the commotion was about. And was it my imagination, or was that a photographer and a reporter standing next to the doors? This was getting too amazing for words!

The moment Dad and I stepped outside, the kids all began pointing and murmuring, wondering who this obviously important man was who had just unlocked the doors of the romantic-looking landmark theater . . . and maybe even wondering who was the very well-dressed, sharp and glamorous redheaded girl? I giggled and hoped they'd think maybe for just a split second that I was a celebrity here for the ribbon-cutting ceremony.

As Dad and I made our way through the crowd to the big bow in the middle of the ribbon, the crowd actually moved apart for us. Kids were totally looking at me and then whispering to each other. Even though half of me wanted to tell them that I was just a regular kid and that the big, friendly looking guy happened to be my dad, the other half of me really wanted to be a famous actress . . . even if it was just for a little while.

Suddenly, all heads turned away from me and started pointing down Beacon Street. I shielded my eyes and squinted to get a better look. Whoa. Just when I thought this morning could not get more exciting, what should pull up right in front of the Movie House, but a white stretch limousine!

Now the crowd was really going wild. Everyone was

shouting things like, "Who has a pen?" "I don't know who's in there, but I want an autograph!" I didn't say anything myself, but thought how funny it was that people went so nuts over stars and autographs. When I became famous, I'd make sure not to forget how important it was for fans to have their picture taken with *moi*.

The driver got out first and walked around the back of the limo. He swooped down his arm, opened the door, and out stepped Mr. Von Krupcake wearing his fedora hat. "Ahem," announced the driver. "It's my pleasure to introduce the one and only Walter Von Krupcake."

"Huh? Who's Walter Cupcake?" asked a little boy behind me.

"Don't you know? He's the Krupcake King!" answered an all-too-familiar voice. "He helped my dad redo the Movie House for camp."

I shook my head. Sooo typical. Sam the Know-It-All strikes again. I decided it was best to stay incognito (that means in disguise . . . another great word nerd word from the brilliant Charlotte Ramsey!) as long as possible. People would definitely know soon enough that Mr. Know-It-All was my little brother.

Mr. Von Krupcake whispered something to the driver, whose face instantly turned white. "I'm sorry, sir!" he gasped and dove inside the car. When he emerged, he was carrying something shiny—something red and gold. "Ladies and Gentlemen!" shouted the driver. "Let me present . . . the Krupcake King!" He stood on his tiptoes and placed something on Mr. Von Krupcake's head. It was the huge crown from his commercials. Once the crown was secured, everyone started oohing and ahhing. Sometimes people just needed a little help remembering who was famous, I guess.

The driver—who'd let the limo door fall shut after waiting so long—jumped at the sound of banging within. Was that knocking and clattering coming from the *limo*? The driver mumbled an apology and threw open the door. A hush fell over the crowd. Everyone's eyes were glued upon the limo, waiting to see who would be the next star to pop out.

Instead of a star, the only thing to pop out was a loud *cough-cough*.

"My apologies again," said the driver. "And last, but certainly not least. Certainly, *certainly* not least, may I present, the Princess of Pastries herself, Mademoiselle Madeline Von Krupcake."

A boot covered in shaggy white fur slipped out of the car, followed by a dainty little hand French manicured to perfection. A girl emerged in silky black pants and a white, puffy, fur-lined jacket, her long blond hair topped with what looked like a real diamond tiara. Even though I loved the crown Ms. Pink gave me . . . how I envied those twinkling jewels on Maddie's head! She was the same angelic little girl from the Krupcake commercials, except now she was my age . . . and very pretty. I could never imagine her going to my school, Abigail Adams Junior High. She oozed a lifestyle of the rich and famous. To top it all off, in her arms was a tiny white dog that looked like a cotton ball with an itsy-bitsy head. I was glad that Marty wasn't here to see it—because he might get jealous. This dog was adorable . . . really adorable.

"Wave to our friends, Fitzy," Madeline cooed into the little pup's ear as she waved his paw at everyone. Fitzy didn't seem too happy about it, but I knew Marty would have been thrilled. Marty was a little like me. We were both kind of showoffs.

Maddie turned to the driver and hissed, "Jeffrey, the Maddiecakes. NOW!"

"Oh yes. So sorry, Mademoiselle Madeline."

What in the world is going on? I wondered. The limo driver dove again through the door behind Maddie, who tried to cover up the commotion by waving little Fitzy's hand at the crowd again and saying, "Thank you for being here. You're all *too* kind."

When the driver reemerged he had a four-foot-long sterling silver tray of individually wrapped plastic cakes. "Voilà! Maddiecakes for all!" Maddie squealed. "My gift to you. Bon appétit!"

The driver looked like he was about to topple over under the weight of the giant tray as he knelt to the ground, balancing one side on his shoulder. Hands reached out and surrounded Madeline, and she looked like she was positively in Seventh Heaven.

"Have a Maddiecake—they're delicious," she repeated, doling out the packages. The Maddiecake was like a doughnut but with no hole, covered with frosting, caramel coated popcorn, and white chocolate chunks. Sweet was one thing, but the Maddiecake looked like a mouthful of cavities.

Pretty soon, everyone was munching away and saying how yummy the Maddiecakes were. Even Sam's face was plastered with frosting. Don't get me wrong—I adore my junk food (Chocolate Gag is, after all, my signature dish). But for some reason . . . I kinda lost my appetite. Maybe Avery's anti-junk-food lectures *were* starting to get to me.

Pretty soon everyone's mouth was white with Maddie-cake sugar . . . except mine and Maddie's. Maddie's picture perfectness was totally off the charts . . . she looked ready to get her picture taken for the cover of a magazine.

Mr. Von Krupcake walked over to Dad and pumped his hand up and down so many times that I was afraid he'd pull it right off. "I hope you don't mind that I took the liberty of arranging a few last-minute decorations," he gushed. "I thought the situation called for just a *smidgen* of pomp!"

If this was just a smidgen, I wondered what Mr. Von Krupcake's real parties were like . . . and if Madeline had been to tons of them.

I brushed myself off and found a place to stand with the rest of the kids who were watching Madeline—totally awestruck. They were so fascinated that no one even noticed a small black car pull up behind the long limo. No one—*including the news crews*—even noticed a very chic woman step out of the car. She had sleek red hair parted to the side, with long bangs sweeping over one side of her face. She reached up and neatly tucked the strands behind her ear with a sparkling white glove, exposing an even more sparkling diamond earring. She looked around cautiously and quickly tiptoed to the backdoor.

"Who's *that*?" asked the little boy behind me.

I could totally understand not knowing who the Krupcake King was . . . but Artemia Aaron? In the name of Hollywood and film camp, I simply had to say something. But of course, Mr. Know-It-All beat me to it. "Hellooooo?" said Sam. "That's Artemia Aaron! She's like . . . a *world famous* movie director."

"No, not *her*, Sam," scoffed the boy. (I couldn't believe that we'd been at camp for less than ten minutes, and people already knew Sam's name!) "I meant the girl with the curly red hair. Right there! Is she famous or something?"

As I turned to shake the hand of my new little admirer, Sam burst out laughing. "No way, José! That's my sister, Maeve. She's not famous. She's just my plain, old, annoying sister."

I glared at Sam. "Not famous *yet*," I corrected. "But I most likely will be soon enough." I smiled my warmest movie star smile. "It's never too soon for an autograph—" I started to offer, but the little boy wasn't listening anymore. Maybe some people around here didn't know who the *très* glamorous Artemia was, but *everyone* instantly recognized her son.

"Hey!" cried my almost fan. "That's him! That's . . . that's . . . Apollo Aaron! *Home Unsupervised* is like my favorite movie EVER!"

"COOL!" Sam exclaimed. "Hey, Maeve, can you duck or something? Your hair's blocking our view."

It was time to face the fact that my fifteen minutes of fame (okay, two minutes) were officially over, so I stepped into the crowd next to Sam.

We watched as a tall, tanned boy with light brown curly hair got out of the car. He was wearing jeans, a green sweater, sneakers, and a navy blue Dodgers base-ball cap. But even though this kid looked like he was a regular freshman from Brookline High School, there was no doubt about it—that kid was surely Apollo Aaron the child movie star! He looked up and gave the crowd a shy half-smile. "Oh!" I gasped, catching a glimpse of his dazzling sky-blue eyes. I thought my heart might skip a beat! He had grown up to be sooo cute! *Wait 'til I tell the BSG* . . .

The cameras and kids swarmed around him like bees to honey. Apollo looked totally embarrassed to be the cen-ter of so much fuss. I couldn't understand why he wouldn't *want* to be drooled over. Wouldn't having a bunch of peo-ple whispering about you be really . . . flattering? Artemia, seeing that her son was stuck in the people muck, ran back and took his arm.

She smiled warmly and waved at the crowed, show-ing off her arm-length gloves. "We are so happy to be in Boston!" she called. "And I am very pleased to direct this session of the New York Film Academy Camp!" The crowd erupted into applause and the camera lights flick-ered. *What a star!* I sighed and wished I had thought of elbow-length gloves. *Hmm . . . maybe I should have dressed like Audrey Hepburn this morning?*

Artemia escorted her shy (but adorable) son in through the backdoor of the theater, and the crowd let out a disappointed groan. Lucky for them, there was another aspiring star to take center stage. Only this time, it wasn't me.

Madeline ran into the middle of the carpet, eager to return to her place in the spotlight. "And I am very pleased to be a camper at the New York Film Academy Camp!" The cameras flickered again as all eyes turned to Madeline Von Krupcake. Everyone started to ask her questions and she seemed super confident when she answered. Her dad took a red silk hanky from his jacket pocket and started dabbing his eyes.

Sam pulled my arm. "Wait, I don't get it. Aren't we *all* campers here?"

I shrugged. "That's what I thought." But Madeline was the only camper in a diamond tiara with a stretch limo. She also seemed to be a natural in front of the fans. Not only was she totally glamorous (obviously with tons of famous connections) but what if she was also an amazing actress/singer/dancer? What if this Madeline girl was the serious ack-*tour* that her father had promised?

CHAPTER

6

Freeze and Justify

Sam went ahead with Dad to turn on the stage lights, leaving me alone with the crowd of campers. At first I was kind of overwhelmed by all the kids yammering on and on. I wondered how I'd ever join in the conversation. Then I realized what they were talking about: *our* Movie House! "This place is so cool!" one girl whispered to the boy beside her. "It reminds me of the opera house from *Phantom of the Opera*!"

"Hey," I interrupted. "*Phantom* is one of my favorites. I just love the song, 'Music of the Night.' Don't you?" Suddenly I shivered.

"Are you cold?" asked a boy.

"No, it's just that I hate to think about poor Christine Daaé being dragged down into the dungeons below the theater. I'm an above-ground kind of girl. No bats and creepy crawlies for me."

He stared at me for a moment. Maybe he thought I was

a little weird. But instead, he held out his hand politely. "I'm Mickey."

"I'm Maeve. Nice to meet you, Mickey." I couldn't help but giggle.

"Yeah, yeah, I know what you're thinking. Mickey like the Mouse, right?"

I shook my head as we walked into the stage area. "Nope. I was actually thinking Mickey like Mickey Rooney. He was, like, a big, *big* star back in the day of Judy Garland and Elizabeth Taylor. Ever heard of him?"

Mickey blushed. "Actually, my mom named me after him. She's a big Mickey Rooney fan. I kind of come from a long line of movie nuts," he confided.

"You think that's bad?" I looked both ways like I was about to reveal a very important secret. "My dad . . . owns this place."

Mickey's eyes grew wide. "No way! You're the luckiest person ever!"

I smiled back. I wanted to raise my hand and say, "Thank you, thank you very much," but I knew that the grown-up thing to do was not brag. Besides, hearing all the kids going "ooh" and "aah" as they first entered the theater was already making the skin on the back of my neck prickle. A few younger kids ran straight up the stairs stage left and poked their heads behind the enormous red curtain. Being around so many people who felt the same kind of excitement as I did when they walked into a theater was seriously bizarre and wonderful. It felt like we were all part of a crazy family of theater groupies.

"People, quiet down!" Dad called, but everyone just continued talking. All the kids had gathered around Madeline. The girls especially were asking her all sorts of questions, like where she got her furry boots (Gucci) and her bag (Prada) and her cute little Fitzy (a Pomeranian from Paris). One girl even asked her if she was friends with Hilary Duff, and I think Maddie said that she wasn't best friends with her, but they were definitely close.

The only person who didn't look like he'd been hit by Cupid's Madeline arrow was Apollo Aaron, who was busy moving around heavy boxes and showing the younger kids how to turn on some of the fancy lights. *That's weird.* I thought. *Considering Madeline and Apollo are both a part of the whole Hollywood scene, I figured the two of them would be the best of friends already.* But Apollo seemed more interested in setting up the stage and Madeline seemed more interested in showing off Fitzy.

Artemia click-clacked her way to center stage and clapped her hands together. "Attention, set! QUIEEEET!" she hollered. Whoa, so *that* was how you commanded an audience as a famous and successful director! I sure had a lot to learn. The kids hushed and immediately scrambled to find seats in the front row of the theater. "Welcome, young actors and filmmakers, to the New York Film Academy's Boston winter camp!" The room started clapping and hooting—we were all so excited to just be there.

"First of all, this film is going to be created entirely by the people in this room—from the script to the filming.

We are going to have videographers, grips, light technicians, set designers, costume designers, editors, makeup artists . . . every single job that needs to be filled in order to make this movie happen is going to be performed by the members of this camp."

"What about the actors?" I blurted. Oops. I totally forgot to raise my hand, but it just slipped out. Artemia hadn't mentioned anything about actors when she went over the jobs, and that was extremely important to me, obviously.

Artemia smiled. "The people at camp who want parts in the movie will have the opportunity to audition," she assured us.

I heard a lot of people around me breathe sighs of relief. I looked around at the room full of wannabe ack-*tours*. For the first time in my life I was worried whether I, Maeve Kaplan-Taylor, would actually "cut the mustard," as my dad used to say. I started to bite my nails and then remembered my perfect silvery manicure. I quickly sat back on my hands.

Artemia went on, "But just because you're an actor doesn't mean you won't be getting your hands dirty. Even the lead actors will have other jobs, such as settings, props, costumes . . . you get the idea. I am thrilled to be directing the production, but I'll need assistant directors. And you should all know that there is no easy job in the movie production world. By the time camp is over, all of you will learn that each person on the set matters when it comes to making a movie . . . which is amazing since we only have ten days to get this done. But believe me, we will get this movie done, and it will be one fabulous movie. And speaking of a fabulous movie, I'm sure you all read the part in the brochure that the plot of the movie is going to come from one of your ideas."

I felt butterflies in my stomach. Just wait until Artemia heard about *Boston Holiday*! She'd be *so* impressed.

"Now I have a question," Artemia boomed. "Who can tell me when film camp started?"

A few kids' hands shot into the air. "Ooh, ooh, pick me, pick me!" begged a girl. She reminded me a lot of Betsy Fitzgerald—the resident over-achiever of Ms. Rodriguez's class. She always went way out of her way to do extra credit assignments and was totally obsessed with her college applications even though it was like *Hello? We're only in seventh grade here!* Betsy was kind of nice, but she just got way too intense about school.

"Yes," Artemia called on the Betsy-clone sitting near the center.

"Camp started at exactly 9 a.m. this morning," the girl pronounced in a know-it-all voice.

Duh, I thought. *Everyone knows that.*

But Artemia didn't say "Exactly." She just raised her eyebrows and smiled a little. "Anyone else?" she offered.

"It starts right now?" another kid in the crowd peeped.

"Well, that's one way of looking at it . . ." Artemia scanned the crowd once more.

Very slowly I felt like my hand was being pulled up by an unstoppable force.

"Yes, Maeve." She nodded. (I couldn't believe she actually remembered my name!)

"Well I guess this is the first official *day* of camp . . ." I began, "But for me, I started thinking about film camp as soon as I found out about it," I admitted.

I bit my lip waiting for Artemia's response. "Very good!" she said. "New York Film Academy Camp started the moment every single one of you wrote your name at the top of the application form. You see, in the movie business, a film doesn't start with the script, or when the film starts shooting . . . it starts out as something very small, like a little tiny seed of a dream or an idea. Yes, Madeline?"

I hadn't even noticed that Madeline had her hand wiggling in the air. "Artemia, I was just thinking that for me, film camp started even before we had a film camp. See, this whole film camp was partially my idea. I had the seed of a dream for having a New York Film Academy Camp right in my hometown, Boston."

Artemia nodded. "Very good, Madeline. Without vision we'd never have the incredible art and movies that we're fortunate enough to have. Thank you for your passion. So I hope that you all possess the same attitude as Maeve and Madeline and have done some good brainstorming already. Now who's excited?" Artemia asked.

All the kids started clapping quietly.

"C'mon . . . I said *excited*! Now let's try that again. Who's excited?"

This time everyone cheered and stomped their feet. I caught Sam out of the corner of my eye whooping and shaking his head around so that his crazy, blond hair stuck out everywhere. He looked like a cross between Tweety Bird and Huckleberry Finn. I wanted to laugh. Even if it did mean I'd have to put up with a little bit of annoyingness, it might end up being kind of fun having Sam around.

"I have something else to say," Madeline announced and without waiting to be called on, continued, "Daddy's seed of a dream is going to be the most unbelievable film camp ever! He's going to—"

"Maddie, wait!" Artemia interrupted.

"But, Artemia!" Maddie had this totally stunned look on her face, like no one had ever told her to "hold her horses" before. I'd heard that one all the time.

Artemia said very primly, "Your father hasn't finalized this with me yet. I don't want to get peoples' hopes up."

Madeline smacked her lips shut and pretended to zip them tight and throw away the key, but the damage had been done. It was obvious peoples' hopes were already up. Way up. Everyone was chattering about what they thought the Krupcake King's seed of a dream was . . . the seed that was going to make this the most unbelievable film camp ever.

"Hee hee, ha ha, it's okay, Artemia! It's okay!" Mr. Von Krupcake had the absolute strangest laugh *ever*. I turned to see him huffing and puffing as he ran down the aisle of the theater. "They'll find out soon enough." Then Mr. Von Krupcake did something really *strange*. Mr. Von

Krupcake turned around and tried to lift himself right onto the middle of the stage. Since the stage was pretty high, though, he didn't quite make it on the first try. He just kept jumping until Dad leaned down and helped hoist him over. In his gray suit and big mustache, I thought that Mr. Von Krupcake sort of looked like a walrus. I could hear some of the other kids snickering quietly. I am proud to say I resisted the urge. First, it wasn't polite to laugh at people. And second, Mr. Von Krupcake had just fixed up the whole Movie House, which was like beyond nice. So, no matter how funny he looked, I just couldn't laugh.

"Now, now, quiet down everyone, quiet down." Again Artemia's movie-director voice hushed the room of bubbling chatter. "I know all this news is a lot to take in. But we can't afford to lose a minute of time. Like I said before, film camp has *already* begun. Everyone form a circle here on the stage."

I squeezed my hands together and took a seat. I loved theater games!

"This activity is called 'Freeze and Justify.' It's really simple. Two people get in the center of the circle and act out a scene. They continue on with the scene until someone sitting in the circle shouts 'Freeze!' at which point the two people freeze. The one who shouted 'Freeze' taps one of the players on the shoulder and takes his or her place in the same position. Then the new player begins a new scene with a new scenario. Any questions?"

I saw a hand shoot up from the back.

"Yes, Sam? Do you have a question?" Artemia knew

that Dad had made special arrangements for Sam to be at camp even though he was way younger than the rest of us. Of course, being young had never stopped Sam from talking before.

"I have a comment AND a question."

Oh great. I thought.

Artemia smiled. "Go ahead, Sam."

Sam cleared his throat. "First of all, I wanted to say that I'm the designated filmotographer."

I glanced nervously at Artemia, who was still smiling just as sweetly as ever. "That's fantastic, Sam. We're very pleased to have you. Now what's your question?"

"My question is about the game. How are we supposed to know what kind of . . . of . . . scenario to act out?"

I banged my hand on my forehead, embarrassed that my own flesh and blood would ask such an obvious question. *It's called* IMPROV, *Sam!* I wanted to yell.

"That's a very good question. Sam, the purpose of the game is to get the creative juices flowing. You learn how to play around with the first thing that pops into your head. It's a great way to brainstorm. Yes, Madeline?"

Madeline stood up and bravely walked into the center of the circle. "'Freeze and Justify' is one of the most basic improvisation games. Improvisation is a performance given without preparation," she explained. "I play it all the time in acting class. Would you like me to volunteer to go first?" The Krupcake Princess sounded like she was twenty years old.

It seemed to me like she'd already volunteered by

walking herself into the middle of the circle, but Artemia nodded politely. "Thank you, Madeline. How very courageous of you." My mouth felt dry. I felt like an amateur and not an actor.

"And I was thinking maybe Apollo would like to go first as well. I know *he* knows this game!" Madeline waved at Apollo, who was back shrinking into the folds of the curtains and pretending to fix a light. "Come on, Apollo. Let's show them how it's done."

This was the one second when Artemia's patient smile disappeared. "Oh, um, I don't think . . . Apollo?"

Apollo didn't answer but put the light down and shoved his hands in his pockets. He trudged, slouched over, to the middle of the circle staring at the floor the whole time. I mean, I knew that the wood floor was refinished a week ago, but it couldn't have been *that* interesting to look at.

"Sure, whatever dude," Apollo mumbled. Why wasn't he psyched about being the first person to go? Wasn't he a real actor?

"All right, fabulous. Apollo, I already have a brilliant idea. Just play along," Madeline instructed.

Apollo threw his shoulders back and took a deep breath. He looked like he didn't know what to expect. I didn't blame him. I was beginning to think that Madeline Von Krupcake would do just about anything to capture everyone's attention.

Madeline leaned over and whispered something into Apollo's ear.

"Huh?" Apollo said in a regular volume voice.

"Please lie down and CLOSE YOUR EYES!" Madeline ordered. Then she smiled sweetly. I wished all the BSG were there because I could not figure out this girl.

Apollo laid flat on the stage with his eyes closed. Madeline bent over him and pretended to dab his face with a facecloth. "Johnny, Johnny, please wake up!" Madeline said in a thick Southern drawl. "Oh, Johnny, I can't hold it in anymore. I know I'm just your nurse, and I know you've been in a coma for three months, but they've been the most magical months of my life. It's this war, Johnny. This terrible war. Oh, Johnny, I know how crazy this must sound. I know you'll never walk again. Why, you might not ever wake up from this coma. You don't even know who I am. But I know that you are a good person even if you can't wake up." Madeline put the back of her hand against her forehead and pretended to look faint. "I just hope someday you'll be able to see the face of the beautiful nurse who saved your life."

Madeline collapsed on the stage in a fit of hysterical crying. It looked pretty real, too. She even sniffled and wiped her nose. Gee, she was good . . . *really* good.

Then I had an idea. "Freeze!" I shouted.

Madeline stopped fake crying and Apollo, well, he kept lying there in exactly the same position. I got up and tapped Apollo's shoulder. "Hope you don't mind if I take your place," I told him.

"Be my guest!" He bolted upright and gratefully slipped out of the circle.

Madeline didn't look quite as grateful that I'd interrupted her scene, but "freezing" was half the point of the game. The other half was "justifying" that your idea was creative. I hoped I'd be able to pull it off.

I scooted into Apollo's exact lying-down position and took a deep breath. Then I began to crab-walk backward as Madeline stared. "Get down!" I cried, tugging the fur on her boots. "Stop drop and roll, remember?" I started coughing as loud as I could, and suddenly Madeline got it and started coughing too.

"There's smoke everywhere!" she hacked. "I'm afraid! I think it's coming from the kitchen. You weren't baking again, were you?"

We were now both crawling around on the stage pretending to push clouds of smoke away and coughing our most blood-curdling coughs. I put my hand over my heart. "Oh, sister, I admit it! I was the one baking. I promise—I'll never cook again!"

Now the whole circle of campers started laughing. I couldn't believe it—the kids really thought we were funny. Madeline and I were a hit!

"Freeze!" another camper squeaked. Just my luck—the little squeak of course came from Sam, and of course he tapped Madeline's shoulder and squirmed into her position—crawling on the wood next to me.

"Sam!" I hissed under my breath.

"You *have* to," he whispered back, and I knew he was absolutely right. No matter what Sam's made-up scene was, I had to play along. And knowing Sam, there was pretty much only one scene that *he* liked to act out.

"Over there, Peter!" Sam pointed at an invisible spot toward the back of the stage. "I see Charlie at five o'clock."

"Who's Charlie?" I asked.

Sam rolled his eyes. "No, Maeve! Charlie's supposed to be the enemy. You know, like when you're playing Army?"

Now Artemia was the one to shout. "Freeze! Sam, once you start acting out a scene, you can't break character. Maeve isn't Maeve anymore . . . she's Peter, okay?"

Sam nodded sheepishly.

"But Maeve and Maddie, I mean, Madeline, you two had it exactly right. Great job, girls. And Sam, wonderful try. You'll get the hang of it in no time. Now we'll take a quick break for water and snacks and meet back here in five."

I smiled, so relieved that I'd been brave enough to say "Freeze" and jump right in like that. I felt someone tap my shoulder and I turned. It was Madeline.

"Nice job," she said. "I wasn't sure anyone here would be able to keep up."

I couldn't believe her confidence in herself. And in me.

"Thanks," I told her. "You were really good too. I loved your 'Johnny' scene. It was so sad! How'd you come up with that? I mean, you didn't even need Apollo's help at all!"

"I know," Madeline announced proudly. "I've taken lots of acting classes, so I'm kind of an expert. I'm Madeline

Von Krupcake, by the way." (As if I didn't already know.) "But you can call me Maddie." She held out her hand very properly.

"Maeve Kaplan-Taylor," I shook her hand firmly. "But you can call me Maeve."

"Maeve, it's very nice to meet you, darling. I think this is the beginning of a beautiful friendship."

I nearly fainted! She was quoting *Casablanca*—one of my all-time favorite movies.

"I think you're right." I laughed.

"C'mon. Let's go see if Artemia needs our help for the next activity. Maeve, we are so going to *rule* this camp."

"I know! I already have a fabulous idea for the film!" I boasted.

"Maeve, you are too much!" Maddie strutted to the back of the stage where Artemia was standing. Fitzy yipped and took off behind her, and then I went behind Fitzy, feeling only a tiny bit silly that I was following a dog. Maddie tossed her shiny blond hair over her shoulder, and I did the same thing. Her hair swished from side-to-side, while all my curls did was bounce up and down. Still, I felt like all the campers were looking at me with total admiration. Like Maddie said, it was the start of a beautiful friendship. Wait until the BSG heard about this!

CHAPTER

7

Makeovers and Muffin Tops

On Wednesday morning, I got up while it was still dark out. Maddie told me that if I ironed my hair, I could get it as silky and straight as hers. But since my hair is naturally curly, I was going to need a lot of time.

Maddie was right though. After thirty minutes and only a few teeny tiny "ouches" from the straightening iron, my hair looked like it was something out of a shampoo commercial. I ran my fingers through the long red strands (that's one thing curly-haired people can *never* do) and it felt *glorious*. I looked like Ariel from *The Little Mermaid*. She was one of my favorite red-haired heroines.

Wednesday was Jeans Day—Maddie decided that on Tuesday. I slipped into my cutest pair with a black long-sleeved shirt on top. Maddie said that if you wanted to be taken seriously in the theater, then black was the only way to go. I glanced longingly at the pink shirts and dresses that seemed to be screaming my name from the closet. *Sorry, guys. Maybe another day*, I thought.

When I checked my reflection in my dresser, it was like a different person was staring back at me—someone with very serious clothes and long, long shiny hair. I looked like I could be about three years older. It was amazing what a little hair and costume work could do!

I was ready thirty minutes *ahead* of schedule. When I got downstairs, Mom was so startled she dropped her empty toast plate on the floor. "Whoa. Who are you, and what have you done with my daughter?"

I tossed my hair over my shoulder. "Please. This is theater, Mom. I'm like a caterpillar turning into a beautiful, acting butterfly."

Mom ran her fingers through my hair and smiled lovingly. "Well I thought the old caterpillar was a beautiful actress just the way she was."

"I think she looks pretty," Sam piped in. I couldn't believe my annoying little Army-obsessed brother would actually be able to come up with such a nice compliment. I ran over to give him a hug, but he pushed me away with a big "Yuck!"

"Aren't you going to have some cereal?" Mom asked, still staring at my hair.

I shook my head. "No time. I have to go. I told Maddie I'd meet her at camp early today to practice our scene."

"All right," Mom agreed. "Let's head downstairs to the Movie House together."

Looking around, she asked "Where did Sam go?"

"He must have gone down already," I answered as I primped my hair. I simply could not believe how fabulous it looked. Shampoo commercial here I come!

Typical early-bird Sam was waiting by the theater door, his camera ready. As soon as Mom got into her car and pulled away, I told Sam to go on inside and meet Dad. "Why? Where are you going?" Sam asked suspiciously.

I told him the truth. "I've got to run to Montoya's super quick."

Sam squinted and folded his arms decidedly. "Fine. On just one condition."

I groaned. "Yes?"

"Can you bring me back a muffin too? Please? The kind with the cinnamon chips—it's my favorite."

"Fine," I agreed.

Sam shook his finger. "And don't forget, Mrs. Franken-butterfly." Sam turned on his heels and I zipped down to Montoya's.

It was a very sunny warm day for February, so I wore my enormous white sunglasses right into the store. When I wore sunglasses inside, I felt like a real celebrity trying to stay away from all the pesky cameramen. Thankfully the pesky cameraman at my house (Sam) was going to camp with Dad that morning.

"Wow, Maeve, you look so . . . different," said Nick Montoya when I got to the front of the line. "What's up?" Nick was in Ms. Rodriguez's class with me at Abigail Adams Junior High School. His family owned Montoya's Bakery, and the

BSG loved meeting there for delicious drinks and pastries. Nick had dark hair and was cute enough to be a teen star. Too bad he wasn't into acting. (True confession—I used to have a crush on Nick at the beginning of the year, but it didn't work out—he just wasn't a true romantic . . . like me.)

"Good morning, darling," I greeted him with a little wave.

Nick looked behind him then his eyes widened. "Oh wait, are you talking to me?"

"Well of course I am, darling! Who else would I be talking to?"

Nick looked way confused. "I dunno. You usually don't call me 'darling' so . . . I wasn't sure."

"Yes, I picked it up from Maddie. Isn't it divine? Everybody feels special when they're a 'darling,' don't you think?"

"Sure, I guess. So what can I get you?"

"Two hot chocolates and two of your fabulous blueberry muffins, darling."

Nick nodded, looking impressed. "Wow, Maeve. Hungry much?"

I tipped my head forward so my huge glasses slipped down my nose. "Please, darling. They're not *just* for me. It just so happens that I'm getting breakfast for Madeline Von Krupcake . . . THE Krupcake Princess," I said for emphasis. "She loves Montoya's."

"That's funny," Nick said as he placed two warm blueberry muffins in a white bag. "I don't think I've ever seen this Maddie person in Montoya's."

I nodded. "That's because she's never been in Montoya's. Maddie has this weird condition where she *can't* wait in lines."

Nick raised his eyebrows. "Oh really?"

"Yeah. I saw her faint once when she had to wait in line for the bathroom. She's very fragile."

Nick put two cups and the white bag of muffins on the counter. "Well, it's really nice of you to get her breakfast then."

"That's what friends are for," I handed Nick five dollars. "Do you know what the kids at camp call us? M&M! Isn't that fabulous?"

"Oh I get it. M&M because Maddie and Maeve."

"And because we're both sweet as M&Ms," I added. "Now have a good day, darling. I must run. Film camp awaits, you know." I pushed my bag over my shoulder and grabbed my stuff.

"Hey, Maeve," Nick called behind me. "Have you talked to any of the, um, other BSG lately . . . isn't, um, one of them going to someplace cool during vacation . . . like um, Montreal or something?"

Oh yeah. There was one *more* reason why Nick and I would never work. It was pretty obvious that he had a major crush on my friend Charlotte. They would probably be a better match anyway, as they both loved travel and adventure so much. Don't get me wrong, I loved travel and adventure too . . . as long as I was watching it on a big screen with a bag of popcorn in my lap.

"You mean Charlotte?" I asked. I wanted to wink but

Nick was already turning reddish. "As a matter of fact *yes*! I just got a postcard from Charlotte yesterday. Oh I miss that girl so much . . ."

"Me too," Nick replied. "I mean, I miss all our friends who are on vacation."

I smiled and nodded. *Typical Nick.* I thought. *Good at soccer . . . not so good at being romantic.*

"Well, I must be off. Film camp awaits. Ta-ta, darling!" I waved Nick good-bye and dashed out the door.

It wasn't easy to carry two cups of hot chocolate, a bag of muffins, and my big, giant purse up the slippery side-walk of Harvard Street. Plus, I was late . . . which meant I had to *run.* By the time I arrived at the Movie House, I was panting and my light pink parka had dribbles of chocolate all over it.

I reached the door just as Maddie's white stretch limo pulled up to the front. Maddie had told me that it was sim-ply the *only* way to get around.

I dabbed off my coat as I waited by the doors, eager to see what breathtaking designer outfit Maddie would be wearing today. "Good morning, darling!" she sang as she trotted over. Maddie had selected a pair of jeans with gold stitching all over the pockets. They sort of reminded me of how Katani liked to jazz up her old jeans with beads and ribbons. But, to be completely honest, it looked like Mad-die's jeans could have been straight off the fashion run-way. She never wore the same piece of clothing twice.

Maddie linked her arm with mine and helped herself to a hot chocolate. "Thank goodness you remembered. I'm absolutely famished. The only thing I want right now is a banana muffin and hot chocolate."

I felt myself getting warm. "But I thought blueberry was your favorite."

Maddie laughed and smoothed out her black ruffled blouse. "Blueberry muffins are so last week, darling. I was talking to my friend Mary-Kate last night, and she and I both agreed that banana muffins are the new blueberry."

How did I miss that? I wanted to throw out the muffins as quickly as possible, but Maddie grabbed the bag right out of my hands. "Oh well. I suppose blueberry will just have to do." She peered into the bag. "Yum. I'm going to have the muffin tops. You can have the bottoms. I hate the bottoms."

I felt a little pang as I watched Madeline pop off the moist muffin tops and leave me with the dark, waxy bottoms. It didn't quite seem fair . . . but I didn't say anything. I guess it wasn't her fault that she didn't like the muffin bottoms.

"Come along, Maeve. We don't want to be late for warmups."

Since the first day of camp, Maddie and I got to lead the morning warmup exercises. I wasn't sure how we got that job exactly, but I was learning that when you hung out with Maddie, people pretty much started thinking that you knew as much about stuff as she did. It was just one of those things.

We burst through the doors of the theater and all the kids who'd been chatting got very quiet and turned to watch us stroll down the center aisle. "M&M . . . M&M . . ." they whispered to each other.

"I like your jeans, Maddie!" peeped a short girl as we passed.

Maddie smiled to herself. "Gucci, darling."

"Your hair looks so pretty, Maeve," said a tall girl with curly hair.

"Pantene, darling," I told her. It was so inspiring to be admired like a real starlet. Maddie told me that the first step to landing a lead role was *acting* like the lead. She had so much great advice.

We took our rightful places in the center of the stage and waited as the other kids moved the boxes and props into the right places. "Never do the work of a grip . . . or else that'll be the job you get stuck with," Maddie warned. Hey, *not* getting my hands dusty and musty was fine by me. She and I took our nail files out of our purses, clicked them together, and laughed. Then we just relaxed and filed while the other campers scurried around.

It seemed like Apollo wasn't afraid of getting stuck as a grip though. Whenever I saw him he was always untangling wires, repairing equipment, or helping the younger kids. "Okay, let's swing this over here, Sam," I heard Apollo shout from backstage. Sam and Apollo appeared from behind the curtain hauling a large, worn-out sofa. "Wow, Sam, you are one strong dude," Apollo complimented.

Sam looked overjoyed. "Thanks! I've been doing my pushups before bed. Just like you told me." Sam spotted me and looked excited. "Hey, Maeve, can I have my muffin now?"

Oops . . . I felt my cheeks burn and then thought of something. "Um . . . uh . . . don't you mean *please* can I have my muffin now?"

Sam held out his hand. *"Please?"*

"Um . . . I sorta forgot. Sorry, Sam."

"But you said you'd get me one!" Sam objected. I wasn't really sure what to do to about that. Unfortunately, at that exact moment, even Sam's new pushup routine wasn't going to stop the sofa from slipping out of his sweaty little hands and landing on the wooden stage with a ginormous "THUD!"

Looked like my big-sister mistake was saved by the couch. "Nice going, Sam. Dad's going to be sooooo mad if you scratch the stage—he just refinished it!" I reminded him.

"Hey, maybe if you guys actually did some work—like helped us out—then the couch wouldn't have fallen," Apollo said in an aggravated tone.

"Yeah!" Sam yipped.

Who did Apollo think he was that he could tell *Madeline Von Krupcake* and *Maeve Kaplan-Taylor* what to do? Just because he didn't want to be a star anymore didn't give him the right to act so high and mighty, I thought.

Maddie just started laughing though. She wasn't bothered at all. "Why, Apollo, you're terrible!" she squealed. "I'm a *thinker* not a *laborer*. Apollo, you know that."

"Besides, we have plenty of work to do," I added.

"Yeah!" Sam chirped. "On your *nails*."

I glared at Sam. I couldn't believe how my own little brother could be so disloyal, saying that in front of Apollo. Worst of all, Apollo burst out laughing.

Maddie rolled her eyes. "Speaking of thinking, I'm going to go talk to Artemia about an idea I had in the shower this morning. Picture it, Maeve—our faces on a billboard outside the Movie House. Fabulous, right?"

"Fabulous," I agreed, although I felt kind of funny about the whole idea. Maybe it was a little too much?

"Now you boys can just keep doing, well, whatever it is you're doing. I need to find Artemia." She was always going to find Artemia and telling her about her ideas. Maddie skipped down the hallway and left me sitting alone in the middle of the stage with my nail file. I was the only person not moving things around, and suddenly I started feeling a little silly. I glanced back at Apollo trying to drag the old couch with Sam huffing and puffing on his end.

"Hey, Maeve. Can you give us a hand?" Apollo asked.

With all my heart I really did want to get up and make it a little easier for Sam . . . but what if Maddie came back and saw me working like a common camper? Even though I knew Sam needed me, I couldn't risk losing Maddie and going back to being just a camp nobody.

"No thanks. I'm a thinker not a laborer," I replied in my sweetest voice.

"A thinker not a laborer?" Apollo dropped the couch and folded his arms. "Dude, what's up with that? What're you, some kind of Maddie-clone?"

"I—I—I . . . That's not a very nice thing to say!" I finally exclaimed.

"He's kind of right, Maeve. It seems like ever since you and Maddie started hanging out, all you do is copy everything she does. I mean . . . you even dress like her," Sam pointed out.

"I do NOT!" I protested, even though it didn't take a genius to figure out that we *were* both wearing jeans with a black top.

Apollo looked at Sam and the two of them burst out laughing. "No offense, little dude, but I think your sister is morphing into Madeline Von Krupcake Part Two. Hey I just got a good idea for a sci-fi movie . . ."

Sam giggled. "I gotta get my tape!" He tore off the stage to rummage through his equipment.

I huffily got up and marched right over to the end of the couch that Sam had not-very-expertly been trying to carry. "Look, I'm just trying to be taken seriously around here . . . as an ack-*tour*."

Apollo lifted the arm of his couch with a loud, "Mmph!"

"And just because I'm becoming more mature . . ." (I pronounced mature like ma-*tour*) ". . . doesn't mean I'm turning into Maddie!"

"Maeve, just because you act the way you *think* a movie star would act *doesn't* make it right."

"Easy for you to say," I griped. "You don't need to worry about how to act, 'cause you're already a movie star."

"Yeah right," Apollo mumbled. "Ex–movie star. Ex. That stuff is so not for me."

"Well that stuff IS for me, and excuse me if I want to try as hard as I can to become a movie star." I was getting really fired-up now. I couldn't believe that Apollo was saying this to me when he had no idea how serious I was about my dream.

"All I mean is, you can be a movie star and NOT be a clone of Maddie."

"I'm NOT a clone!" I insisted.

"I know!" Apollo exclaimed. "Because if you *were* a clone, you wouldn't have helped me carry this couch across the entire stage."

"Huh?" We stood—out of breath—on the other side of the stage. I'd been so wound up that I'd lifted the couch and hadn't even realized I was doing it. Weird. Maybe helping out was one of those things that just came naturally to me.

Right at that moment, Maddie pranced back into the theater and slammed her cell phone shut. "Maeve, darling, I have the most fabulous news. Daddy says you can sleep over our house tonight, and we won't take no for an answer."

I didn't think I could take no for an answer either! Maddie's house wasn't just a house—it was a mansion. I'd heard Dad go on and on about it after his meetings with Mr. Von Krupcake. "Well, I guess . . ." I began.

"Good, it's settled."

"I was going to say, I need to ask my parents first."

Maddie laughed. "As if they'd say no. This is a big opportunity for you, Maeve." Maddie squeezed my hand and giggled. "Trust me. We're going to have so much fun!"

I felt myself burst into a smile. After that invitation, there was no doubt about it. Madeline Von Krupcake really liked me. Madeline Von Krupcake was my friend.

CHAPTER

8

Living La Dolce Vita

I showered and packed up with lightning speed. Once the water hit my head, it was curly Maeve all over again. But Maddie had promised that I didn't need to worry about looking glamorous or anything. "The theme of the night is comfy and casual," she assured me before we left camp.

The drive to Maddie's was positively torturous! I couldn't wait to see her house, but Mom was in turtle driving mode. She kept slowing down and gushing, "Wow, Maeve, look at this house! Isn't it spectacular? I forgot how much I love Beacon Hill."

I had to admit, I loved Beacon Hill too. It was one of Boston's loveliest and oldest neighborhoods. The streets were all one-way and really tiny, running up and down a hill that overlooked the Boston Public Garden. Smack in the middle of Beacon Hill was the State House. I thought Massachusetts had the most beautiful state house ever, even though

I'd only seen the state houses in Vermont, Connecticut, Rhode Island, and Florida (Orlando is a total must-see). But what I liked best about the Massachusetts state house was the gold pine cone on the top of the dome. Ms. Rodriguez told us that the pine cone symbolized the importance of the lumber industry to the early New England economy.

"Look, Mom, there's Louisberg Square. That's us."

Mom turned right on a narrow street lined on both sides with brick townhouses. I instantly felt like I was back in time, or in an old movie—like *My Fair Lady* with Audrey Hepburn (even though it was supposed to be in London, I think).

"Number 7 Louisberg Square. Here we are," Mom said and whistled. "Your father was right. This place really is something."

I just gulped. Maddie's house was a huge brick mansion on the corner, probably the biggest house on the street. It was surrounded by a tall iron gate covered with ivy. Mom pressed the button on a little box on one of the tall posts in front.

"Name?" said a man's voice.

"Carol Kaplan. I'm Maeve Kaplan-Taylor's mom. We're here to see—"

BZZZZZZ!

The gates split and slowly opened up to a crescent-shaped driveway. "Whoa. Toto, I have a feeling we're not in Kansas anymore," I breathed.

We pulled up to the front door and I felt myself shaking as I gathered my things.

"Don't be nervous, sweetie. I'm sure the Von Krup-cakes are just like us . . . only . . ."

"Richer?" I offered.

"Now, Maeve, that's not very polite," Mom reminded me. "You know better than to judge people by how much money they have."

I'd heard that whole "it's what's on the inside that counts" speech like a million times before.

"It's not a bad thing, Mom," I assured her. "I think Maddie's . . . fabulous. Ta-ta!" I quickly kissed Mom on the cheek and got out of the station wagon. I really wanted Mom to drive away quickly before Maddie noticed that the car that took me here was definitely not a stretch limo with a chauffeur.

I rang the doorbell and in about ten seconds the door opened. "You must be Maeve," said a gorgeous Orlando Bloom look-alike in a suit. "We've been expecting you."

And you must be my future prince, I thought, feeling myself blush a little. Thank goodness "Yes, I'm Maeve," was about the only thing I could squeak out.

"Pleased to meet you, Maeve. My name is Kenneth. I'm Mr. Von Krupcake's personal assistant," he said in a British accent. "If there is any way I may be of service to you during your stay, do let me know."

"What does a personal assistant do? Is that like a but-ler?" I asked. *Way to be a total ditz, Maeve. Butler? Oh no . . .*

But Kenneth just smiled kindly and explained, "Some-thing like that. I run Mr. Von Krupcake's household and arrange some of his business affairs."

I nodded. It was probably better for me to just smile and stop talking. Kenneth was too dreamy—Maddie had to be the luckiest girl ever. Still, I couldn't imagine asking him to do anything for me. It just seemed so weird! "Thanks, Kenneth," I managed to say.

"Miss Madeline is upstairs. I shall show you to her wing." Then Kenneth started to grab my black velvet sleepover bag right out of my hand.

I tightened my grip and cried, "What are you doing?"

Kenneth seemed just as startled as me then he started to chuckle. "Oh no, I'm sorry, Maeve. I was going to carry up your bags for you. You are the guest of honor."

I wanted to shrivel up and disappear on the spot! Wow, talk about not being used to the life of luxury. I'd have a thing or two to tell the BSG after this for sure!

I followed Kenneth through the front hall and up a long, winding marble staircase. The walls were covered with large oil paintings that were full of color, just like the ones I'd seen at the Museum of Fine Arts in Boston. At the top of the staircase, in a fancy gold frame, was the largest portrait of all. It was of Maddie in a long purple dress holding Fitzy in her arms. Purple velvet drapes hung on either side of the picture. "We close the drapes when it gets too sunny so the paint doesn't fade," Kenneth explained.

We walked down a long, lavish hallway. It felt like it went on forever. Finally we got to a large door with a gold plaque on it that said "Madeline" in script. Kenneth rapped on the door and I heard Maddie's voice chirp, "Enter."

When Kenneth opened the door I gasped and covered

my mouth with my hand. Madeline's room made my pink palace seem like a shoe box. First of all—it wasn't just a room, it was a . . . hotel suite fit for a princess.

Maddie was sitting cozily on a green satin sofa next to two matching chairs and a coffee table. There was a sterling silver tea set on the coffee table and two plates— cookies and scones on one and cheese and crackers on the other. Steam was even rising from the teapot.

"Maeve, darling. You're just in time for cocoa," Maddie said, patting the couch beside her. She took a sip out of her cup with her little pinky sticking straight up in the air.

Seriously, I could not believe her room. Right then, I really did feel like Little Orphan Annie seeing Daddy Warbucks's mansion for the first time. I used to think that canopy beds were the ultimate in dreaminess . . . *until* I saw Maddie's bed. It was humongous and draped in luxurious fabric right smack in the middle of her room. But the best part was the lace veil that hung from her ceiling and covered her bedposts like a curtain of mist. It reminded me of the dreamy bed in the movie version of *The Secret Garden*. I always thought that kind of bed was so romantic, but I'd never seen one in person until now . . .

Maddie had the most spectacular view. Her enormous windows opened up to a balcony that looked right over the Boston Common and the Massachusetts State House with its gold dome. I could imagine rehearsing lines out there on a sunny day with my big sunglasses. Maybe I'd be practicing a song and a cute boy walking on the sidewalk below would hear my voice and become completely enchanted. Anyway . . . a girl could dream.

"Now, Maeve darling, come over and have a cup of this delicious hot cocoa," Maddie called.

Kenneth poured a stream of creamy chocolate liquid into a porcelain tea cup, scooped out a dollop of whipped cream from a silver bowl, and plopped it in with a little splash. "I've got to go help your father now, Miss Maddie. He's organizing a Krupcake convention in Baltimore. Call down when you two are ready for dinner."

Kenneth waved and shut the door behind him.

"So, darling, what do think of my little home?" Maddie tucked her blond hair behind her ear and smiled sweetly.

"*Little home?* Maddie, this place is huge! The hallways go on, like, forever."

Maddie shrugged. "I guess it just seems little compared to our cottage in the Hamptons. Maeve, have you been to the Hamptons? It's so fabulous."

I shook my head. Why did Maddie always call things "little" or "cottage" when what she really meant was just the opposite?

"Now, Maeve, that outfit, it's *really* not quite right." Maddie looked disapprovingly at me. She had told me that the dress code for the night was comfy-casual, but here Maddie was wearing a short, cream-colored dress with a pearl necklace and pearl earrings. A white fur shawl rested over her shoulders. Meanwhile, I had thrown on a terry-cloth pink sweat suit. I should've known that in the Von

Krupcake household, comfy-casual meant a whole other league altogether.

"I'm sorry . . . I left all my dresses at home . . ." I began.

"Well, that little jogging ensemble you have on will simply not do. We're just going to have to find you something more suitable, I suppose." Maddie pressed a button on what looked like a TV clicker resting on her coffee table. Two large doors in front of us split open, revealing another room filled with clothes and accessories. The sides of the room were lined with shelves of shoes—so many shoes it looked like a department store. The room was mostly a closet that seemed to stretch back to infinity. Maddie pressed another button on the clicker and suddenly, the closet started *moving*.

I gasped and Maddie giggled. "Daddy designed it like a dry cleaning place. Isn't he too brilliant?" she sighed and pressed a button that made the closet stop. "There. I have the perfect frock for you." I loved the way she said "frock." Maddie just had the cutest way of saying things.

Maddie floated over to the rack and my heart nearly skipped a beat. Maddie walked straight up to a long pink satin gown with a thick pink belt and enormous bow in the back. It looked just like the famous one from this old movie I saw once—*Gentlemen Prefer Blondes*.

But instead of grabbing the glorious pink dress, Maddie grunted and reached in *behind* it. "Come on, I know it's around here somewhere," she said, groping through the fabric. "Ah-hah! Here we go!" Maddie pulled out a garment zipped in a plastic dress bag and skipped back over to the loveseat.

"Maeve, this is going to look *darling* on you. It's just like the dress Audrey Hepburn wore in *Breakfast at Tiffany's* . . . and I know Audrey's your idol."

I felt positively tickled. Maddie was such an amazing friend. She even remembered who my all-time favorite actress was. With her perfect, pearly nails, Maddie unzipped the bag and out fell . . . a black, checkered piece of fabric. The material looked totally dull, and there wasn't even a waist on it. This dress did NOT look anything like *Breakfast at Tiffany's* . . . except for maybe the breakfast *tablecloth* at Tiffany's.

"Voilà! Isn't it darling?" Maddie gushed and thrust the dress at me.

"Um, it's okay . . ." I began hesitantly. I didn't want to be rude, but this dress was so not my style.

"Try it on!" Maddie insisted.

"Well, it looks a little long actually. I was thinking maybe I could try that pink dress over there . . ." I pointed nervously at the fab gown with the ginormous bow.

Maddie threw her hand over her mouth and laughed—hard. "Oh, Maeve, you are just the most adorable thing! That pink dress is a collector's item. It's from a famous movie. Oh dear, of course you can't wear that to dinner, silly. Now be a lamb and put this on. It's a genuine Chanel."

I didn't care *who* it was. The dress was absolutely hideous. I looked over and saw Maddie's concerned face. I knew she was only trying to be helpful so I swallowed and slipped the dress over my shoulders. Maddie buttoned the back and sighed. "There. Perfect. Go look in my mirror."

I tiptoed across the room. I *had* to tiptoe, because the dress was so narrow that I couldn't take normal-size steps. Finally, I reached the little platform in front of a three-way mirror. I suddenly felt dizzy.

"You see? Classic glamour," Maddie declared.

Classic glamour? No way! It was a classic glamour DON'T. I could just see me now in the back of *Glam-girl* magazine in this drape-y disaster with a black line covering my eyes (that's what the editors did to protect the innocent). And I WAS totally innocent . . . how was I supposed to know comfy-casual meant black tie? But I just swallowed and echoed, "Classic glamour."

"Come now. Let's go to dinner!" Maddie flounced over to her intercom and pressed the button. "Kenneth, we're ready now. Announce us to Mummy and Daddy."

The intercom buzzed and Kenneth's voice crackled through: "Of course, Miss Madeline."

Krupcake Dining Etiquette 101

The dining room was gorgeous—like, castle gorgeous—with a long table that could've sat thirty-ish people . . . maybe more. The centerpiece in the middle was a marble sculpture of a plate of Krupcake's Pies and Cakes. The table looked especially empty because only four people were there—Maddie, her parents, and me-the girl in the tablecloth dress. Kenneth pulled out my chair and I sat down, but I wasn't sure what to think of the bowl of green liquid in front of me.

"Cold cucumber soup," Kenneth whispered when he saw my confused look.

I nodded. Now I really wasn't sure what to think. *Cold* soup? We didn't eat cold soup in the Kaplan-Taylor house, but my parents always told me try new things at least once to see if I liked them. I wouldn't let Mom and Dad down, even if this soup did look like my face cream.

Mr. Von Krupcake was at the head of the table with Mrs. Von Krupcake beside him. Lucky for Maddie she looked just like her mom . . . who could have doubled for Grace Kelly with her pretty blond hair and sparkling almond eyes.

"Darling, this is Mr. Taylor's daughter, Maeve," Mr. Von Krupcake said. "She's the one I was telling you about . . . the girl with the big red curls."

Without thinking, I reached up and stroked my hair. *Was that supposed to be a good thing or a bad thing?* I wondered, finally taking a tiny sip of the soup. It wasn't bad, but the whole "cold" part kind of freaked me out.

"You're right, Walter. She looks just a bit like a precious Little Orphan Annie. How charming. Maeve, I'm Maddie's mother, Clarissa Von Krupcake. Maddie tells me you want to be an actress too."

"Oh my gosh, yes. It's been my dream for as long as I can remember. My dad owns the Movie House so—"

"How fortunate for you that you can have a mentor like my Maddie around," Mr. Von Krupcake interrupted.

"You must feel lucky to have the opportunity to work with a real professional."

"Yeah, it's cool." I gave Maddie a smile.

"Our little Krupcake Princess!" Mrs. Von Krupcake squeezed Maddie's hand. "Darling, how *do* you deal with all the autographs? It must be so exhausting."

Maddie nodded sadly. "I despise the paparazzi. They are soooo intrusive," she lamented.

Wow! I hadn't seen any kids ask Maddie for her autograph, but I didn't say anything. Maybe I had missed all of that while I was helping Apollo move the couch.

"Maddie's agent is going to have so many auditions lined up for Maddie after they see her work in film camp. You know what would be the perfect part for you, darling?"

"What?" Maddie asked in a pouting voice, still acting wounded over the hounding hoards of paparazzi.

"*Regally Blonde*—you could play Elle Woods's more beautiful and wealthier younger sister," Mrs. Von Krupcake decided. "Walter, you should call Reese and see if she'd be interested in collaborating. Matt Damon could write the script and set it right here in Boston."

"Hee hee, ha ha, how divine!" Mr. Von Krupcake clapped enthusiastically.

I was speechless. The Von Krupcakes just threw names around as if they could make this stuff actually happen. Maybe they could. All of a sudden, I was starting to feel like the most boring, ordinary person in the world. Maybe becoming an actress wasn't about hard work, talent, and dedication. What you really needed to make a movie wasn't a dad who owned a movie house—it was a dad who could buy a movie empire. After all, I was just Little Orphan Annie with the big red curls . . . while Maddie was a princess who could sail right through to Hollywood. Suddenly, all I wanted was to go home and snuggle into my bed in my own very pink palace . . . even if it was more like a pink shoe box compared to Maddie's room.

"Speaking of divine," Maddie began, "Maeve, you simply must visit our cottage in the Hamptons over the summer!"

Suddenly the gray cloud that had formed over my head totally disappeared. Did somebody say the Hamptons? *Beaches and movie stars and shells . . . oh my!*

". . . Oh, it's sooo fabulous, Maeve. You have NO idea. All we do is swim, play tennis, go to parties, sunbathe on the gorgeous beaches, and eat at the most expensive restaurants. Plus, it's where all the big celebs go on vacay." (Of course, I already knew that. I always kept up with my celebrity gossip magazines.)

As Kenneth served the main course (a delicious beef tenderloin with roasted potatoes and grilled asparagus), I imagined lying on the beach wearing a pink, polka-dot bathing suit, a big straw beach hat, and my oversized Jackie O glasses, all while sipping a strawberry smoothie. I would so enjoy the life of luxury. The photographers would flock to get a snapshot of the blonde and red-haired society girls—and future movie stars *extraordinaire*. Count me in.

Maddie took a bite of her beef tenderloin. She was so dainty and graceful, I wondered if she'd ever been to one of those fancy finishing schools, like rich girls in the movies. I tried my best to copy how she was eating . . . it was good practice for my future Hollywood galas.

"Last year Apollo and Artemia stayed with us during July and Apollo taught me to surf. I was a natural. Maybe he'd teach you too, Maeve," said Maddie.

"Oh, I don't know." I remembered how disappointed Apollo was in me today. His idea of a life of glamour was very different from Maddie's . . . but Maddie's seemed way more fun. I was all about meeting famous people and sunbathing and going to parties with former child stars! The BSG were never going to believe this. Never.

When we finished up with dinner, Kenneth wheeled in a tray with a three-tiered cake. "Chocolate fudge," he announced to Mr. Von Krupcake. "As you requested."

"Marvelous!" Mr. Von Krupcake exclaimed, cutting a hefty slice, and placing it in front of himself as he licked his lips. "Hee hee, ha ha! This looks *delicious*."

Mrs. Von Krupcake grabbed the plate from his hands. "Darling, you forgot your manners. Guests first." Mrs. Von Krupcake smiled fondly at me and pushed the huge piece of cake in my direction. "Here you go, Maeve. It's our own family speciality. The Von Krupcake signature Über Duber Decadent Chocolate Cake!" she whispered.

I took a small bite of the purest, richest morsel I had ever tasted in my life. "Oh my goodness!" I gasped. "This is the best chocolate cake I have ever had."

The Krupcake King beamed as I took another bite.

"Me next!" Maddie pleaded.

Mrs. Von Krupcake shot her a stern look. "Madeline, you know you can't have this. Chocolate cake gives you headaches, remember."

"But, Mummy . . ." Madeline whined.

"Darling, we must watch our health now," Mrs. Von Krupcake said with a smile.

Maddie looked sad. I didn't blame her. I took one more big bite and then put my fork down. I didn't want Maddie to feel bad that she couldn't have any cake. It must be horrible to be allergic to something so heavenly.

"Stop pouting, Maddie." Mrs. Von Krupcake raised her eyebrows.

Suddenly my delicious chocolate cake didn't taste that delicious anymore. Especially when I saw how Mr. Von Krupcake was digging enthusiastically into his piece while Maddie sat looking at him sadly.

"Come on, Maeve. Let's go!" Maddie huffed. She pushed her chair into the table and grabbed my arm . . . kind of hard.

"Now, darling, don't *be* that way!" Mrs. Von Krupcake called. "Kenneth will bring you some grapes." But Maddie was already stomping out of the room with me hopping around in the world's ugliest dress to keep up. I looked back at Maddie's parents. Mr. Von Krupcake was still eating and Mrs. Von Krupcake was still picking. Neither of them seemed bothered by the weirdness at all.

CHAPTER

9

The Princess and the Pea(brain)

Guess what, Maeve?" Maddie whispered. We were finally in our pjs, all cozy in Maddie's king-sized bed with the glorious lace veil around it. It was like being in another world.

"What?" I asked.

"Well I've been giving this a lot of thought, and I realized that you and I have more in common than anyone else I've ever known," Maddie confessed.

I felt so touched. "Wow, Maddie. I know. We DO have tons in common. I mean, we both want to be movie stars . . ." I started, but then I wasn't sure what to say. *Besides the movie star thing, what else do Maddie and I have in common?*

Maddie continued. "So I decided that you, Maeve Kaplan-Taylor, are my new best friend!"

I was silent.

"Well . . . how cool is *that*?" Maddie pressed.

Okay, on one hand it was pretty cool that a famous person like the Krupcake Princess wanted to be my best friend. But on the other hand, I already had best friends . . . four to be exact. I didn't want to be disloyal. But on the other hand, if there was one thing that the BSG taught me, it was that you can always open your heart to new friends. The more the merrier . . . right?

"That's awesome!" I said. "You really want to be best friends . . . with me?"

"Well, of course, silly! We're practically soul mates already." Maddie giggled.

I smiled my kindest smile. "Cool."

"Do you know the *first thing* best friends do?" Maddie asked, her eyes gleaming.

My throat felt dry. "What?"

"Tell each other all their secrets!" Maddie exclaimed. "So let's start with an easy one. Who do you like?"

My heart fluttered a bit. "Who do I like?"

"Yeah. And not just as a friend. Who do you *like* like?"

I took a deep breath and thought about all the boys I'd had mini-crushes on this past year—Nick, Dillon, Riley, Matt the tutor . . . There were a lot, but there honestly wasn't one totally special person I could name at the moment.

"I dunno," I said. "There's not really anyone right now."

"Come on, that's not true!" Maddie accused. "Do you

like Apollo? 'Cause if you do, that's okay. But you should know that he and I . . . well . . . we kind of have a thing."

That was sure news to me. Apollo was obviously cute, but hello? I barely knew him! "Maddie, I don't like Apollo," I promised. "Not like that . . . besides he's older than I am."

"Swear on our friendship?" Maddie asked, holding out her pinky for me to shake.

"Swear on our friendship," I assured her.

"Good. Then I *know* you're telling the truth. So next question. What's your fabulous idea for the film?"

Talk about flattering! "You really want to know?" I asked, suddenly wondering if my idea—that last week had seemed soooo brilliant—would sound silly to the worldly and sophisticated Madeline Von Krupcake.

"Of course I want to know, Maeve! That's what best friends are for . . ." She squeezed my hand reassuringly.

"What best friends are for," I repeated.

Maddie nodded enthusiastically. "So come on . . . spill it," she ordered.

"Well have you ever heard of *Roman Holiday*?"

Maddie shook her head.

I smiled. "Okay, let me explain . . ." I told Maddie all about the classic film and my idea for *Boston Holiday*—right down to the secret romance between Princess Sophia and the reporter. "And listen, here's the best part of all. The reporter would secretly be a kung fu champion who has to protect Princess Sophia from kung fu fighting bad guys. We could have *awesome* kung fu choreography around all the famous Boston landmarks." I took a deep breath and looked up nervously. "Well . . . what do you think?"

Maddie put her hand to her chest. "Oh, Maeve. It's a fabulous idea!"

"Really?"

"Of course, darling! A classic movie set right here in our very own Boston? It's brilliant—just brilliant. Artemia will love it."

I almost wanted to cry out of joy. Maddie seemed to know all there was to know about movies. This was definitely a good sign.

"Hey can I ask you a question now?"

Maddie sat up and twirled a strand of golden hair around her finger. "Of course. Anything."

I smiled and leaned in. There was something I had been wondering about ever since the first day of camp. "So what's the big surprise your dad planned?"

Maddie opened her mouth when suddenly the intercom buzzed. "Ten o'clock. Bedtime, Miss Madeline," said Kenneth.

Maddie sighed. "Oh well. Looks like that'll have to wait 'til the morning." She yawned, clapped her hands together, and the lights in her room instantly went off.

"But," I began.

Maddie giggled and put one finger over her lips. "Shh! We're very strict about bedtime at my house. Sweet dreams, darling."

I didn't want to disobey the rules, so I snuggled into her feather-stuffed comforter and pillows, feeling very much like the princess from *Boston Holiday.* "Sweet dreams, Maddie," I whispered. "I'm glad we're friends."

"Best friends," Maddie added. "Good night."

"Oh Wouldn't It Be Lovely?"

All night long I had the most wonderful dreams about what the surprise would be. My imagination was going crazy. One dream was about a week-long cruise after camp was over. Another was that Maddie and I were cast in a real Hollywood movie, with Artemia directing. I woke up to the sound of a little dog barking. "Mmm . . . Marty . . . shh . . ." I mumbled as I groped around to give my furry little buddy a good morning hug.

"Who's Marty? Is he your *secret crush?*"

I bolted upright. Maddie Von Krupcake was sitting next to me with her hair in curlers stroking Fitzy the Pomeranian. For a split second I forgot that I was sleep-ing over at the Von Krupcakes' and thought I was back in the Tower with the BSG. Maddie pressed the clicker and Kenneth's voice sounded through the intercom. "Ready for breakfast?"

"Yes, Kenneth. Now. I'm starving. So tell me, Maeve, who is Marty?"

I laughed. "Marty's my dog. Well, me and all my friends' dog. He's the BSG mascot."

"What's the BSG?" Maddie gave me a weird look. If she wasn't one of my best friends, I would've been afraid to answer.

"Um . . . the Beacon Street Girls . . ." I said softly.

Maddie suddenly burst out laughing. "You are just too cute Maeve—I can't even stand it."

I wiped the sleep out of my eyes. "How am I cute?"

"I don't know. You're just so . . . commonplace . . . with your little club and your little sleepover parties."

I was beginning to get that horrible boring and ordinary feeling again.

"We aren't *that* cute," I said quietly. "Hey, Maddie . . . now can you maybe tell me about the surprise?"

"Well . . . maybe I can give you a clue. Tell me honestly, have you ever been to a real red carpet event?"

"Um, besides the first day of camp . . . no."

Maddie threw a satin robe over her shoulders and squeezed some lotion on her hands. "The first day of camp doesn't count," Maddie pronounced as she walked over to the bookshelf that went all the way up to the ceiling. Maddie climbed a ladder to reach whatever it was that she was looking for. "All right, Maeve, since we're best friends, I'm going to show you my most prized possession," she said, climbing back down.

In her hands was a giant black book. "I've been going to red carpet events my entire life. Every socialite and actress absolutely must keep a scrapbook of all the amazing things she does and all the fabulous people she meets." Maddie threw the book on her bed and plopped down beside it. "It's like a portfolio, sort of."

I reached out to open it, but Maddie yanked it back. "Don't touch," she ordered again. Maddie opened up the book to the middle and pointed to a cutout magazine photo of her with a gorgeous blond man in a tux. "That was at the premiere of *Wyoming Rodeo*," she informed me.

My jaw dropped. "Whoa! Is that you with . . . Keith Ridger?" Keith Ridger was a big-time, A-list Hollywood star—talented and adorable. I read somewhere that his nickname in Hollywood was Brad Pitt Jr.

Maddie shrugged like it was no big deal. "Yeah. Keith said he'd love to work on a movie with me someday. Isn't that just too much?"

I nodded and tried my hardest to smile. Keith Ridger was as dreamy as dreamy could get—especially with his Western accent. I had been hopelessly devoted (tragically, a one-sided romance) to Keith ever since I saw him in his breakout movie *Kiss Me, Karen*. I couldn't help feeling just the tiniest (okay maybe not-so-tiniest) pang of jealousy, but I knew that as a best friend it was my job to be supportive. "Too much," I echoed.

Maddie flipped the page. "Oh and here's one of me with Venice Doubletree."

"The famous hotel heiress?" I gasped.

Maddie tilted the book in my direction. "See for yourself." Sure enough, there she was standing with her arms wrapped around the willowy bleach-blond model/ socialite. "Venice and I are totally best friends," Maddie added. I looked at Maddie and wondered how an eighteen-year-old celebrity would want to be best friends with a twelve-year-old.

There was a knock on the door and I heard Kenneth announce, "Breakfast is served."

"Enter," Maddie called.

"Good morning, Miss Madeline. Good morning, Miss Maeve," Kenneth said cheerfully as he opened the door and smiled. And for the record, he had a smile that could melt any girl's heart.

"Morning, Kenneth," I said with a huge grin. "What's for breakfast?" I asked when I noticed the cart with two silver platters on top.

"Belgian waffles with whipped cream and strawberries," he answered, dramatically lifting the silver cover. My mouth instantly watered when I saw the stack of thick, piping hot waffles and bowl full of sugary strawberries. "And the tape you requested, Miss Madeline." Kenneth took off the second cover to reveal a DVD.

Maddie leapt off the bed and snatched up the movie. "Look, Maeve! It's *Roman Holiday*! Daddy had his people buy it this morning and bring it over."

"People being me," Kenneth added with a wink.

"I thought maybe you could use a little inspiration," Maddie said with a shrug.

"Wow, Maddie, that's so nice of you." *Maddie really is a sweet girl, once you get to know her*, I thought.

Maddie ran over to her enormous flat screen TV to pop in *Roman Holiday*. I had to admit, I was a little surprised at how eager she was to learn more about my idea. Who knew that I had such a natural flair for movie ideas?

Kenneth carefully prepared our waffles. "Lots of strawberries," I mouthed. (I do love those little berries.) As Maddie fiddled with the TV, I stared at the scrapbook.

Who else is in here? I wondered. Without even thinking I flipped it open to the front. *"What?"* I whispered to myself. One person on the very first page was obvious—President Bill Clinton. But who was the little girl standing next to him? Okay, maybe little would be the wrong word. The girl looked about seven maybe, but she was kind of chubby, and it didn't take the fashion brain of Katani to know that the leopard print leggings were a big mistake. Her hair was brown and frizzy and she wore a pair of thick dark glasses.

Suddenly a hand reached out and slammed the book shut. "What are you doing, Maeve?" Maddie cried.

"Huh? I—I—I was just looking."

"Well don't!" Maddie snapped. "Why would you want to look at my cousin anyway?"

"That's your cousin? Wow, she looks nothing like you."

Maddie huffily sat back down on the bed as the movie started to play. "Thank goodness. Why do you think we're not close, Maeve? Ugh. She's terrible and I don't want to talk about it."

"Okay," I agreed . . . definitely not wanting to talk about it either. I didn't know what to say because I didn't know what I had done wrong.

"Now, let's eat, shall we?" Maddie asked.

"We shall," I said quite properly if I do say so myself. But I was starting to think that all of the Krupcakes, including my new best friend Maddie, were kind of weird.

Kenneth pressed a button that dimmed the lights and

closed the drapes. *These people and their buttons!* I thought. But I had to admit, I was impressed. *Breakfast in bed? Watching any movie, at any time, right in your own room? A spinning closet? KENNETH!* I really did feel like Audrey Hepburn in *My Fair Lady*. There was no doubt about it—this was definitely the life for Maeve Kaplan-Taylor. My mind was filled with fantasies about what life would be like if I were this rich. I would build a fort for my brother in the backyard . . . I would give my father a new car and take my mother shopping for the most glorious clothes ever . . . My guinea pigs would have a gold cage . . . I would have a pink fur bedspread . . .

If I were as rich as Maddie, I wouldn't have a care in the world. Why, in Maddie's gorgeous bedroom, I couldn't even remember what my cares used to be. *Oh well*. They probably weren't that important anyway.

"What Do the Simple Folk Do?"

The next day after film camp, I was invited back to the Krupcake palace. I wanted to stay for dinner, but Mom put her foot down. She said I had to be back at 6 o'clock on the dot for a family meal. When Maddie's chauffeur dropped me off that evening, I couldn't help feeling a little disappointed. Was my apartment always so itsy-bitsy?

As soon as I walked in, there was a camera in my face. "She DOES exist!" Sam gasped.

"Sam, go away!" I begged, remembering Maddie's paparazzi aggravation.

"Well look who's finally decided to grace us with her

presence," Mom said as she stirred the pot on the stove.

"Okay . . . look, Mom, I know I've been gone for a while . . . but I did call . . . and you *did* say it was okay to go to Maddie's after camp," I pointed out.

Mom walked over to the table with a casserole bowl of macaroni and cheese.

"Well, that was very sweet of you," Mom remarked, "but it would be nice if we could spend a little time together, Maeve."

"Yeah!" Sam piped.

"Hey, no comments from the peanut gallery," I quipped, sounding exactly like Dad. I wasn't sure what the peanut gallery was, but I knew it had something to do with when you talked about things that were plain old none of your business.

"Maeve," Mom warned quietly, "be nice to your brother. He just misses you."

I sighed and stared at the huge bowl of yellow noodles. "Do I seriously have to eat this, Mom?" I whined. After the beef tenderloin last night, I wasn't sure if I could ever put a macaroni noodle in my very sophisticated mouth again.

"This is not a restaurant, young lady," Mom replied, looking kind of surprised at me. "Since when do you not eat mac 'n' cheese?"

I tossed my hair over my shoulder and said in a bored voice, "You guys are so cute."

Mom and Sam looked at each other and then at me. "Cute?" Sam did not sound happy.

"Yes. With your little mac 'n' cheese and your little

video camera. It's all so . . ." I tried to remember the word Maddie had used. ". . . commonplace."

"Commonplace?" Mom's voice was making me a little nervous, but I tried as best I could to be as dignified as Maddie. "Maeve, maybe if this dinner is too 'common-place' for you, you should just go up to your room."

I stood up and pushed in my chair. "Fine. You can send my dinner up to my room. I'll have anything—besides mac 'n' cheese."

Mom stared at me for a while like I had three heads. So did Sam. Then the two of them began to giggle. The giggles started out like quiet little snorts at first but soon Mom and Sam were out-of-control laughing. "Whew!" Mom said when she started to calm down a little. "That was a good one."

"What's so funny?" I demanded.

Sam shook his head and squealed . . . being as annoying as he possibly could.

"News flash, Princess Maeve. The maid is off today. Now go upstairs and clean your room. You can come back down when you can behave like a normal human being," Mom said sternly. "GO."

I marched to my bedroom. Why was my star-power attitude getting me in trouble? It worked for Maddie . . . why not me? Life was so unfair sometimes. I couldn't wait until I had my own personal suite of rooms at the Beverly Hills Hotel.

10

Et Tu, Madeline?

Something huge was happening first thing Friday morning at camp—FINALLY. And that something huge was the pitch meeting. That was where everyone got to propose their ideas for the movie. And after watching *Roman Holiday* at Maddie's, I was totally pumped for it.

"Okay, kids, circle up. We have a big day ahead of us," Artemia called, clapping her hands. Today Artemia wore a sleek suit and looked—as usual—straight off the pages of a fashion magazine.

Everyone hustled onto the stage. Maddie and I sat next to each other and I reached over and squeezed her hand. "Are you excited?" I whispered.

Maddie nodded but didn't look back at me, and she let go of my hand really quickly. If I didn't know any better, I would've guessed she was nervous. But come on. Madeline Von Krupcake was totally a professional, and professionals NEVER got nervous.

Artemia took a sip of her soy cappuccino and began, "So far we've learned a little bit about acting. We've learned a little bit about equipment and jobs. And we've learned a little bit about team—" Artemia paused and looked slightly annoyed. "Apollo, care to join us?" she asked.

Apollo was perched on a ladder switching a light bulb. He sighed and stepped down. "Fine . . . but Mom, Mr. Taylor *did* ask me to help out with this stuff."

Maddie rolled her eyes at me and whispered, "I don't care if she IS his mother! If Apollo doesn't watch it, he is SO not going to get a speaking part. He's a total fox, too. Major tragedy."

I nodded. "Major."

"As I was saying, we've learned a bit about teamwork. Which means . . ." Artemia looked at every camper with a smile. ". . . it's time for us to make our very own movie!"

Everyone clapped and hooted. Even Apollo looked excited. (Take it from me, once you get bitten by the movie bug, it doesn't just go away.)

"So, who'd like to share an idea for the movie?" Artemia glanced around the circle and made eye contact with me. "Anyone?"

My heart started beating faster. I wanted to share. Definitely. But I sort of, kind of didn't want to share *first*.

"I've got an idea!" volunteered a girl across the circle.

"Yes, Rebeccah," Artemia said.

"So it's like there's this girl, right? And she's really rich and engaged to this guy who's kind of mean but also rich. And she's going on this huge cruise ship. And when she's on the boat she meets this really poor, really cute guy. And he's an artist and they fall in love. But then, the boat hits an iceberg . . ."

"Isn't that the same plot as *Titanic*?" shouted a boy.

Rebeccah looked crushed. "Oh . . . *no wonder* Mom said it sounded familiar."

Artemia nodded. "Don't worry, Rebeccah. Wonderful movies have been made using classic formulas. Remember *West Side Story*? You know, that's *Romeo and Juliet*? Just make sure if you borrow ideas that you make them your own. That means original," she advised. I felt like I was going to burst with my own fabulous plot, because I was pretty sure I had made it my own. *Boston Holiday*—a creative takeoff—was definitely going to be the hit of the day. "Who else would like to share?"

Sam waved his hand and shouted, "Ooh, ooh, me, me!"

Now my heart was pounding for a different reason. I never had any clue what Sam was going to say. And mostly I could be pretty sure it would embarrass me.

"What about if we do a movie where a spaceship lands in Washington, D.C.? And then the FBI, and the CIA, and the Army need to figure out a way to attack the aliens. But the thing is—the aliens . . ." Sam said, looking excitedly around the circle, "are disguised as humans. Cool, huh?"

I couldn't believe it. Some of the kids were actually looking excited about this. Personally, I was *not* a fan of alien movies. I mean, come on . . . little green dudes coming to earth in a flying saucer? Please. Movies about romance were way more realistic.

"I like your creativity, Sam," Artemia said. "But we also need to consider our limitations as a production crew. For example . . . we aren't shooting in Washington, D.C. And special effects—like UFOs—can be difficult. Still, great thinking, Sam. You have a wonderful imagination."

Then I knew. It was time for me to give the campers a taste of REAL movie brilliance. I slowly raised my hand just as Artemia turned to glance in my direction.

"Go ahead," she said.

I took a deep breath, but at that very moment Maddie began to speak.

"Thank you, Artemia." Maddie stood and walked right into the middle of the circle and stood next to Artemia—cool and confident as ever. "I have an idea for the most fabulous movie ever," Maddie announced.

The campers started whispering to each other, hanging on Maddie's every word.

What's going on? If Maddie has such a fabulous idea, why didn't she tell me about it at our sleepover? Was my new best friend breaking the number-one rule of best friendship and keeping a secret from me? I wanted to think no . . . but something funny was definitely going on.

"Ahem!" Maddie made sure all eyes were on her. "I call this movie . . . *Boston Holiday.*"

WHAT? I suddenly felt dizzy.

"Go on," urged Artemia, looking intrigued.

"Like Rebeccah's idea, it's based on a classic movie—*Roman Holiday.* Except it's original too, like you said. It would be set in modern times, in our very own city of Boston."

I couldn't believe my ears. I tried to give Maddie a look, but she wouldn't even turn in my direction.

"The main character is called Princess Sophia. She and her father are from the country of Tazmundo and they go to Boston on a royal visit. But once they arrive, Princess Sophia gets sick of having to do all of her princess-ly duties all the time. Trust me—being a princess is a lot harder than it looks."

The campers nodded at each other. Seriously, it was like they were feeling sorry for Maddie or something. I could tell she loved every second of it.

Maddie continued. "So Princess Sophia runs away and meets this handsome reporter. The two of them go all around Boston and have all sorts of fabulous adventures. Meanwhile, the princess has no idea, but there are bad guys trying to kidnap her. And check it out—here's where it gets *really* cool. I was thinking that we could use Artemia's special talents to incorporate kung fu choreography throughout the whole movie."

Artemia burst into a huge smile, as I felt the tears start to burn my eyes. Maddie had taken my fabulous idea and stolen it. I wanted to jump up and scream, but I was seriously way too shocked to move. Was this really happening to me?

Maddie was wearing her hair in loose blond ringlets. In her white skirt and blouse she probably looked like a perfect angel to everyone there . . . everyone except *me*.

Maddie giggled and twirled her hair around her finger. "There's one more thing that'll make the movie very . . . original. I was thinking the princess might run away with her maid. I sort of imagine her as mousy and little . . . with frizzy red hair and glasses. She'd be a funny sidekick for the beautiful princess, right?"

"I like what I'm hearing, Maddie," Artemia said. "I'm very . . . impressed."

Maddie shrugged and waved the compliment away. "Well I can't take all the credit. Maeve did help. A little." Maddie looked at me and gave me her sweetest smile. I did *not* smile back.

"Does anyone else have anything they'd like to share?" Artemia asked. "Maeve?"

My throat felt like it was made out of sandpaper. "No," I said softly.

Artemia looked suspicious for a second. "Anyone else?"

Everyone shook their heads. "I like Maddie's idea," one girl offered.

"Yeah," another boy agreed. "Kung fu fighting in Boston sounds awesome. Imagine all the cool stuff we could do!"

Pretty soon everyone was babbling to each other about how amazing MADDIE'S idea was. If only I had a friend there to talk to . . . just someone who would believe me when I said the idea was mine and not Maddie's. But I had been so busy thinking Maddie was the coolest girl ever that I hadn't even bothered to make friends with anyone else. Now I was back at zero. Maddie was definitely not my best friend. In fact, she wasn't my friend at all.

"Well then, it's settled." Artemia clapped her hands.

"We'll begin working on *Boston Holiday* immediately. Maddie, thank you for your contribution. For those of you who want to act in this movie, keep in mind that auditions will be held on Monday. If you are interested in another job, see me."

Maddie bounced back to her seat and turned to me with a pleased smile. "You see, Maeve, *Boston Holiday* is a complete smash."

It took absolutely all my strength to answer. "You—you—you stole my idea!" I breathed.

"Oh silly, I didn't steal it. I just knew that if you wanted people to do *Boston Holiday* you would NEED me to back it up. Why do you think everyone agreed in the first place?"

"Because it was brilliant?"

"No," Maddie folded her arms. "*Because it came from me.* I hate to break it to you, Maeve, but that's just how things work. If you want to make a movie about a princess, it has to come from me."

I folded my arms. "What makes you so sure you're going to be the princess?"

Maddie began to laugh and then she stopped. "Oh, you're serious? Get real, Maeve. Who else do you think could play the princess?"

I shrugged. "Well, I wouldn't mind . . ."

Maddie snorted and covered her mouth. "I'm sorry, I'm sorry. Maeve, you are TOO CUTE! Silly, why do you think I made up the maid part?" Maddie was laughing uncontrollably now.

I felt so *furious* at Princess Maddie . . . furious . . . like smoke coming out of the ears, cartoon-style furious. It was time for my Oscar-worthy impromptu.

"Thanks so much for thinking of me, Maddie . . . but I'm still going to try out for the princess."

Maddie tossed her hair and pushed out her chest. "Oh yeah?" she sneered.

"Yeah." I stuck out my hand for her to shake. "May the best actress win."

Maddie went to grab my hand, but then at the last minute pulled it away and wiped it on her shirt like she had touched something dirty. "I'm going to go talk to Artemia. Since *Boston Holiday* was my idea, I'm sure she's going to have a lot of questions for me."

Maddie stuck her nose in the air and huffed away. "Oh, and Maeve," she added, glancing over her shoulder. "If you change your mind about the maid part . . . call me."

"Don't hold your breath," I whispered. Let Maddie put on a little wig and be the mousy maid. This was war.

Part Two
Red Fooey Rides Again

11

Bubble Burst

It didn't take long for the news to spread around camp that M&M were O-V-E-R. The only problem was, no one had any clue why. And the rumors were flying. When I went outside to get a drink of water, I could hear some kids talking in hushed voices around the corner. I pressed myself up against the wall and stayed as quiet as possible. "Did you hear?" said a boy. "Maddie and Maeve are in a *huge fight.*"

"No way! What happened?" asked a girl.

"I thought that they were BFFs," said another girl.

"Not anymore," whispered the boy. "No one knows for sure, but I heard Maeve stole Maddie's diary and published it!"

I felt dizzy. *Stay calm, Maeve,* I reminded myself.

"I heard that Maddie has a crush on Apollo and Maeve tried to go behind her back and steal him!"

I put my hand over my mouth. *Yeah, right!*

"Well, I heard that they were going to do a reality show together, but Maddie backed out at the last minute. They don't even want to be taped together!"

"NO!" gasped all the kids.

"Yes."

I tiptoed down the hall to get away from all the whispering. Being the center of gossip wasn't fun at all.

"Hey, Maeve, is it true that M&M *broke up*?" asked a very familiar voice. I turned around to see the black circle at the end of Sam's camera staring me in the face. Behind him, Apollo stood at the top of a ladder adjusting a light, smiling at Sam and laughing to himself. I should've known Apollo would think this was funny.

"No comment!" I huffed and tried to block the lens with my hand.

"Hey quit it! You're going to smudge the glass!" Sam cried.

"Sam, enough taping for now, dude," Apollo instructed. I was surprised. Was Apollo actually on my side in this?

"But I'm the filmotograph—"

Just then the three of us turned at the sound of Maddie's crystal-clear stage voice booming from inside the theater.

"Artemia, you and Apollo *must* come to the Hamptons this summer! It will be sooo divine."

The dream-bubble of Maddie and me on the beach with my pink polka-dotted bathing suit, straw beach hat, and Jackie O sunglasses burst into a million slimy little pieces.

"What're the Hamptons?" Sam whispered to Apollo as he passed him a new light bulb.

"Man, you don't want to know," Apollo replied.

I instinctively put my hand over my heart. "Are you kidding? Sam, the Hamptons are where all the big celebs hang out during the summer. It's like the most incredible place to be. There are parties and beaches and . . . and I'm never going to go . . ." I almost cried on those last words. It wasn't that I really wanted to go to Maddie's "cottage." I mean, not after what she did to me. But still . . . it was the Hamptons.

"Don't sweat it, Maeve. Except for the beaches, the Hamptons aren't as great as you think. It's mostly just a lot of hoity-toities who think that going to the Hamptons is pretty much the most important thing in the world." Apollo demonstrated by pretending to sip out of a tea cup. "Ah, how *delightful!*" he said in a fake accent.

Sam started to laugh, and I did too, remembering how Maddie sipped her cocoa in her bedroom. Maybe Apollo was right.

"Maeve, Apollo, there you are!"

I was surprised to see Artemia holding her director's notebook and standing in the doorway. I was even more surprised NOT to see Maddie. I thought she was super-glued to Artemia! Instead there was another girl with Artemia. She looked like she was around my age. She had long, silky dark hair and cute little green glasses. (True confession—I used to wish I had bad eyesight just so I could get a pair of sophisticated glasses. Alas, I was cursed with perfect vision.)

"Kids, I want you to meet Lizzie Kwan," said Artemia. "Lizzie knows how to work Final Draft—a script-writing computer program. She's volunteered to put together a screenplay for *Boston Holiday*. Apollo, since you also know Final Draft, I thought you could help. And Maeve, since you and Maddie came up with the idea, I was wondering if you'd like to do some more brainstorming as well."

Apollo grinned. "Yeah! That sounds cool. Maeve . . . you in?"

There were so many questions spinning around my head like a tornado. One of them, of course, was if Maddie would be a part of this project too.

As though Artemia was reading my mind, she told us, "I asked Maddie if she had anything else to contribute, but it seems she's not interested in doing any writing."

Maddie waltzed onto the stage and practiced curtsey-ing. "I am an ack-*tour*. My work here," she waved her finger around at us like we were her own little gnomes, "is done."

I tried to totally ignore Princess Krupcake. "Are we allowed to work on the script and still act in the film?" I asked Artemia.

She nodded. "Absolutely. I want you kids to get a taste of as much as you possibly can here at film camp. The more things you try, the better."

Sam had picked up his camera and started rolling again. I knew I had a serious decision to make. I could decide not to work on the film . . . and continue doing everything Maddie did. *Wait. Copying everything Maddie did*, I realized with a sinking feeling. OR I could help Apollo and Lizzie and tell them the rest of my idea.

Decision? This was a no-brainer.

"I'm in!" I exclaimed.

Maddie smiled her sweetest possible smile. "I think the part of the not-pretty redheaded maid is ripe with possibilities, Maeve," she quipped and then whispered with a fake smile, "You should go for it."

I gulped and did *not* smile back. Even though Maddie wasn't as nice as I thought (okay, she was pretty much a Queen of Mean in disguise), she was still a really good actress. Plus she was like Artemia's shadow! Could I ever get the part of the princess over Madeline Von Krupcake? I wanted to so badly . . . but I just wasn't sure anymore.

CHAPTER

12

Boston Brainstorm Bonanza . . .

W hoa, check out the rowers! How are they not freezing?" asked Apollo. He was looking out the window with his mouth completely open in shock.
Oh yeah. I should probably mention that the famous ex-
child star Apollo Aaron was actually sitting in the back
seat of my dad's car. I had to pinch myself a couple of
times to make sure I wasn't dreaming. Dad suggested
taking Lizzie, Apollo, and me on a tour of Boston over
the weekend to brainstorm ideas for the movie. Artemia
thought it was a brilliant plan. And somehow Sam had
managed to weasel his way in . . . with his video camera,
of course.

Dad laughed. "That's the Harvard crew team. They
practice all year long . . . unless the Charles River is
frozen."

Apollo shivered. "I can't believe how cold it is here. Back home, I'd be in a T-shirt right now."

"Where do you come from anyway . . . Venus?" Sam asked. "That's the hottest planet. Even hotter than Mercury, even though Mercury is closer to the sun." Sam was a total math and science brainiac and he wasn't afraid to show it off.

"Nope. Los Angeles," Apollo replied.

"That's where Hollywood is, Sam," I informed him. "Aka—my future home."

"So I guess you really want to be a movie star, huh?" asked Lizzie.

I turned around, as I was sitting in the front seat, and gripped my heart with both hands. "Don't you know? I was *born* for the stage." (True confession—If Apollo and Lizzie hadn't been there, that would've been the point when I broke out in a verse of "There's No Business Like Show Business" but I didn't think that would be the best idea. Especially because there was a one-hundred percent chance that Dad would have joined in, and then we would've really freaked them out. After all, we were the Kaplan-Taylors, not the Von Trapps.)

"So the first stop is Newbury Street," Dad informed us.

"Hold up. What's Newbury Street?" asked Apollo.

"Newbury Street is the awesomest!" I gushed. "The outfits, the stores, the restaurants . . . oh my gosh, it's THE MOST glamorous place to be in Boston. Don't you think, Lizzie? Isn't it the best?"

Lizzie smiled and scribbled something in her notebook.

(*Très* Charlotte of her!) "It's very pretty," she agreed. "I especially like it during the holidays when all the lights are on the trees."

I slipped my large sunglasses down my nose with my finger and said, "Okay, to translate for Hollywood boy in the back seat, Newbury Street is like the Rodeo Drive of Boston . . ." and then I whispered, "Sort of a big deal. It's the place to be seen in the summertime with all the cafés and people-watching."

Apollo looked genuinely horrified.

Dad saw Apollo's contorted face in the rearview mirror and chuckled. "Relax," Dad assured him. "I just figured, since you're writing a script about a princess . . . we might as well go to the princess mother ship."

"Shopping. Shopping. Take me to your leader," Sam sang in a funny alien voice. I gave him a look.

Dad miraculously found a parking space right away and we unloaded in front of J.P. Licks—the famous Boston ice cream store with the Vermont cow design. "Ice cream, anyone?" asked Dad.

We put on our gloves and shivered. "NO!" Apollo looked the most terrified of all. Probably the idea of eating ice cream during the Boston winter sounded as crazy as drinking hot chocolate in the desert.

Dad laughed. "Well I'm craving some Heath bar crunch. And yes, Apollo, I *do* know how cold it is." He went into J.P. Licks while the rest of us stayed in the cold like frozen Popsicles.

"You know," Apollo said, taking a look around. "This

place isn't as bad as I thought. It's actually kind of . . . nice."

"Nice?" I gawked. "Nice? This is the fashion capital of Boston! This is where I get all my inspiration for style. You see"—I linked arms with Lizzie—"I pay close attention to all the hot styles on Newbury Street, and then I go to the discount stores and buy the same stuff but cheaper. No one can tell the difference," I whispered.

It was then that I noticed Sam's camera pointing at me. "Hey, Maeve, what about concentrating on brainstorming for the movie?"

"She is," Lizzie said simply and wrote something down.

"Hey, what'd you write?" I asked.

Lizzie blushed. "Oh it's nothing really. I just thought it would be funny if the maid was a pro discount shopper . . . maybe she could be so good at it, that people can't tell the difference between her and the princess."

Apollo looked up. "Yeah! That's an awesome idea. What should the maid's name be?"

"How about . . . Mauve?" Lizzie offered.

I folded my arms. "No way. That sounds just like 'Maeve.'"

Lizzie looked at the ground. "Sorry. It was the first thing that popped into my head," she explained.

I understood what was happening. Maddie had basically painted the maid part for me, and now it was impossible for Lizzie to imagine anyone else doing it. "You guys, I know Maddie *said* red-haired maid . . . but seriously! The princess part is the one that's perfect for me."

"Okay, so let's come up with a different name then. Something that *doesn't* sound anything like Maeve," Apollo proposed.

The three of us tapped our chins and looked around. Our eyes settled on a sign that read "Sufoo Sushi House."

"That's it!" said Apollo.

"Sufoo!" the three of us chimed at once.

"Sufoo the designer-discount-wearing, bad-guy-brawling, kung-fu-fighting maid. I love it!" I cried, kicking the air to demonstrate.

"Okay, so just who are these 'bad guys' that you and Maddie keep talking about?" asked Apollo. There it was again: you and Maddie.

I couldn't hold it in anymore. "All right. I have to get this off my chest. The film idea, *Boston Holiday* . . . it was mine. Not Maddie's." I bit my lip and waited, hoping that Apollo and Lizzie would believe me.

Apollo started to laugh. "Are you serious?" he asked.

My heart was pounding. "Yeah . . . why?"

Apollo was now laughing so hard that tears were rolling down his cheeks. "Maeve, you didn't have to tell me that! I've known Madeline Von Krupcake for years. That girl hasn't had an original idea in her life."

"Really?" Lizzie and I gasped at the same time.

Apollo nodded. "Oh yeah. That's how she works. Maddie pretends to be your friend, and then she steals your ideas. One minute, it's your idea . . . and then BAM . . . she kidnaps it!"

"Oh my gosh, that's it!" I cried. "The bad guys—they can be kidnappers."

"Oooh, good one," Lizzie agreed. "Kidnappers who are double-crossers. They seem like they're on the king's side, but they're really not."

As soon as Lizzie said "king" one picture immediately popped into my head: the Krupcake King. Then things really started ticking.

"What if the personal assistant is one of the bad guys?" I suggested. I did love that dear Kenneth, but the idea of a double-crosser personal assistant was just too good to be true!

"And the nanny!" Apollo added.

"The nanny?" Lizzie looked shocked.

Apollo shrugged. "There was this one nanny I had when I was little who was grouchy all the time, and her breath always smelled like tuna. It was the worst."

"I think her name should be Nanny Nuna," I suggested. "It has a funny ring to it."

Apollo laughed. "Nanny Nuna. I like that."

Dad came out of the ice cream store looking sticky and full. "How's the brainstorming?" he asked as he beeped open the car.

"Nanny Nuna smells like tuna," Sam told him.

"Sam," I warned, not wanting Dad to think that all we were doing was goofing off. Dad just seemed glad that we were having fun though. "Time for the next stop," he said as we piled into the car. "Beacon Street."

"We're going back already?" Apollo looked seriously

disappointed, but the rest of us Bostonians knew better.

"No, silly. Beacon Street goes aaaaaaall the way into Boston. See?" I said, pointing to a street sign. Beacon Street in Boston was one gorgeous brownstone after another . . . leading right up to Beacon Hill. I trembled a little—out of fright—thinking how close we were getting to Maddie's mansion.

"Hey, there's the *Taj*!" Apollo cried, pointing to the blue regal-looking sign out the window. "That used to be the world-famous Ritz—right?"

"Well, the Boston Ritz-Carlton was the first one ever," Sam stated smugly. "It opened in 1927 and all the kings and queens and movie stars stayed there. And guess what? Back then rooms only cost fifteen dollars!"

I turned around and stared doubtfully at my little brother. "How on earth do you know that, Sam?"

Sam smiled. "I know *everything*."

Dad rolled his eyes. "I told him about it this morning."

"Wait a minute, that's it!" Lizzie cried suddenly. "Princess Sophia and her loyal maid Sufoo are staying at the Taj hotel in Boston—they're on a royal peace trip representing the country of Tazmundo. And the movie starts out showing how glamorous Sophia's life is . . . but Sophia is completely bored and miserable doing everything she's supposed to do."

I gave Lizzie a proud look. "Hey . . . have you seen the original *Roman Holiday*?" I asked. I didn't really know anyone else my own age that was so passionate about old movies. In fact, most of my favorite movies were ones that my friends (including the BSG) had never even heard of.

Lizzie smiled and tossed her long, silky hair over her shoulder. "Please, Maeve. I'm a total movie freak. All my friends think I have the weirdest taste, but I say they have no appreciation for the classics."

My mouth dropped open. Now I was really happy that I was in film camp . . . brainstorming ideas for a movie, meeting other people who were as movie crazed as me . . . what could be better?

I closed my eyes. "I can see it now. Sophia and Sufoo—the beautiful princess and her redheaded maid . . ." I glanced at Lizzie and Apollo and the three of us burst out laughing. "So they're in their gorgeous suite at the Taj, and when Sophia is in the shower—"

"Bubble bath!" Apollo corrected. "A princess would be taking a bubble bath." We stared at him. "What? I grew up in Beverly Hills," he said with a shy shrug.

I grinned and went on. "Obviously I meant bubble bath. And Sufoo overhears the assistant and Nanny Nuna in the connecting room talking about kidnapping Sophia and using her to take over the kingdom of Tazmundo."

"Yeah . . ." Lizzie breathed, sensing my excitement.

"Sufoo has to convince Sophia that she's bored with being a princess, to get her out of the hotel and away from the evil-doers . . ." I said "evil-doers" in a creepy, mysterious voice to really get my point across.

"Sorry to interrupt," Dad said, "but I wanted Apollo to see the Boston Common . . . right over there."

"Huh." Apollo looked kind of bored as he stared out

the car window. "I can see why they call it 'common.'"

I snapped my head around again and glared at Apollo . . . not too mad, but mad enough for him to know not to call the Common common. "I'll have you know, Apollo Aaron, that this just so happens to be the home of the famous swan boats. Ever heard of 'em? Yeah, that's what I thought."

Apollo's mouth hung open for a moment and then he offered, "Okay, but in the winter, no offense, Maeve, the Common just looks like a big fenced-in park."

"But, it would be the perfect place for the first kung fu fight of the movie, don't you think?" mused Lizzie.

"Should I pull over?" Dad asked.

I looked back at the kids and imagined trying to do jump kicks in the park in the middle of a cold, winter day. "I vote no. Too cold!"

The others nodded. "I want to see more Boston!" Apollo burst out.

"See more Boston! See more Boston!" Sam started chanting and pumping his fist in the air.

Before I knew what was happening, we were all in sync with Sam, shouting, "See more Boston!" as loud as we could. Dad didn't mind one bit though. *If he didn't own the Movie House, he would've been a truly fabulous tour guide,* Maeve thought.

Dad led us on a crazy drive, one that made the tiny city of Boston seem like the most exciting place in the world. He looped all around the expressway and over the brand new Leonard P. Zakim Bunker Hill Bridge (isn't that name fantastic?). And the whole way all any of us could do was spill out ideas for *Boston Holiday* like . . . like . . . a big gushing idea fountain.

We drove past Fenway Park and Apollo had the hilarious thought that Princess Sophia could catch a fly ball in the middle of a Red Sox game while Sufoo fends off Nanny Nuna and the assistant, who are disguised as crazed Red Sox fans. Lizzie and I loved that one. Dad bought us a baseball so we could act it out a little. I insisted on being Princess Sophia. Then when Apollo threw me the ball, I got scared at how fast it was going and instead of catching it, dove to the side and covered my head. Avery would've flipped if she'd seen me.

"Stick to the red carpet and stay far, far away from the Green Monster," Sam advised from behind the camera.

"Thanks," I responded with a tone of sarcasm. I did not enjoy being taped at my most un-glamorous.

Then when we were walking in Faneuil Hall—a historic tourist spot with shops and restaurants—a big pink tank drove by and started *quacking* at us. Of course, Dad, Sam, Lizzie, and I knew what was up right away, but Apollo looked totally freaked out. "Whoa, why are all those people quacking at me? Do I have, like, feathers stuck on my coat or something?" He spun around and started batting at the back of his jacket in a furious motion, making me and Sam burst into an uncontrollable fit of Kaplan-Taylor hysterical laughter.

"Stop, stop," I gasped, panting for air. "Apollo, those are the Duck Tours! They always quack at the people on the sidewalk . . . it's part of the fun!" I said as though it made all the sense in the world. People quacking and honking from a brightly colored tank was totally normal, right?

"Hey, imagine how funny it would be if Princess Sophia traded in her tiara for a Duck Tour hat and was all into the Duck Tour, quacking and stuff, while Sufoo was dealing with the bad guys hanging off the back of the tank?" I suggested with a little bit of a devilish grin. I demonstrated doing some kung fu chops off the sidewalk, but had a momentary lapse of gracefulness and fell right-smack on my bum.

I looked up to see Sam's horrid camera very close to my blushing face. "Nice one, Sufoo," Sam jeered.

"Hey, watch it, paparazzi boy," I warned. "And that's Princess Sophia to you, thank you very much."

Apollo, in a very gentleman-like way, bent down and helped me get to my feet. (True confession—I just melt when boys are chivalrous—that means gracious as a Knight of the Round Table. I think it's terribly roman-tic.) Of course then Apollo popped the mood by saying, "Dude, if we *don't* put the Duck Tours into *Boston Holiday* it would be a big mistake."

"Huge," I agreed.

"Mammoth," Lizzie added. Was she a word nerd *and* a movie nerd? No wonder I liked this girl!

"There's one more place we need to see, I think," Dad remarked, leading us back to the car.

"Aw, really? But I'm hungry," Sam griped, "and my

shoulder is killing me." No wonder Sam's shoulder was hurting—he'd been in paparazzi mode 24/7!

"Then stop videotaping me and all my embarrassing moments!" I demanded with my hands on my hips.

Sam turned on the video and pointed it at me. "Hey, it's not my fault you're embarrassing."

I fumed for a few seconds but decided I'd had enough of fighting with Sam. I was actually having too much fun. "Where are we going Dad?" I was dying to know.

"It's a surprise," Dad replied.

"Ooh, surprises are the *greatest*," Lizzie cried, giddy with excitement.

"Not me," Sam blurted. "I want to know NOW!"

"Me too," I admitted. Sam and I were having one of those moments where it was obvious how we were related . . . absolutely no patience whatsoever.

Dad shook his head and continued to drive through the busy Boston traffic. I think he enjoyed torturing his kids, or at least teasing us a little.

Apollo turned his Dodgers hat backward and shrugged. "It's all new to me." He seemed very relaxed. I wondered if it was his laid-back California attitude coming out.

"See, Maeve and Sam. You gotta be more like Apollo. Go with the flow, dude," Dad uttered in a fake-surfer voice. "How am I doing, Apollo?"

Lizzie giggled as Sam shook his head and I buried mine in my hands. But Apollo made a fist and held it up for Dad to tap. "Right on, dude," Apollo said with an approving nod.

"Whoa, dude, what do you know? We're already here," Dad announced in the same goofy way. I was about to die of embarrassment. Then it occurred to me where Dad had taken us, and all at once I forgave him for all his strange dad behavior.

"Chinatown!" I breathed and gazed up at the green shelled rooftop of the tall gate, decorated with gold Chinese characters. "Dad, you are a complete genius!"

"I know," he answered. "I figured a little kung fu inspiration couldn't hurt. Along with . . . moo shu pork and scallion pancakes?"

"Mr. Taylor, you're the man!" Apollo exclaimed.

"Yeah, Dad, you're the man!" Sam echoed.

As we strolled through the streets of Chinatown, I was completely wowed by the store windows. I loved how all the outfits were such vibrant shades of color and embroidered with gold. "Probably at the end of the movie Sufoo should get a cool kung fu costume," I thought out loud, then added. "A discount one, of course."

The rich smells of Chinese food cooking in fryers wafted up from a little basement restaurant—The Dragon Hop. "This has the best egg drop soup in the city," Dad explained.

As we sat down at a table and started to read our Chinese horoscopes, Lizzie looked like a light bulb had suddenly blinked on over her head. She got out her notebook and started scribbling.

"What?" I asked.

She continued scribbling and scrawling until finally

she dropped the pencil and collapsed back in her seat. "Okay, I've got it. Sufoo lives in Chinatown and is trying to be a clothing designer. But her day job is being a maid at the Taj, where she picks up on the styles of the rich and famous." Lizzie spoke quietly even though we were the only guests in the dimly lit restaurant. It felt very official that way.

"I really like where you're going with this, Lizzie," Apollo encouraged.

"So she's putting mints on the pillow in the hotel when she overhears the nanny plotting with the evil assistant. Turns out they know kung fu and have been secretly training in Boston for months! But here's the catch—Sufoo has been training too."

"With her gorgeous kung fu instructor!" I added.

"Exactly!" Lizzie answered with a wide smile.

"Name?" Apollo asked.

I tapped my chin. "Well, in the movie he was played by Gregory Peck, so how about . . ." I waved my hand in the air and said dramatically, "Grego."

"Grego . . . I like it," Apollo decided. "Short, sweet, and simple."

"So Sufoo brings Grego with her and pretends he is a reporter, when really he's there to protect the princess. But then he ends up falling in love with her, and Sufoo saves the day! What do you think?"

Just then, the waiter came over with a three-tiered pu-pu platter. I grabbed an egg roll and took a bite. "I love it," I started to say, but then realized how hot the food was and had to spit it out into my napkin. Ick! Definitely not my best Princess Sophia moment. And even worse—Sam had the camera rolling again.

"Can you *not*?" I begged. "How am I ever going to be the princess, if all the tape shows is me acting like a total slob?"

"You know," Apollo began, digging into a chicken finger, "I think Sufoo is a way cooler part than the princess."

I gave him a look. "Puh-leease."

"No really," Apollo insisted. "Think about it—you'd get to fight, and wear cool costumes, and be the hero in the end. Plus it would be, like, totally hilarious."

Lizzie nodded. "If I was good at acting, I'd definitely want the Sufoo part. It's so original!"

"But Sufoo doesn't get to fall in love," I pointed out. "Not very romantic."

"Blah!" Sam frowned. "Romance is gross, dude." He looked up at Apollo, probably hoping that Apollo would agree.

Apollo put his fist out and tapped Sam's. "Gross for kids." He laughed and then looked back at me, suddenly seeming very serious. "Maeve, if you want to have fun, you should really think about trying out for Sufoo."

"No one could do it like you," Lizzie added.

I felt a little uncomfortable. It was weird—why was everyone trying to talk me out of the princess part? Did they think I was not in the same league as Maddie? I had to prove that I was talented enough to be the lead in this film.

❁ 142 ❁

"No way. I'm trying out for Princess Sophia," I insisted as the waiter plopped a plate of crackling, glistening scallion pancakes in the middle of our table. I stabbed one with my fork and added, "Period, final, the end!" and took a huge bite. "OUCH!" I cried.

"Hot?" asked Dad with a smirk.

"Uh-huh." I reached into my water glass to grab a handful of ice.

"Wow. You are going to be one awesome princess," Sam teased, patting my shoulder. Then he neatly cut a piece of pancake, blew on it, and took a long, satisfied crunch. I glared at Sam, who looked back with a huge smile and pronounced, "Dee-lish."

CHAPTER

13

Downward-Facing Dog

B e online, be online!" I pleaded out loud as I clicked the enter key over and over again. Seriously, I adored the Internet, but why was it that whenever I *really* wanted to get on, it seemed to take forever? I had yoga class in fifteen minutes and there was something really important I had to talk to my friends about. "Come on, BSG, you've *got* to be online!"

Finally the computer made a chortling noise and my buddy list popped up. I was overjoyed. The very top of my list said "Chat Room BSG (5/5)." But then . . . the tragic reality: everyone had put up away messages. Life was too cruel sometimes.

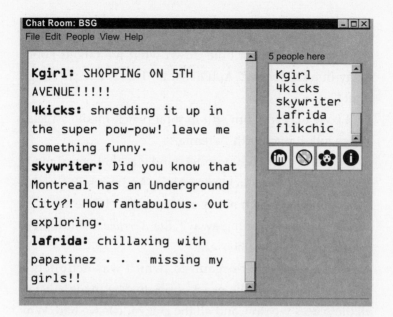

Kgirl: SHOPPING ON 5TH AVENUE!!!!!
4kicks: shredding it up in the super pow-pow! leave me something funny.
skywriter: Did you know that Montreal has an Underground City?! How fantabulous. Out exploring.
lafrida: chillaxing with papatinez . . . missing my girls!!

"Oh, Izzy, I miss you too!" I sighed as I stared at the front page of my notebook. I'd written a note to myself on it and the very sight of it made me feel positively nauseous. "Write sceens 1 and 2—hotel and runing away." I chewed on my thumb. How was I supposed to write an outline of the first two scenes tonight? Apollo was going to do 3 and 4, and Lizzie was going to do 5 and 6. It seemed simple enough, except for one thing: I was probably the worst speller in the history of the world.

At first, I was really excited to start this project after our exciting field trip around the city. But then there was the conversation about the outline I had with Apollo and Lizzie.

"Can we do it on the computer?" I'd asked Apollo.

"Nah . . . just scribble down what we talked about today in a notebook," Apollo said. "This is a *really* rough draft."

Lizzie agreed. "I'm still in total pencil mode. At least 'til we talk it over with Artemia."

But what they didn't understand was that pencil mode for me was pretty much impossible. An impossible nightmare. I looked down at my notes again: "Write sceens 1 and 2—hotel and runing away." *Ew. Terrible.* I shuddered. I knew that couldn't be right.

Lizzie was super-organized, which was definitely a plus, because I was the exact opposite. She made a list of all the places we saw, and all the crazy ideas we had. Why did I have to be dyslexic? It was *so* unfair.

Thank goodness I was allowed to bring my laptop into school with me. Without my spell-checker, I'd be totally lost. But out in the real world, did I really have to abandon my trusty computer and go back to being Maeve the terrible speller? Just when Apollo was finally starting to think I was smart (after a little bit of a bumpy start with Maddie), did I really want to go back to feeling stupid? No way.

I went over to my desk and stared at my face in the mirror. "Hair, A-plus," I said in my most confident voice, twisting a silky red ringlet around my pencil. "Skin . . . A," I decided. Some girls weren't crazy about a few little freckles on their noses like I had, but I happened to like my freckles. My mom and dad said they gave me character. "But spelling . . . ugh. D-minus."

I rested my chin in my hand and blinked back the tears that were clouding my A-plus-pluses. What was it that Dad said about my eyes? Then I remembered it with a weak smile: "Those baby blues speak for themselves." He was always so nice and encouraging and made me feel tons better when no one else could. I sniffled, picked up my cell phone, and dialed Dad's number. He would know the perfect thing to say.

After only two rings Dad picked up. "Hi, Maeve."

"Hey, Dad," I sniffled.

"Sweetie? Is something wrong?"

I gulped. "Well . . ."

"Maeve . . . talk to me, kiddo," Dad encouraged me just a little. He always had so much love and patience that I stopped trying to hold back my tears, and let them drip down my cheeks in a steady drizzle. "Sweetie, what is it?" Dad asked again.

"I—I—I . . ." I sputtered. "I'm supposed to write this outline for the movie, and we aren't allowed to use a computer, and I have to do it in a notebook, and I know that when I do it's going to be just awful, and Lizzie and Apollo are going to know what a terrible writer I am, and they'll think I'm totally stupid. Oh, Dad, this is horrible! I might as well quit right now. I know—I'll just be a mime."

"Maeve!" Dad sounded shocked.

I glared at my reflection in the mirror and miserably added, "They'll probably WISH they had Madeline Von Krupcake in their group instead of me. Dad, believe me . . . I can't do this."

"I'm sorry, may I ask who's calling?" Dad asked. "This must be some kind of prank, because the Maeve Kaplan-Taylor I know is probably the most talented, creative person in all of Massachusetts. No, in all of the United States of America."

Dad was so obviously just trying to make me feel better with his huge exaggeration that I giggled unexpectedly and it came out as a loud snort. "Was that . . . laughter?" Dad prompted.

"Actually it's called a sniggle . . . technically speaking," I said, dabbing the saltiness out of my long eyelashes.

"Maeve, what do you suppose would happen if you came in tomorrow with an outline that you made on the computer?" Dad asked.

I considered that for a sec. "Probably Lizzie and Apollo would think I was too dumb to write without a spell-checker," I moped.

"Sweetie, did you ever think that maybe Apollo and Lizzie would be really impressed that you went above and beyond on the outline?"

"Huh? What do you mean?"

"Well, a computer printout is much easier to read . . . and much more organized. And if that's how you feel most comfortable presenting your ideas, I think it's absolutely fine. Kiddo, I know you're self-conscious about having to use your laptop to organize ideas, but the truth is, it's the end result that matters. When everyone sees all your cool ideas, I promise they'll be impressed."

I got up from my desk, wedged the phone beneath my ear, and started my pre-yoga stretches. It was important to warm up before my lesson. Plus, I was suddenly feeling a little bit brighter. "Really?"

"Absolutely. They're going to think that you're a super hard worker . . . and they already know how talented you are."

"Wow, Dad, thanks." I began doing one of my favorite yoga poses—the tree. It was when I bent one leg and placed my foot on my knee with my hands pressed together above my head. It was very good for improving balance.

"There's one more thing," Dad added. "Maeve, remember, perseverance is what it's all about."

It was hard to answer while I was standing in "tree" but I managed to admit, "Yeah . . . I guess."

"Maeve . . ." Dad warned.

"All right, all right. I'm getting to work."

"Balderdash," Dad scolded. "I'm not convinced. You can do better than that. Now say it again, but this time, make me believe it."

I sighed, put the phone on speaker, and placed it on the floor as I transferred my yoga position to downward-facing dog. Red curls toppled onto my pink rug and I felt my cheeks warm as the blood rushed to my head. "I can do this!" I shouted.

"And what does 'smart' rhyme with?" Dad asked.

When the word popped into my head I was appalled. "Daddy!" I gasped.

Dad laughed. "I was thinking 'heart.'"

"Oh yeah."

"So repeat after me. I've got heart."

"I'VE GOT HEART!"

"And acting is my art."

"AND ACTING IS MY ART!" As I shouted the last part my hand slipped and I toppled to the floor. Luckily, my rug is very thick and very soft.

Except for my sore ankle, I had to admit—Dad's cheer-up strategy worked. I felt a lot better. Who cared how I wrote my outline . . . as long as I wrote it. "You're the best, Dad. I need to get my stuff ready for yoga now. I love you. Thanks for taking us out today—by the way."

"You're very welcome. Love you too."

We hung up and I felt a tiny pang of sadness that Dad wasn't home now, right down the hall like the old days. But I knew he was there for me all the same.

"Heart, art," I said in a low voice. "Heart, art," I repeated a little bit louder. "Heart, art, smart. SMART, HEART, AR—"

There was suddenly a loud "THUNK" sound right outside my door, followed by the pitter-patter of little footsteps. I dashed over and threw the door open. "Hello?" I called, but there was not a person in sight. The only traces that anyone had been there were the small footprints left in the hall rug . . .

I had a sinking feeling that a certain member of the paparazzi was at it again.

CHAPTER

14

The Entourage

"Saaaaam! Will you please hurry up!" I hollered as I waited anxiously by the kitchen door.

"Oh no. Don't tell me you're turning into a Maddie-clone again!" Sam warned, marching into the kitchen. Lately he had traded in his Army clothes for a style that he deemed "way totally cooler." Today he was wearing loose-fitting jeans with a backward baseball cap. I was pretty sure whose "way totally cooler" style Sam was trying to imitate. "I got two words for you, Maeve. Get real." He was even beginning to sound like his new idol.

"Today, I shall only be addressed as 'Your Highness.'" I pointed to the pink tiara I had crunched into my curls.

"No way, dude," Sam replied in his best Apollo voice.

"Way, *dude*," said Mom, giving me a warm smile. "Your sister is doing a little method acting right now. She's already in character for the big audition."

❀ 151 ❀

I nodded. "Thank you, Mother," I said in my most regal voice. Mom and Sam had actually been really awesome last night. They stayed up for two hours running lines with me until I felt totally prepared. Sam even videotaped it so I could see how I'd look on film. All my hard work had definitely paid off. "I am the great Princess Sophia," I declared with confidence. "You may kiss my hand."

"And I think that's just wonderful," Mom said, sweetly running her hand over my head. "But if you think your brother and I are kissing your hand . . . you're dreaming!"

That comment made me break character and my mouth break into a smile. "Fine." I giggled. "I'm sooo ready for this audition, though. Can we go?"

Sam spun around and pinched his arm. "Wait a minute. You're ready to leave the house before me? This IS weird."

When we got to the theater, my heart was racing at a hundred miles a minute. Even though I loved auditioning, I always got nervous right before. My drama coach said that those were called "healthy nerves." *Channel your nervous energy into positive energy*, I reminded myself.

Sam looked up at me with a mischievous smile. "Scared?" he asked.

"Never," I promised, giving Sam a look that meant I was in no mood to be teased.

"Good," Sam answered. "Because I think you're the best actress in the whole world!"

I looked at Mom, who just shrugged. Sometimes little

brothers could surprise you by saying the nicest thing and make you feel totally guilty for ever thinking of them as an annoying pest. Then other times . . .

"Last one to the theater's a rotten egg! Haha, that's you, Maeve," Sam suddenly cried. He took off with his large camera bouncing by his side.

Never mind about that feeling guilty thing . . . I thought.

"Break a leg today, sweetie." Mom kissed me on the cheek.

"Pheeeeeeew," I exhaled a deep yoga breath to calm myself. "Oh, dear me, aren't these little Swan Ships the most dee-lightful vessels?" I recited one of the Princess Sophia lines I'd memorized.

Mom smiled. "You've got it, Maeve! Now go in there and show that pastry puff princess who's boss!"

"You got it!" I gave her two thumbs up.

I shook out my curls and smoothed my purple blouse outlined with pink ribbons. (I thought it was my most princess-y looking choice!) Confidence surged through every part of me. I knew in my heart that I could play the lead role in this film. *Even better than Maddie!* I realized with a little jolt.

I was one of the first people at camp that morning. I was about to pull open the door to the Movie House when I heard a loud screeching behind me and I turned with a start.

It was a huge white stretch Cadillac Escalade. That car looked like it was straight out of a rap music video. I did a quick spin around just to make sure I wasn't secretly being filmed or "punked" maybe, but there didn't seem to be any lights or cameras. I wondered who was in there. Maybe it was a famous hip hop star! The driver got out and jogged to the back door . . . which—might I add—was VERY far away.

Oh my gosh! This Escalade limo didn't belong to a rap star at all. IT WAS MADDIE! Yikes, I couldn't believe this Krupcake Princess. One limo was bigger than the next. Today, Maddie had her hair pinned up in large curlers and was wearing a long pink bathrobe. And she wasn't alone. The next one out of the limo was a man with a Mohawk and a large cosmetics box—the makeup artist. A short, stocky woman with purple spiky hair and platform shoes clomped out carrying a blow-drier. She must have been the hairdresser. An older gentleman in a black beret was next, prompting Maddie with lines. Just when I thought the parade had to be over, a girl wheeled out the longest rack of outfits I'd ever seen. I gulped. I wished the BSG were here to see this. Maddie brought an entire *entourage*.

The Madeline fame train rushed inside, with Maddie's crew buzzing around her like a swarm of bumblebees. I tried to open my purse to get out my lip gloss and noticed my hands were shaking.

Take a deep breath, I told myself. I slowly walked over to the bench outside of the theater to sit down and chill. How could I . . . how could *anyone* possibly compete with *that*? Maddie had a personal drama coach and a whole TEAM to help her look like Princess Sophia. And what did MKT have? Well, Mom, Sam, Dad, two adorable guinea pigs . . .

and a room full of very loyal and attentive stuffed animals. It would just have to do.

"Hey, Maeve, you pumped for the big day?"

I looked up. Apollo Aaron was bouncing down the street with three folding chairs slung over his shoulder. He was wearing his blue Dodgers hat backward with a few curls spilling out under the sides. *Gosh, he is cute!* I immediately pushed the thought out of my head though . . . Apollo was my friend.

I smiled weakly. "I think so, I guess."

Apollo tapped his fist against mine. "Yo, you're gonna rock out, Maeve! Feel good?"

As I was an actress, I acted brave for Apollo. "Totally!" I assured him. But as soon as he disappeared into the backstage of the Movie House, the only thing I "totally" felt was *totally* sick to my stomach.

I sat back on the bench and watched the cars whiz down Harvard Street. I liked how my curls blew against my cheek. It was nice and very peaceful. The bench was so soothing, maybe I could just lounge out there and skip the audition altogether. *Bad attitude, Maeve*, I scolded myself. I looked at my watch. It was time to go in, but now I was a little afraid. This was not like me . . . not like me at all.

"Hey, there's my girl!" Dad greeted, poking his head out the door. "I've been looking everywhere for you. I thought you said you were going to come in early and run lines with me?"

I turned to Dad—my face cursed with tragedy. "Oh, Dad, I completely forgot . . . I *was* here early!"

"And . . . what happened?"

I sighed. "Maddie happened. Did you see her limo?" I was using what Mom would call my woebegone voice. "She's got an entourage, Dad. Like a real movie star. I'm talking makeup artist, hairdresser, drama coach, wardrobe . . . I'm toast!"

Dad grinned. "Now there's my little drama queen!"

I stood up, pushed my purse up my arm, and placed my hands on my hips. "Hey!" I said, outraged.

"I mean that as the best of compliments," Dad promised, putting his arm over my shoulder. "You don't need an entourage to shine on stage. Remember—cream always rises, Maeve. It always rises."

He looked at me, and I could see he really did believe in me. I held up my head and informed him, "That's Princess Sophia, to you."

15

Eavesdrop Soup

I was practicing writing my autograph in the steam of the bathroom mirror. "Maeve Kaplan-Taylor," I whispered to myself. It looked really fabulous in big, loopy script. There was no doubt about it—my audition that day had been a smashing success. It made me tingle all over just remembering it. The lines poured out of me so naturally, I felt like I really was Princess Sophia.

Knock, knock.

The hairbrush dropped from my hand and clattered on the black-and-pink checkered tiles. "Don't come in!" I shouted. I was in my pajamas and everything . . . but still, couldn't a girl get a moment to herself?

Then it happened again. *Knock, knock, knock.*

There was only one person in my house who was rude enough to knock after you told him to stop. "I SAID don't come in . . . *Sam!*"

"Maeve, this is an emergency. You need to report to

my room . . . STAT!" Sam commanded in a hushed voice. "Stat means now, by the way."

I groaned and cracked the door open, expecting to see a camera poking in my face. But surprisingly, there was no camera. Sam was standing in the hall, holding a pair of binoculars, his little eyebrows furrowed.

"What's up?" I asked.

"You gotta hear this! Artemia and that Krupcake King dude are talking outside. It's about *you*." Sam grabbed my hand and began to drag me down the hall to his room.

"Me?" I gasped. "Wait, Sam, are they talking about the auditions?"

Sam bonked his forehead. "Well, duh!"

"SAM, why didn't you say something?" I cried, sprinting past him and into his room to the one window that overlooked Harvard Street. His room was the complete opposite of my pink palace. It was filled with toy soldier armies positioned in front of castles and Lego planes that Sam had built himself.

"Careful, Maeve. Don't mess up *anything*," Sam warned.

"Relax. I'm trying my best here!" I had to tiptoe around all the little Army figures so I wouldn't knock anything over. It was like being in a weird cartoon movie.

Sam and I sat on his bed and peered out the window. "Check it out," Sam pointed and handed me the binoculars. I slowly rose up so my nose peeked right above the ledge and tilted the binoculars toward the street below. It was times like this that I felt lucky to live above the Movie House.

"Do be reasonable, Walter," Artemia was pleading.

"I'm always reasonable!" Mr. Von Krupcake growled. "Is it not reasonable to expect that the most educated, most experienced, and most rigorously trained actress should play the lead role of the princess?"

"Madeline is an extraordinarily talented young woman," Artemia agreed. "She is certainly destined for a successful career on Broadway."

I lowered the binoculars and looked at Sam in horror.

"Just listen," Sam hissed, jabbing me with his elbow. He propped the binoculars back up to my eyes.

"But this is film camp . . . not theater camp. Maeve Kaplan-Taylor's audition translated very well to film. I think she should play the princess." There it was. The nicest compliment I could have gotten from the world-famous Artemia Aaron. I gripped Sam's arm and squealed. I was going to be Princess Sophia. My life was now fabulous beyond belief.

"Shh!" Sam reminded me that we were supposed to be spying. Spying meant not making a peep.

Below, Mr. Von Krupcake threw his arms in the air. He looked so mad, he was spitting. "Little Orphan Annie!? You can't be serious, Artemia."

"I *am* serious," Artemia began in a strained voice. "I work for the New York Film Academy, and it is my job to do what's best for the film. Madeline was very good. In fact, she would be my second choice for the role. But I have to be honest . . . Maeve is my first. She had the stronger audition for Princess Sophia."

"Yes!" I mouthed to Sam. We quietly high-fived, and I began to spin around the room. I was just so happy I couldn't help myself.

"I'm sorry, Artemia. I beg to disagree with you." Mr. Von Krupcake's voice suddenly sounded softer. I immediately leaped back on the bed to hear more. "I saw both of the girls audition, and I found my Maddie's Princess Sophia much more compelling than Maeve's. My Maddie was born to play the princess. She already had the crown."

Artemia took a deep breath. "I told you. Madeline is a great actress. However—"

"I don't think I'm making myself clear, Artemia. If you were to give the part of the princess to Maeve Kaplan-Taylor I would feel very, very disappointed. I would feel so disappointed that I'd probably have to ask Ross Taylor to pay me back for all those repairs I made to the Movie House."

"Walter, you can't do *that*. You told Ross that you were more than happy to make the repairs," Artemia said in a stern voice. "You told him it was a *gift*."

Walter scratched his chin. "Well, yes . . . I did, didn't I? Good thing I never signed a contract. Hee hee, ha ha. Then I'd really be in trouble! I'll have my lawyer straighten this whole mess out first thing tomorrow. I just hate dealing with money, don't you? It can get so . . . unpleasant. Well, I'm sure Ross will understand the pain and torment I'm going through. After all, he is a father."

"Please, Walter, you wouldn't do that to Ross Taylor . . ."

Artemia sounded nervous at first then she folded her arms. "Wait a minute. Are you trying to blackmail me, Walter?"

"Of course not, darling. You cast whoever you like in the role of Sophia."

Artemia nodded. "That's right. Casting is my decision, and I work for the film camp . . . not *you*."

"The repairs to the Movie House are between Ross and me. These are, after all, troubled times." Mr. Von Krupcake's voice got quiet. "Ever since the Atkins Diet, pastry sales just aren't what they used to be. Oh well! Have a good night, Artemia. I look forward to seeing the cast list in the morning." Mr. Von Krupcake tipped his feathered fedora hat. "Oh, and Artemia . . . I trust that you WILL make the right decision." The Von Krupcakes' limo pulled up to the curb. He got in, slammed the door, and the car zoomed away, leaving Artemia alone in the street.

Sam shook his head. "Now I see where Maddie gets her bad attitude. It must be genetic," he murmured.

I think my brother was trying to be funny, but I couldn't laugh. I swallowed. "Oh, Sam . . . this is terrible."

"Tell me about it. You knocked over all my Star Wars dudes!" Sam pointed to a pile of toys that hadn't survived my dancing episode.

I sighed and bent down to pick up the action figures. "Sam, this is serious. Mr. Von Krupcake could ruin the Movie House. What are we going to do?"

"Mom, wait up!" boomed a male voice. I jumped back on the bed and peered out the window. It was Apollo.

"This is totally bogus. See! What did I tell you about the Von Krupcakes?"

"Oh, Apollo," Artemia put her arm around her son. "Look. This is a lot more complicated than it seems."

"No way!" Apollo shook his head. "Come on, what's wrong with that dude? He saw the auditions. Maeve was so much better than Maddie . . . it's not even funny."

"You're right. Maeve was better. But Maddie was good too."

Apollo looked at his mom. "So what're you going to do?"

Artemia shrugged glumly. "I don't know. If I give the part to Maeve . . . well . . . I'm afraid of what Mr. Von Krupcake might do."

"Me too," Apollo agreed. "For the Krupcake King he's not very sweet, huh?"

"Very funny," Artemia said in a serious tone. "Well, I suppose I'll just have to sleep on it."

My heart was pounding like a drum. There it was—my dream come true—dangling right in front of me. But suddenly it didn't seem all that important anymore. "Sam, I'll be back." I jumped off the bed and ran—actually more like hop-scotched really because of all the toys on the floor— out the room.

"Where are you going?" Sam shouted after me.

"If Mom asks, just tell her I went outside for a breath of fresh air," I replied.

I pulled on my jacket as I scuttled down the stairs. I opened the front door with all my might and sprinted down the block to the place where Apollo and Artemia were talking underneath a dim streetlamp. I knew what I had to do.

"Maeve!" Artemia seemed surprised to see me.

"Hey, y'all!" I tried to look cheerful, but it was pretty obvious that cheer was the last thing on anyone's mind. "I sort of, kind of, accidentally overheard you guys talking . . ." I began shakily.

"What part of the talking?" asked Artemia.

"Um . . . all of it."

Artemia shook her head. "You kids. I don't know what I'm going to do with you!"

I looked up meekly. "I know, I know, but there's something really important I have to tell you."

Artemia and Apollo froze, waiting to hear what I had to say. Harvard Street was so still and empty—it looked like the set of a movie. Secretly, I loved being center stage . . . but it just wasn't about that right now.

I took a deep breath. What I had to say next was not going to be easy. "You should let Madeline play Princess Sophia," I told Artemia. My voice broke a little. "If you don't . . . well . . . I just don't want Mr. Von Krupcake to do anything mean to my dad. It's just not worth it."

Apollo looked at me. "What are you saying, Maeve?"

I sighed. "I know I auditioned for the part of Princess Sophia, but I'm bowing out."

Artemia bent down with her hands on her knees. "Are you sure? Casting this movie is my decision, Maeve. Not Mr. Von Krupcake's, you know."

I nodded. "I'm sure." I wiped away just one teeny tiny tear from my eye and put on my best smile. "It's not that big of a deal. Someday, I'll have plenty of starring roles." I bit my lip and hoped that saying the words out loud would make them true, but inside I felt like my heart was breaking into pieces.

Apollo raised his hand like we were in school. "I have an idea," he announced.

Artemia and I slowly turned and at the same time said, "Yeeeeeees?"

He sighed. "Okay, okay, just hear me out. I said it before and I'll say it again, Maeve. I think you should think about trying out for Sufoo. I'm telling you, it's a way more interesting part than the princess. Think about it—why would you want to be a boring old princess if you could be a weird kung fu fighting little maid?"

"Sometimes the supporting actor is the role that makes a movie outstanding," Artemia added matter-of-factly.

I thought about this and then remembered something. "Like how Anita and Bernardo in *West Side Story* won the Oscars for Best Supporting Actress and Actor even though Tony and Maria didn't?" I asked in one giant breath.

Apollo raised one eyebrow (*How do people do that?*) "Okay, since I've been in Boston, I've seen a lot of ducks. A LOT. And I gotta tell you . . . you're one odd duck, Maeve Kaplan-Taylor. That's a good thing, by the way," Apollo assured me. I think he was impressed. See, when it comes to math facts and science facts . . . they are soooo not my thing. But movie trivia? I happened to be an expert extraordinaire.

"Hold on though. Let's just say I did want to try out for Sufoo. The auditions are over now . . . and I didn't try out for that part. It doesn't seem fair for me to get it." What was wrong with me? First I was giving away Sophia and now it was Sufoo? *BE QUIET, MAEVE!* I scolded myself.

"You're absolutely right, Maeve," Artemia agreed. "It wouldn't be fair to just give you the part. But . . . do you know what directors do when they want to see an actor try out for a different part?"

I searched my brain. Oh, this one was so obvious, it was right on the tip of my tongue.

Apollo raised his hand again. "I know, I know!" (I could see why he and Sam got along so well.) "Hold a callback?"

Artemia looked at her son, smiled, and shook her head. "Thank you, Mr. Hollywood. Yes, that's right. We'll hold a callback for the part of Sufoo tomorrow. And Maeve, I shouldn't be telling you this but . . . I think your name might just be on the list," she whispered and winked.

I smiled. "Well . . . no offense, but I don't have time to sit around and chit-chat, kids. I've got to get my beauty sleep. Looks like I have a big audition in the morning to prepare for!"

Apollo clapped his hands. "Boo-yah! Does this mean what I think it does?"

I pressed my lips together, bowed, and did a chop-kick toward the door. "If you'll excuse me, there's a kung fu fighting weird little maid whose audition lines I absolutely *must* learn. Ta-ta, darlings!" I blew them a kiss, bowed again, and dashed up the stairs to my house and shut the door.

"Sweeeeeeet!" I heard Apollo holler. "She's going to be the best kung fu fighting weird little maid EVER!"

I opened the door to our apartment a crack. "Hey . . . don't get my hopes up!" As I ran up the stairs, super excited to start a new acting project, I suddenly thought of one more thing. I ran into Sam's room—totally knocking down his Star Wars dudes all over again.

"Hey!" Sam sat up in his bed.

"I'll fix them, Sam." I struggled to open his window. Artemia and Apollo were almost at the corner. "Artemia!" I called, just loud enough to get her attention, but quiet enough to not wake up the entire block. "I was thinking . . . please don't tell my dad about this. He would feel just terrible . . . if he knew."

She waved and smiled. "Of course, Maeve. I completely understand. Your secret is safe with me."

CHAPTER

16

Stealing the Show

O nce we started working on the movie, film camp
instantly became the best thing that ever happened in
my whole life. People really got into the whole *Boston Holiday* idea. Lizzie Kwan even brought in her copy
of *Roman Holiday* for us to watch. Dad screened it in the
Movie House—obviously—and, also obviously, got the
famous Movie House popcorn machine going. (Watching
classic movies *without* buttery, delicious popcorn would
be just . . . well . . . wrong!)

Right away I learned some good news and some bad
news. Good news first. I got the part! Not of Sophia, of
course, but of Sufoo. And the other good news was that
Apollo was one hundred percent right. It was even more
fun than I had anticipated. I mean, maids usually reminded
me of dusting, vacuuming, and other cleaning-type things
that I really do *not* enjoy. Who would've thought that playing a maid could be so much fun? And not just fun . . . *a*

blast. Turned out I had a lot to learn about acting after all.

My yoga came in handy too. Take it from me—you needed to be pretty flexible to do a lot of those high kung fu kicks and lightning fast spins. I practiced all my moves before *and* after camp. I really wanted to know all of Artemia's choreography by heart.

Now for the bad news. If I thought Maddie was annoying *before* she got the part of Princess Sophia, afterward she was seriously a nightmare. A year ago I saw the musical *Phantom of the Opera* by Andrew Lloyd Webber when it came to Boston—totally awesome musical BTW—and there was this song in it called "Prima Donna." In operas, "Prima Donna" means the first lady or the lead role. The song's basically about this Carlotta woman who was the star of all the operas and forced everyone to treat her like a queen. She was not nice AT ALL. (Later on in the play, the Phantom makes her croak like a frog in the middle of her singing! It's hilarious.) Anyway that pretty much reminded me of how Maddie was acting all week, minus the frogs . . . unfortunately.

As a dedicated observer of movie stars, one of my favorite columns in *Teen Beat* was the one called "Prima Donna Behavior." That's when people in Hollywood spilled their secrets about the crazy things that movie stars do. One of my favorite stories was about a famous actress who would only wash her hair with bottled water. When I told my friend Katani about that she got so mad. "There are people who need water to drink!" she'd fumed. So believe me, I knew a Prima Donna when I saw one.

The very first second she got out of her limo, Maddie announced, "Now that I'm a movie star, you can't expect me to go anywhere without my entourage." That was how she began every sentence: "Now that I'm a movie star . . ." It was extremely annoying.

She reminded me of those dolls that played a recording when you pulled their string. "Now that I'm a movie star, I can't be seen without makeup, darling," and "Now that I'm a movie star, you can't expect me to walk! *Darling*, call the driver." Nobody really knew what to say to Maddie, including me. Even the girls who used to be part of her fan club were no longer impressed. When Maddie was on the set, we all knew to stay far, far away.

I was super relieved that the other lead actors didn't also turn into major Prima Donnas. (Were boy Prima Donnas called Prima *Dons* or Prima *Donalds*?) Artemia gave the part of Nanny Nuna to Rebeccah Fullerton. Rebeccah turned out to be a really fun girl. She was two years older than me, and had a few big parts in real high school plays. She could dance and sing and was a very outspoken contributor to camp, which I thought was totally awesome. Her amazingly colorful outfits and upbeat attitude had earned her the cutest nickname: "Snappy Turtle."

The Evil Assistant (Apollo suggested that this part would be more treacherous without a name) would be played by Mickey Snyder, a large boy who wanted to be a playwright. He was a little bit braggy, but overall nice. He had helped Lizzie out with a lot of the script-writing. But it turned out he could act, too.

Grego—the kung fu instructor, reporter, and the (*sigh*) romantic lead—went to a boy named David Dell. David was by far the funniest actor. During improv, he would make all the kids laugh to the point of tears—which is the best kind of laughing. David wore thick, tortoiseshell glasses and was about the height of Henry Yurt (who might be the shortest kid in my whole grade), but when he acted, he honestly changed into a whole other character. Best of all, he was a wonderful dancer. Two thumbs way up in my book. I was sure that he'd make a perfect Grego. Maddie, on the other hand, wasn't so sure.

We taped the first scene in front of the Taj hotel. It was double the fun, because all the strangers and guests of the hotel were totally curious about what was going on. They all whispered and stared, wondering if we were famous actors and if this were a real Hollywood movie. *Someday,* I thought dreamily.

The scene we were doing was actually the one I'd out-lined on my laptop. (BTW, Dad was right—Apollo and Lizzie were impressed that I typed it.) It was the big escape sequence when Princess Sophia fled from the hotel with Grego. Our super, dramatic idea was that Grego could give Sophia a piggyback ride while Sufoo went down the fire exit, fighting bad guys the whole time.

Apollo was ready to tape our big escape scene, when David Dell raised his hand. "Hey, I have a little problem. I was thinking . . . maybe we should change this piggyback part," he suggested. "Like, we could just run instead . . ." David stretched his mouth into a funny smile and tilted his head at Maddie. My jaw dropped as I realized what the problem was: Maddie was at least a foot taller than David. There was no way he'd be able to give her a piggyback. Everyone around us giggled. Maddie was not pleased.

"You expect me to run? In these shoes?" She was outraged. "*I'm* the princess and the script says *you're* going to carry me out. It makes perfect sense. Now can we start already?"

All eyes turned to David. "Okie-dokie, chokie. Let's give it a shot." He turned to Rebeccah and Mickey. "Do me a favor. When you guys try to chase me, don't try too hard."

I covered my mouth, trying not to laugh. David was too funny.

"Scene one, take one. ACTION!" Artemia shouted.

Maddie straightened her crown and began, "Oh Grego, I can't leave this hotel. Not yet. I'm not ready! All I've known my whole life has been wealth, luxury, and privilege. How do you think I could possibly survive in the cold, outside world of commoners?"

"You must, your highness. This hotel isn't safe!"

Maddie clomped out the door in her high-heeled shoes and dramatically pretended to faint. "I can't go, Grego. You and Sufoo must leave. Save yourselves. Don't worry about me."

David stomped his foot. (In the movie, Grego and Sufoo didn't want to scare the princess, so they hadn't yet told her that the bad guys were none other than her very own Nanny Nuna and the assistant. It was part of the suspense.) "Well if you won't leave . . . then you leave me no choice. I'm going to have to *take you*!"

*"Scene one, take one. ACTION!"
Artemia shouted.*

I held my breath as David charged at Madeline, hoisted her on his back, and tried to gallop down the stairs of the beautiful, old hotel. "Oof!" he grunted. His face was pink.

"Faster, faster!" I heard Maddie whisper as David limped by me. But the faster he tried to go, the more he had to stoop over. Pretty soon he was slumped over like Quasimodo from *The Hunchback of Notre Dame,* dripping with sweat. "I said go faster!" Maddie shrieked.

"He's not a horse, you know," Rebeccah informed her. I liked that Rebeccah wasn't afraid to put Maddie in her place.

"This is as fast as I go!" David groaned. He stopped at the bottom of the steps, wavered to the right, caught his balance, wobbled to the left, caught his balance again, and then started crumbling. "Tiiiiiiiiiiiiiiiimberrrrrrrrrrr!" David shouted as he went down.

"Cut!" cried Artemia.

We ran out and huddled around Maddie and David. Maddie quickly got up and collected herself, dusting off her coat. David just lay there like a pancake. "David, David, are you all right?" I asked.

He couldn't answer, he was shaking so hard. I dropped on my hands and knees. "David, answer me!"

He shook his head and looked up with a huge smile on his face. Laughing hysterically, David banged his fists against the sidewalk. "Please tell me that'll make the final cut!" he finally gasped.

"This is awful!" Maddie spewed. I took a step back. Maddie was furious and madder than a hornet. She shook her finger in frustration. "Hey, you, stop that!" I looked to see who she was shaking her finger at. *Oh no . . .* This was not good. Not good at all.

"Were you . . . were you . . . taping me? Did you tape me *falling*? Give me that camera!" Maddie glared at Sam. He clung to his camera, staring at Maddie with huge, bugged-out eyes. Sam shook his head.

"I said *give me that camera*!" She took a giant step toward Sam.

"Easy there, girlfriend!" I cried and jumped in front of Maddie. "He's just doing his job."

Maddie tucked her hair behind her ears. "And what, might I ask, is his job?"

I frowned. *Hello?* Did Maddie really not know? "I'm the filmotographer! Duh!" Sam blurted.

"He's documenting our experience at film camp." I smiled. "Which means . . . he's taping our most embarrassing moments."

Maddie's lip trembled. "Why . . . AAAHHHHH!" she shrieked.

Beside me, David snorted to keep down a giggle. Not laughing was next to impossible.

Maddie breathed out of her nostrils and tried her best to act calm. "Now that I'm a movie star . . ." she began in a wounded tone, ". . . I shouldn't have to tolerate this *abuse!*"

Artemia sighed. "Now Madeline, that's a bit of an exaggeration. David didn't mean to fall. It was an accident. Remember, we're not using stunt doubles."

Maddie glared at David, who was grinning and rubbing his scraped elbow. "This is ridiculous. David is just too short to play Grego. If I'm supposed to be in love with Grego, he needs to be tall, and strong, and dashing, and David's, well let's face it, none of those things." She shrugged at David and patted him on the head like a toddler. "I'm sorry, darling, but it's true."

My jaw dropped. How could Maddie say those things to someone? It was like she had no feelings at all. *Ice Princess Sophia*, I thought.

"So it's settled then. Apollo will play Grego, and David

can go play with the camera. Shoo, now. Run along," Maddie instructed. Apollo turned white—no, *green*. He suddenly went into a violent coughing spasm. He was quaking so much he had to put the camera down.

"Apollo!" Maddie squeaked. She fluttered over to him and whacked him on the back. "Darling, are you all right? Will somebody get Apollo some water? NOW!"

As one of the campers dashed over with a cup, Maddie purred, "See, darling? We're going to make an excellent team."

Apollo gulped down the water—every little drop of it—before he could manage to spurt out an answer. "Maddie, I told you. I'm done with acting. Finished. *Finito*. I WANT to be the cameraman."

Maddie was shocked. She grabbed Apollo's arm and squeezed it. "You can't be serious. EVERYONE wants to be a star."

We didn't make a peep as we waited anxiously for Apollo to speak. "Look," he said sharply. "My answer's no. N-O. I don't want to be a star. I like shooting and setting up scenes. Besides, David got the part of Grego fair and square. He deserves to play the lead."

Now all eyes were on Maddie. No one knew what would happen next. Even David Dell looked intrigued. People just didn't say "no" to Maddie. Forget *Boston Holiday*—this drama was better than a movie!

"Hey, I have an idea," Rebeccah volunteered. "David can still carry Maddie out of the hotel. But we're going to need Maeve's help."

Artemia raised her eyebrows. "Maeve?"

"Why not? I'll try anything once."

Maddie folded her arms. "Typical has-been." She sneered and huffed away.

Rebeccah's idea was nothing short of genius. She showed me and David how to make a seat for Princess Sophia by gripping our fists into a tight square. That way, Maddie could sit primly and properly in the middle—even more like a princess. The best part of all was that Artemia taught us that a series of kung fu punches made the perfect transition to the fist-seat.

"Now let's take this from the top," Artemia clapped. "Scene one, take two—"

"Wait," Apollo interrupted.

Maddie tapped her foot. "What *now*?"

Apollo ran over to me. "Okay, Maeve, I want you to leap in the air and do a high kick. Then do a hip hop spin and punch the air the whole time. Just keep kicking and dancing and doing your thing. When we're done I'll edit the scene so you'll move in slow motion and then pause it when you're suspended in the air, like in my mom's movies. You know what I mean?"

"Do I! I've only watched *Kung Fu Crazy*, like, a billion-gazillion times!" I exclaimed. I could see why Apollo wanted to shoot. He had vision. Maybe he would be a famous director someday.

Artemia looked proud of her son. "That's a great idea! Maeve, can you do that?"

"Sure!" I rolled up the sleeves of my costume—a kung

fu outfit that Ms. Pink had specially made for me . . . in a shade of vibrant, flamingo pink.

I slapped David Dell five. "This is going to rock," I assured him.

He looked slyly at Maddie, who, thank goodness, was busy getting primped by her makeup artist. "Are you sure you're going to be able to do this carrying thing? Take it from me . . ." He glanced over again at Maddie, leaned in, and covered his mouth. "She's pretty heavy."

"It's true," I said, flexing my arms in my best body-builder-woman pose. They weren't what I'd call bulging with muscles. "Maybe Maeve Kaplan-Taylor might not be able to lift her . . . but I have a feeling Sufoo can."

David grinned. "Right on."

"Places!" Artemia called.

I hurried over to my mark in the Taj lobby, while David and a not-so-happy Maddie dashed to the hotel elevator. As Apollo walked by adjusting his camera, I tried to get his attention. "*Pssst!* California boy, over here!"

He looked back at me.

"Thanks," I whispered.

"Hey, *de nada.*" Apollo shrugged, smiled, and went back to the camera. I sighed. Some people were so naturally cool. How they managed it was beyond *moi*.

"Now from the top," Artemia instructed as she sat down in her director's chair. "Scene one, take two. Aaaaaaaand ACTION!"

CHAPTER

17

The Trouble with Eavesdropping

*T*en minutes 'til shooting, Ms. Kaplan-Taylor," calls a *voice.*

Shooting? But I'm not ready yet! My hair is a mess . . . "Renaldo! And where is Julia—my makeup artist? And the gown—it's blue . . . I hate blue." Suddenly the trailer door flies open. "Ms. Kaplan-Taylor, Ms. Kaplan-Taylor. We're here, we're here!"

I sigh, feeling calm and cared for. "You guys are too good to me. I should buy you a gift. How would you like your own convertible?"

"TOTALLY, DUDE!"

I sat up with a start and blinked. I was in the back seat of Dad's car, and . . . oh no. I wiped my eyes and groaned. "Sam, you didn't . . ."

Sam lowered his camera. There was a big, silly smile

plastered on his face. "Did you know that you talk in your sleep, Maeve? And did you know that you say some pretty funny stuff too?" Sam pinched his nose and squawked, "Where is Renaldo? Where is Julia?" He started to giggle. "You know, you're a better actress sleeping than you are when you're awake. I mean, you sounded just like Maddie."

"I was *dreaming*," I huffed, feeling my cheeks burn. Why did my brother always seem to catch me right in the middle of my favorite Maeve in Hollywood dreams? "Can you drop the camera already . . . pleeeeease, Sam?" I couldn't help whining, I was so tired.

"Sure. But first, who's *Renaldo*?" Sam asked, using the same high-pitched voice. I reached over and grabbed his jacket.

"I SAID drop it," I warned, shooting him my best impression of Mom's I-am-really-not-amused look.

We were parked outside the Boston Common, and it was the last day of *Boston Holiday* shooting. After filming for days, I was totally zonked. There was a big difference between my dream of being in a movie and my reality of being in a movie. It was more work than I had ever imagined.

Artemia made sure that all the campers got a taste of the different tasks that came with making a movie—set design, schlepping stuff, running lines, shooting the same scene over and over again, more schlepping, moving stuff—I wanted to sleep for a week. No wonder it cost so much for a movie ticket!

But I couldn't sleep. I had to make Sufoo shine . . . over and over again. And then I had to do my second job, which was to count and gather ALL the props after every shoot. When she noticed how tired we were, Artemia declared, "Welcome to the world of independent film."

"Artemia made sure that all the campers got a taste of the different tasks . . . design, schlepping stuff . . . "

I'll take the world of Hollywood with limos and stuff, thank you very much! I thought.

Today we were filming the very last scene of the movie:

the Parasol Fight Scene. It was the trickiest one yet. I had to learn how to fake sword fight with my pink umbrella against Nanny Nuna and her red umbrella. David, with a green umbrella, got to fight the Evil Assistant with a blue one. "Think *Singing in the Rain* meets *Kung Fu Crazy*," Apollo told us. "It'll be awesome."

I was excited, but still I yawned. "They haven't started filming yet, have they?" I asked Sam.

He shook his head. "Nope. Maddie isn't even done setting up the props. It takes her forever."

Even the Krupcake Princess had another job—putting all the props exactly where they were supposed to be *before* the scenes. That was called continuity. If someone didn't do that, then when you went to film again, things could be out of place and the audience would see it. Maddie had asked Artemia if she could be in charge of bringing Maddiecakes as refreshments instead, but Artemia said no—no way. "Maddiecakes aren't going to give you young people enough energy to shoot this movie," Artemia had told her.

"But Artemia," Maddie said with a smile, "everyone knows that Maddiecakes are filled with Vitamin L-O-V-E." Everyone could tell that Maddie was mad, but she was really good at pretending she wasn't. She knew better than to talk back to Artemia. In fact, Artemia was the one person who kind of mellowed Maddie out. Artemia was like a general . . . a nice general who made sure everyone did their jobs. Katani would have loved her. Katani loved people who were organized and got the job done.

I opened the car door to get out. "Where's Dad, Sam?"

"Let me see . . ." Sam reached into his backpack and pulled out a pair of binoculars. I had to admit—he could be pretty handy to have around. "Hmm . . . Dad is at two o'clock. Precisely."

I folded my arms. "Translation please . . . for those of us who don't speak Army geek?"

Sam pointed. "Right over there by the Frog Pond. He's talking to Artemia."

"Good job, Sam. Let's go."

Artemia and Dad were in the middle of the park by the Frog Pond, which was my favorite part of the Boston Common. The Swan Boats—these boats that look like huge swans—were across the street in the Boston Public Garden. Sam and I used to ride them all the time when we were little. They were another Maeve-approved favorite landmark.

Sam and I walked around the little shack where you could rent skates or use the bathroom. Artemia and Dad were standing on the other side, so busy talking they didn't notice us.

"I'm telling you, Ross," Artemia was saying, "she's really making this film come to life."

I put one finger over my lips and reached out my arm to block Sam from walking. "Shh!" I crouched down outside the ladies' room. I wasn't eavesdropping on purpose this time . . . well, maybe a little. But I was too curious. *Who's making this film come to life?* I had to know.

"That is very nice to hear. You're not just saying that?" Dad asked.

"Why would I just say that?" asked Artemia.

"Well, you know, her father happens to be a pretty important guy around here," Dad remarked. "Kind of a big deal."

Sam nudged me. "They must be talking about the Von Krupcakes," he whispered. With a sinking heart, I realized he was right. No father was a bigger deal than Maddie's.

"That's true," Artemia was saying with a laugh. "But no, I am very serious. Giving her that role turned out to be the best thing we could've done for this movie. What a lovely surprise, right?"

"Absolutely," Dad agreed. "Remember how worried we were at first?"

"I know! It seems so foolish now. With all her knowledge and experience, I can't believe we doubted for even a moment that she would be anything less than a real pro," Artemia declared.

I looked at Sam and gulped. *So Maddie had been the right choice for Princess Sophia all along.* How could the universe be so cruel? I almost cried. I had wanted to be Princess Sophia so badly. And now I was just a funny maid who was good at kung fu and dancing. This was a real tragedy.

"I have worked with a lot of actors in my day, Ross," Artemia continued. "And Maeve has been not only an amazing talent but also a delight. She's a great sport."

"No way!" I breathed. "They're talking about me!" I

started to do a silent victory dance. "Go Maeve, it's your birthday. Go Maeve, it's your birthday . . ." I whispered as I boogied around in a circle.

"Ugh!" Sam gulped. "You better stop or I'll laugh and then we'll blow our cover!"

But I couldn't stop. I was too elated. I grabbed Sam's hands and swung him around with me. "C'mon, this is HUGE! Go Maeve, it's your birthday, Go Maeve, it's—"

The door of the ladies' room suddenly rattled and we heard the scampering of feet running away. Sam and I froze. We weren't alone.

CHAPTER
18

The Saboteur

"Hey, Kaplan-Taylor dudes!" Apollo jogged over to us. "I've been looking everywhere for you guys. It's time to start. Maeve, are you okay? You look a little . . . pale."

"Who me? Pale? Nope. I am A-okay. Swell. Fantastic. Cool as a cucumber. See?" I did my best kung fu chop. "Lights, camera, action. Let's get rolling!"

Apollo looked worriedly at Sam as if he didn't know what to make of my little performance. "I think your sister might need a vacation."

We followed Apollo back to where the rest of the campers were getting ready for the shoot. Maddie was sitting in a chair running lines. She wouldn't would even look in my direction—big surprise there. (True confession—I was a tiny bit jealous of her Princess Sophia wardrobe.) I looked down at my cheesy kung fu clothes and over again at Maddie's special, sparkly, spanking-new designer dress . . . courtesy of Krupcake's Pies and Cakes Incorporated, of course. Artemia said the extravagant clothes were not necessary. Maddie said they most definitely WERE. She told Artemia they helped her get in character. The princess clothes were in.

Maddie's dress today was a strappy gown in robin's-egg blue satin, bespeckled with rhinestones. I had to admit, she looked really, truly gorgeous . . . and also—without a jacket—really, truly cold. In fact, her lips were blue, and she was shivering. I took pity on her. After all, the show must go on and I wouldn't want our leading lady to turn into an ice sculpture. "I have an extra sweater in my bag if you want it," I offered.

Maddie glared at me but didn't say a word.

"Maeve-a-licious!" Rebeccah greeted me with a wave. "I missed you, girlfriend." I spun around, happy to see my friend. My fellow campers had started to call me "Maeve-a-licious" ever since I had brought in a super-sized bag of my favorite candy—Swedish fish.

"Snappy Turtle!" I waved back. "Love the costume." Rebeccah was wearing a swirly red skirt with a crisp white blouse with her trademark pearls. Her golden curls had been pinned into two Danish buns on either side of her head. It was Princess Leia meets wicked Nanny Nuna— totally fabulous.

Mickey was in a black tuxedo and he had a fake goatee glued to his face. He pretended to buzz in on an intercom. "Attention: Call off the search party. The Sufoo is alive. Repeat, the Sufoo is alive."

The kids giggled, but Artemia, who was walking toward us, wasn't pleased. Unfortunately, Mickey's joke wasn't the problem. "Maeve, where have you been?" she asked, folding her arms. "You know how important it is to be punctual for your shoot. This is the last day of filming, and everyone else has been waiting here in the park . . ." Artemia tapped her foot. "Do you have something you'd like to say?"

I felt my cheeks burn. I didn't mean to be disrespectful or anything. This Maddie situation was just really getting to me. I cleared my throat and said as graciously as I could, "I'm very sorry, everyone. It won't happen again."

"Okay, we've lost enough time. Let's get started. Places!" Artemia ordered.

Rebeccah and Mickey, as Nanny Nuna and the Evil Assistant, hustled over to their marks behind trees.

I took my place on top of the hill, right next to Maddie and David. "Sorry, guys," I mumbled. "I guess I blew it."

"Don't sweat it, Maeve. Artemia's been in General mode all day," David told me.

"Last day of filming is always the worst. It's like crunch time panic," Apollo agreed. "Everyone goes kind of nutty . . . even the director of *Kung Fu Crazy*."

I turned to Maddie and offered a smile. Maddie glared at me so hard I was afraid daggers might come out of her eyes. "Well, well, well. Look who it is . . . the best thing that ever happened to this movie."

My stomach flipped.

"Maddie, are all the props where they need to be?"

Artemia shouted from across the path. "Parasols in place?"

"Of course, Artemia," Maddie yelled. "They've been exactly where they need to be for ages. Unlike certain *maids*." Maddie looked at me like I was mold on cheese. I felt very grateful that my BFFs were Katani, Charlotte, Avery, and Isabel. They never made me feel like cheese mold. I hate feeling like cheese mold.

"And ACTION!" Apollo clicked the black-and-white scene board and the cameras started rolling.

Maddie ran down the hill, stumbling in her sparkling ball gown. Just as planned, Nanny Nuna and the Evil Assistant popped out from behind the trees with their colorful umbrellas outstretched. "I knew it!" Nannie Nuna cried. "She IS the real Princess Sophia!"

"I can't believe we ever confused her with that weird little maid in her tacky imitations!" cried Mickey, the Evil Assistant. "They were so obviously designer knockoffs."

I almost shouted, "Sufoo is not tacky!" I was becoming quite fond of Sufoo. She had spunk, that little maid.

"Now is the perfect chance to kidnap Princess Sophia for good!" Nanny Nuna tossed her umbrella in the air like a baton, caught it, and jabbed the air. "En garde! Let the games begin!" she shouted and then promptly fell backward and rolled down the hill. Artemia yelled cut as everyone on the crew laughed. I felt bad for Rebeccah, but a whirling twirling Princess Leia clone with a Mary Poppins parasol was actually a pretty funny sight. Artemia thought it was so cool that she decided to keep it in the film.

Finally it was Maddie's/Princess Sophia's turn. She let

out a blood-curdling shriek and fainted right in the middle of the park. I had to give Maddiecakes credit—she was superb at fainting. She looked like a real damsel in distress.

Nanny Nuna and the Evil Assistant ran out, picked Maddie up by her arms, and dragged her away. That was my cue.

"Not so fast, Nuna!" I hollered.

"Drop the lady!" David/Grego commanded. He picked up his green umbrella from behind a bench. "Or else."

"Hah!" the Evil Assistant replied. "Or else what? You're just a reporter. You don't stand a chance."

"That's what you think!" I shouted and charged down the hill, straight toward the bush where my pink umbrella was stashed. I reached down into the bush and groped for the umbrella handle, but strangely, there was nothing plasticky to be found. Finally, I felt something smooth. I grabbed and yanked with all my might. Instead of pulling out my trusty pink parasol, I found myself tugging at a sticky plant root. "Eeek" I yelled as my feet went out from under me and the bush snapped back like a boomerang.

"CUT!" shouted Artemia. "Maeve, WHAT are you doing?"

I pushed myself off the ground and tried to pick the leaves out of my curls. "This can't be right. My umbrella . . ." I walked around the entire bush. "It's not here . . ."

Maddie re-awakened from her faint, pointed at me and laughed. "Silly, forgetful little Maeve. I JUST told you. Artemia wanted your umbrella in *that bush over there*. The one closer to Nanny Nuna. It makes for better choreography."

My mouth hung open in shock. Maddie NEVER TOLD ME about the prop change. I looked at Artemia with desperation. Surely there had to be some mistake.

"I did tell Maddie to switch bushes." Artemia crossed her arms. "Maeve, let's get going now."

"But—" I felt horrible. I could tell she was annoyed.

"No excuses. Now we're just going to have to take it from the top. And Maeve . . . try to be more professional."

I glared at Maddie and trudged back up the hill. "It wasn't your fault. You didn't know," David said sweetly.

"Try telling Artemia that," I sighed. "And to think . . . before this she thought I was good!"

David rolled his eyes. "Maeve, you *are* good. Artemia knows that. See . . . look."

Apollo Aaron had put down his camera and was giving me two thumbs up. As the cameraman he was very good at hand signals. He pointed to Artemia and waved his hand. I knew what that meant: "Forget about it." Then he slowly rotated his finger around the side of his head— the universal sign for "cuckoo, cuckoo."

David grinned. "One little slip-up doesn't mean you don't rock, MKT. Now let's finish making this movie."

And when Artemia yelled ACTION, that's exactly what we did.

CHAPTER

19

It's a Wrap . . . with a Surprise Ingredient!

ere we are. Home sweet home . . . right, Maeve?"
Mom joked. We were pulling into the Von
Krupcakes' driveway for what I hoped would be the
last time.

"It's not as sweet as it looks." I mumbled. I was glad
my mom didn't hear me. She hated when I made catty
remarks, but I'd had just about enough of Maddie Von
Krupcake and her mansion, and her way too sweet (even
for *me*) Krupcakes.

The driveway was crowded with cars full of parents
and kids. All my friends from camp were taking pictures in
front of the Maddiecake fountain. They seemed to be having a lot of fun as they huddled together saying cheese for
the cameras. Mom parked and she and Sam eagerly hopped
out. I sat in the back seat of the car and took a deep breath.

"Maeve, come on. It's freeeeezing out, and I want to see the mansion!" Sam shouted. "Wow! Check out that gargoyle on the top."

I almost said, "It's a warning—keep away—danger within." But I didn't. I held up a finger. "I'll be there in a sec."

Mom blew me a kiss and she and Sam disappeared into the crowd.

"Okay. Deep yoga breath," I whispered out loud. "This is going to be fun. Parties are always fun. You're Maeve Kaplan-Taylor, the queen of parties." But no matter how many times I reminded myself, I was still too freaked to get out of the car. After everything that happened between me and Maddie, going back to her ginormous house just didn't feel right . . . even if I was technically invited. *Maybe I can just stay in the car until this whole wrap party thing is over*, I thought. Then I shook my head. *Snap out of it, Maeve! This attitude is soooo not you!*

Suddenly, a gloved hand tapped on my window, startling me so much I jumped in my seat. "Hey, Sufoo. You don't expect me to go in there without my weird little kung fu fighting compadre?"

It was David. And even though his glove was wooly red instead of crisp white . . . I couldn't have asked for a nicer, nobler escort. He opened the car and held out his arm. "After you, me lady," he said with a bow.

I curtsied. "Why, thank you, fine sir."

David put his hand on his hip, and I looped my arm into his. In perfect step, we walked to the grand front door of the mansion. It was so nice to have a drama buddy.

Then on the steps, I started feeling a little queasy again. I was afraid that Maddie would open the door and slam it right back in my face. "Wait . . ." I begged. But it was too late. The wooly red finger was already pressing on the bell. "Oh no . . ." I groaned. Of course, I should have known better than to assume Maddie would actually open the door of her house herself.

"Miss Maeve!" It was that handsome Kenneth! "What a pleasure it is to see you again." He took my hand and properly shook it. "And who is this dashing young man?"

I beamed proudly at David. His glasses made him look particularly intelligent today, I thought. "This is David Dell. He played Grego, the romantic lead in our movie."

"Very nice to meet you, David. I'm Kenneth, Mr. Von Krupcake's *personal assistant*." David looked at me and I curtsied again. (True confession—I was *loving* the whole curtseying thing!) "And Maeve, welcome back. It's a rare treat for me to see such a delightful friend of Maddie's return to the house. Actually . . ." Kenneth said, scratching his chin, "it's a rare treat for any of Maddie's friends to return to the house ever. Oh well. Enjoy the party."

David and I locked eyes. "Now why doesn't that surprise me . . ." David whispered.

I giggled. "Shh!" I guess I wasn't the only victim. Suddenly, I felt a little better. There was a whole group of us out there who had been Maddie-slammed. Maybe I should start a support group. I could call it Victims of Maddie United.

The mansion was swarming with kids and parents. Everyone was all dressed up—the girls in pretty dresses and the boys in suits and ties. *What is it about wearing suits that always makes boys look ten times handsomer than usual?* I wondered. I smoothed down my own rose velvet dress with the satin trim. I had been so proud of that dress when my mom and I first bought it. But after I'd seen Maddie's closet full of designer duds, I wondered if maybe the dress was a little babyish or something. Just as I was about to lose my courage again, David whispered, "Your dress is pretty." Thank *goodness* there were still knights in shining armor left in this world.

David and I walked down a long hallway filled with photographs of the Von Krupcakes posing with celebrities. "Look, there's Maddie with the Queen of England!" David gasped, pointing at one. "She's riding through the streets of London . . . wow."

"If you think this is something, you should see her bedroom," I told David.

David raised his eyebrows. "Whoa! You've seen Maddie's bedroom?"

I made an embarrassed face. "Um . . . Maddie and I kinda sorta used to be friends, in the beginning of camp . . . remember?"

David covered his mouth. "Whoa . . . I almost *forgot* about the famous M&M. It seems so long ago."

I thought about that. It did seem like ages ago since my brain had been hijacked by the super-fabulous Maddie Von Krupcake express.

When we reached the end of the hallway, David stopped at the very last picture. It was a tiny one with a worn-out gold frame. "Maeve . . . is it just my imagination, or is that . . . *Apollo*?"

I leaned in to get a closer look. *It sure looks like little Apollo Aaron*, I thought. *In fact, if I had to guess . . .*

"Hey, that is me!" Apollo was standing behind us holding a cup of fruit punch. In his black suit and purple tie, he looked like a real, live movie star. I started to feel a little shaky and hoped I wasn't coming down with another Maeve-crush. Talk about bad timing! "That was taken at the premiere of *Home Unsupervised*. Boy, am I glad that's over with!" Apollo laughed.

"Boy, do I wish I were you." I sighed. "I mean me, but my own age, and starring in a real Hollywood movie. I mean . . . oh . . ." I knew I was blushing.

"It's cool, Maeve. You'll get there someday." Apollo's eyes twinkled. "Maybe even sooner than you think!"

"I have a question. Who's that girl standing next to you, Apollo?" asked David Dell. The three of us leaned in to get a closer look at girl in the photo. She looked sort of familiar. There was something about that frizzy brown hair and those leopard tights . . .

"Hey, I know who that is!" I announced, suddenly remembering. "That's Maddie's cousin. She didn't tell me her name."

"Cousin?" Apollo choked. "Cousin? Who told you that's Maddie's cousin?"

I shrugged. "Maddie did . . ."

Apollo started to laugh so hard fruit punch shot right out of his nose. (So much for my crush . . . that was a close call.) "That's not Maddie's cousin! That's MADDIE!"

David and I gasped. "NO WAY!"

Apollo nodded. "Way. That was before the Maddiecake commercials. She looked a lot different back then, huh?"

I blinked. Could it be true? "But . . . but . . . she said . . ."

"I told you Maddie wasn't totally honest."

David rubbed his eyes. "But how is that even possible?" He seemed absolutely astonished.

I knew it was my job to explain this one. I gently rested my hand on his shoulder. "David, never underestimate the power of a makeover." I examined the picture again. "And the power of braces and a straightening iron."

"Want to hear the weirdest part of all?" Apollo asked. "Back then, Maddie and I were friends. Good friends. Seriously, we had a lot of fun together. We went surfing and . . ." he paused. "She liked to collect bugs." My eyes almost popped out of my head. Maddiecakes liked to collect bugs? That made no sense at all.

"But," Apollo continued, "when she changed on the outside, something changed on the inside too. She was still nice enough to me and all . . . but it was just kind of . . . fake."

"She turned into an ice princess," David observed.

"Exactly!" exclaimed Apollo.

"No, seriously, she turned into an ice princess. Look!"

David pointed to the center of the ballroom in front of us. My mouth hung open in shock as we watched Kenneth and Mr. Von Krupcake wheel in an enormous ice sculpture of Maddie dressed as Princess Sophia. A sparkling icy crown adorned her head. In one of her hands was a shimmering parasol, and in the other—a Maddiecake. The three of us couldn't contain it anymore and burst into laughter.

"Come on," I motioned to the boys. "Let's get this party started."

Just as we entered the ballroom, the lights went dim and Mr. Von Krupcake, in a white suit with thin red stripes, huffed into the middle of the room and clinked his fork against a glass. "Welcome, one and all, to the Von Krupcakes' humble abode. Everyone here today deserves a round of applause." A ripple of clapping erupted around me. I scanned the room and saw all my friends cheering and smiling. Rebeccah Fullerton, in a vibrant red dress, was leading Mickey Snyder in a funny little waltz. Sam was holding hands with Mom and Dad at the same time . . . which made me smile on the outside *and* inside.

"I know that each person in this room worked very hard to make *Boston Holiday*. And if there's one thing we believe at Krupcake Pies and Cakes Incorporated, it's that people should be rewarded for hard work. That's why I've decided, as the grand finale for this film camp experience . . ."

I glanced over at Madeline. I had to say, she looked lovely in her diamond tiara and a purple taffeta ball gown as she stroked Fitzy in her arms. Suddenly she burst, "That's the surprise! We're going to HOLLYWOOD!"

The room started bubbling with whispers. Was this some kind of joke?

Artemia darted to Mr. Von Krupcake with a look of panic on her face. "Walter . . . are you sure about this?"

"Of course, Artemia, darling. In exactly three weeks, the New York Film Academy is having a film festival in Los Angeles. And your wonderful film, *Boston Holiday*, is going to be screened at the festival, and . . ." Mr. Von Krupcake paused. It was so quiet I could hear my own heartbeat. "I am personally chartering a jet from Boston to L.A. You and your families will all get the chance to attend a Hollywood red carpet premiere!"

It wasn't a joke! Everyone cheered at the top of their lungs. You would think we'd all just won an Oscar or something. Every person in the ballroom was going crazy, jumping up and down and hugging each other. Well, except Maddie. I mean she wasn't hugging a person . . . she was hugging her precious little Fitzy instead.

Meanwhile, I thought that I was literally dreaming. Stuff like this—celebrity directors, being friends with cute, sort of grownup child stars, and *RED CARPET PREMIERES*—happened to other people . . . really rich and famous people . . . people who were NOT Maeve Kaplan-Taylor. And yet here I was, with one of my biggest fantasies actually coming true! I had to remind myself to breathe, but it was hard. I could practically *feel* the red carpet beneath my feet already!

Mr. Von Krupcake barked, "But this movie, this *Boston Holiday*, would not have been so magical, so wonderful, so *MAGNIFICO*, without the talent and inspiration of someone very, very special. Someone close to my heart." Maddie started to strut into the center as he continued, "I am pleased to introduce you to—"

"Jerry Sherlock, president and founder of the New York Film Academy," Artemia interrupted, rushing to Mr. Von Krupcake's side. "Jerry is a well-known Hollywood and Broadway producer, and without his generosity and support, this Boston chapter of the New York Film Academy Camp never would have happened . . ."

"Artemia, what in the name of Maddiecakes do you think you're doing?" Mr. Von Krupcake snarled under his breath. "This is my Maddie's big moment."

"Uh-oh . . ." I murmured. Madeline Von Krupcake looked very upset. I don't know why, but I started feeling a teensy bit bad for Maddie. I wondered if she knew that being the center of attention *all the time* wasn't such an awesome thing. I wouldn't have traded places with Maddie right then for all the diamond tiaras in the world.

Artemia pointedly ignored the Krupcake King and gestured a kind-looking bearded man to the middle of the room. Mr. Sherlock acknowledged the claps and cheers of the campers and cleared his throat.

"Thank you, Artemia. Thank you, everyone. I'm honored to have been a part of this amazing project—and I want to thank ALL the talented members of our wonderful camp."

"I was in the middle of making an important party toast," Mr. Von Krupcake hissed at Artemia and Jerry. His voice was getting louder. "And I am the party host. It is *most* rude to interrupt the party host in the middle of a party toast."

"Don't worry," Apollo assured me. "My mom knows how to handle this type of thing." Apollo and I squeezed around people to get a little closer to the middle. (Like I could BEAR missing a single drop of real-live drama?)

Artemia gently put her arm on Mr. Von Krupcake's shoulder. "This might be your toast, and you might be the host, but I am the director of this film camp. And, Walter . . . everyone here worked very hard."

He turned red as a beet. "True, but my Maddie—"

"Worked just as hard as everyone else," Artemia pronounced. "Now on with the party!"

The room went back to loud, excited chatter, but Artemia and Mr. Von Krupcake weren't done yet. Apollo motioned at me and we found a space next to the ice sculpture. Good thing too, because now Mr. Von Krupcake was whispering in an angry voice.

"Artemia, I think all the kids in this room would be *very disappointed* if I had to cancel the trip to Hollywood . . ."

She smiled. "They certainly would. Which brings me to my next point . . ." Artemia reached into the crowd and took the hand of a dashing man in a black tux. "Walter, have you met my husband? This is Ansel Aaron, Esquire, Attorney at Law."

Ansel Aaron, Esq., grabbed Mr. Von Krupcake's hand.

"Wow, it's an honor to meet you, sir. Your public promise to take everyone to Hollywood was just lovely. Why, you've just entered into a verbal contract! And it seems you have about . . . well let's see . . . at least a hundred witnesses. Ha . . . ha . . . You are truly a generous man, Mr. Von Krupcake."

"That's my lawyer," Artemia said, looked fondly at Ansel. Except for his silver hair, he looked just like Apollo.

Apollo nodded at me. "That's my pops."

Mr. Von Krupcake tried to clink his glass again, but it was clear the moment had passed. Artemia and Ansel left the Krupcake King trying to console a very annoyed Pastry Princess in the ballroom. No one was really paying attention to the Von Krupcakes though . . . we were too busy discussing our trip to Hollywood.

"Maeve, David, Apollo!" Lizzie Kwan called. She and Rebeccah ran over to us panting. Lizzie looked positively adorable in a green skirt with matching pumps.

"Maeve-a-licious, brace yourself," warned Rebeccah. "This surprise just might be system-overload for you."

I glanced at the ice sculpture. "Lizzie, at this point *nothing* about the Von Krupcakes surprises me."

"But this has nothing to do with the Von Krupcakes," Rebeccah protested. "Okay, so check it out. My best friend from school, Piper, has a cousin, Zoe, who's in . . . brace yourselves, people . . . GIRL AUTHORITY is here . . . at OUR PARTY!"

"No way!" David cried.

My hand flew to my heart. "I love Girl Authority!

Their song 'Girl Authority Theme' is, like, my favorite jam right now!" I raved.

"Well then you are going to love this news," Lizzie said.

"Wait, wait! I want to tell!" interjected Rebeccah. "Piper told Zoe about this party and Girl Authority wanted to come. You guys, *they're here now.* They're going to perform in," she looked at her watch, "well, any second now!"

"You're kidding me!" I shrieked.

Lizzie shook her head, rattling her two pigtails. "Nope. They're really here. When we asked Mr. Von Krupcake if it would be okay, he was more than happy to, um, what did he call it? Oh yeah, make a few minor adjustments."

Rebeccah giggled and confided, "He had a rising stage installed in the middle of the ballroom, and a—"

Lizzie poked her. "Rebeccah! Don't ruin *all* the surprises!"

Rebeccah clasped her hand over her mouth.

"I just can't believe this," I confessed.

Lizzie looked exasperated. "Maeve, how many times do I have to tell you? Girl Authority *really is here.*"

I shook my head. "No, I just can't believe that something this HUGE is about to happen and the Von Krupcake clan has nothing to do with it."

David pretended to tremble. "Creeeeeepy . . ."

"You guys are too much." Rebeccah gave me a hug. "Okay, kids, I gotta run. It's time for my big announcement!"

Rebeccah ran in front of the grandiose ice princess, her

dress swishing and swooshing all the way. "Ladies and Gentlemen!" she shouted. I was so proud of her—loving the spotlight, she was a gal after my own heart. "I am pleased to introduce the ultimate authority on girl power, coolness, and unbelievable singing. Like you and me, they come from Boston, but they're known all over the country. Let's give it up for . . . Girl Authority!"

A large disco ball descended from the ceiling and the music blasted. Neon lights of every color whirled around the ceiling, as a circular, spinning stage began rising right out of the floor. On the stage were the nine girls of Girl Authority—looking very stylish and hip-a-licious. Then, just when I thought the scene had reached its peak of awesomeness, fog began to stream out from under the stage. I gripped David and Rebeccah's arms to steady myself. "You gotta love show biz!" I remarked to my friends. "You never know what's going to happen next!"

No one could keep still as Girl Authority rocked out with their jamming cover of "Girls Just Wanna Have Fun."

"I love this song!" Lizzie squealed.

"Who doesn't?" I agreed. "Oh my goodness! Look!" I pointed at Sam, who was involved in some very serious boogying. His whole body wiggled in some kind of earthworm imitation as he sang along to each word. "No fair! Why isn't anyone taping Sam?" I laughed.

Mickey and Rebeccah broke into one of their dances from the movie. David gallantly held out his hand. "What do you say, Sufoo? Let's teach Nanny and Assistant a thing or two about dancing."

I grinned and started freestyle dancing with David. There was only one person in the room who wasn't lost in the incredible beat of Girl Authority's music. Maddie Von Krupcake stood in the corner of the large ballroom, uncomfortably fiddling with her hands. The ice sculpture of Maddie was smiling, but the real Maddie was not. At the cast party, usually the romantic leads would share a dance. But Maddie's romantic lead was dancing with *me*.

"David, wait," I stopped him. "This isn't right."

"Why? You and I are the craziest dancers here, Maeve!" David objected.

I shrugged. "Yeah, but Grego doesn't end up with Sufoo . . . he ends up with Princess Sophia." I glanced at Maddie, standing in the shadows by herself. "Don't you think you should ask her to dance?"

David groaned. "Maeve, are you kidding me?"

"Just for a little teensy bit!" I pleaded. "She looks so sad and I just can't stand seeing anyone look sad. It's just a thing I have."

"NO WAY." David shook his head. "That girl was so cruel to me throughout the entire camp. Even if I asked her to dance, she'd probably say no."

I sighed. "Yeah. I guess you're right." I sadly let go of David's hand and started to walk away. "I'll be back," I told him in my best Terminator voice.

"Maeve, what are you doing?" David called.

"The right thing," I replied and muttered to myself, "Geez, I really *must* be crazy."

I made a beeline right over to Maddie. Even though

we were on the same team in the film, we hadn't really talked since the day she stole my idea for *Boston Holiday*.

"Hey!" I yelled over the music.

She stared at the ground, like I wasn't even there. "Hello? I said 'Hey!' The polite thing to do is say 'hey' back."

Maddie slowly looked up. "What are *you* doing here?"

"I thought maybe . . . you might want company," I answered.

"What?" Maddie shouted.

"COMPANY!"

Maddie cupped her ear. "WHAT?"

"Come here." I sighed. I took her hand and dragged her into the hallway where it was a bit quieter. To my surprise, Maddie didn't resist. What a switch this was from the days when I was following *her* around.

"Why aren't you dancing?" I faced Maddie. "This is Girl Authority. You gotta work it, girl." I offered her a smile.

"Why do you care? I thought you hated me," she grumbled.

"No . . . I don't *hate* you."

Maddie looked suspicious. "Whatever. It's okay if you do."

I sighed. I didn't hate Maddie. I felt sorry for her. Maddie could have her limos, and designer gowns, and fancy ice sculptures. But she was missing something— something huge. I thought of the amazing friends I'd met at camp, and of course, my best friends—the BSG. I wouldn't trade them in for all the glamour and glitz in the world.

"I don't hate anybody," I confessed, remembering a little tip my Dad taught me. "It takes way too much energy to hate, and is soooo not worth it. I was pretty mad at you though."

Maddie squinted. "Is this about that whole stupid *Boston Holiday* thing?"

"Maddie! That wasn't stupid. Not to me. I thought I could trust you. I told you my idea and you stole it. And you didn't even say sorry."

Maddie shrugged. "I know. Honestly, I didn't mean to. It just kind of . . . happened."

"How does that *just happen*?" I demanded to know.

"Well, I wanted to be the one who had the brilliant movie idea. And I did think of a few, I promise. I even wrote them down in a notebook."

"You did?"

Maddie bit her lip. "Well, technically Kenneth did. Anyway, when you told me about *Boston Holiday* I knew it was the perfect idea. I wanted *Boston Holiday* to be mine so badly, and I always get what I want. So . . . I just took it."

"But you just can't do that!" I cried.

Maddie nodded. "I know. It's a really bad habit. It sort of comes naturally to me now." She let out a little heave and a sniffle-snort. It was weird. I felt like I was seeing Madeline Von Krupcake for the very first time.

"You definitely should quit that habit," I told her. "Stop

stealing what isn't yours and meddling with people's lives to get exactly what you want. Seriously. You're going to end up missing out on the most important thing."

"The most important thing?" asked Maddie.

Did she really not know?

"Friends!" I exclaimed.

"Friends?" Maddie looked stunned. She blinked, and I could've sworn I saw a single tear escape out of her light blue eye. "Friends? You really think friends are the most important thing?"

"Well duh, after family of course . . ." I bonked my head as a joke.

"Maeve, you are so cute." Maddie started laughing. She laughed harder and harder. "Friends? Hah. Are friends going to win you lead roles in movies? Are friends going to buy you mansions, and pools, and cars, and tennis courts? Well actually, maybe rich friends will. The point is, I always get what I want, and I'll do anything to get it. It's the best. Don't you see, Maeve?" Maddie threw her Pashmina scarf over her shoulder. "*Everyone* is just jealous of me. I have it all."

It was at that exact moment that I did see, and what I saw was this: Princess Maddiecake was missing out on some serious Vitamin L-O-V-E. "Good for you, Maddie." I smiled my best, most Hollywood-worthy smile. "Enjoy the rest of the concert. Go Girl Authority!"

If Maddie was happy living in her own little fantasy, that was fine by me. I, on the other hand, had a reality to get back to. And my reality didn't just *have* the most important thing—it was chock full of it! That was when I noticed. In the middle of the stage, dancing with Girl Authority and belting out every single word, was my very own little brother, Sam. *What do ya know? Looks like the acting bug is genetic after all!*

As I ran back to the ballroom and back to my friends, I couldn't help but whisper proudly, "I really do have it all . . . and I *love it*!

CHAPTER

20

Hurray for Hollywood!

*T*he sky is a ribbon of magenta and gold as the big, red sun retreats behind the mountains. As if this evening wasn't already perfect enough, tonight there's a full moon. In fact, the moon is SO enormous, I seriously can't tell if it's real. (Around here, you never know . . . it could be part of a set!)

My gown—my incredible, satin, sequined gown—swishes and swirls around me. It's honestly the most beautiful thing I've ever worn in my life. Want to guess what the color is? (Like there's even a question!) Pink . . . pomegranate pink. Now, I know pink and red don't usually go together. That is, outside of Valentine's Day. But don't forget. There's one shade of red that matches with everything: Red Carpet. Look out Hollywood. Make way for the one and only Maeve. (I've been thinking about doing the whole no-last-name thing . . . like Madonna and Beyoncé.)

I wave at my many adoring fans and blow a kiss to my beloved family. Mom looks oh-so-beautiful in her velvet plum dress. Dad and Sam, in their très dapper tuxedos, are oh-so-handsome.

Mom dabs her eyes with a tissue. Ohh . . . She's crying, just a little bit. This is a big night for all of us.

Breathe, Maeve. Just breathe, *I remind myself. As I stroll down the world-famous Hollywood Boulevard, the cameras are going crazy. The flashes all around me are the brightest of bright. No matter how much I want to, I absolutely can't squint. (Rule #1 of being a movie star: You must look paparazzi-perfect at all times.) When I reach my destination, the crowd forms a crescent around me.*

"How do you feel, Maeve?" asks a reporter, holding out a microphone.

"I feel like the luckiest girl in the whole entire world!"

"Maeve!" another reporter calls. "What's it like to walk in the shoes of Hollywood's greatest legends?"

I point my toe and show off my sparkly pink pumps. "It's a little blistery but totally worth it!" I reply.

"Maeve! Maeve! Maeve!" all the people are shouting at once.

Renaldo rushes to my side and shoos away the cameras. "That's enough questions for now. Maeve, sweetie, it's time. Do your thing."

The sight of my name, "Maeve Kaplan-Taylor" (in gold, with its very own tile on the Hollywood Walk of Fame) is almost too much to bear. Renaldo has to steady me so I don't lose my balance.

The cameras snap and flicker as I bend down and squish my hands into the freshly-poured cement. It is cold, wet, and wonderful. Dad's voice booms over all the rest. "This is it! Say cheese, Maeve."

"CHEESE!" I looked up and smiled as Dad clicked the camera. Okay, maybe I didn't have my very own name in the Walk of Fame yet . . . but I did have the next best thing!

"Wow, Maeve. I can't believe your hands are the exact same size as Audrey Hepburn's!" Sam knelt down beside me to get a closer look. "That is *too weird*."

"I know! It must be a sign or something," I giggled.

Hollywood was every bit as glamorous in real life as I imagined it would be. My gown—my incredible, satin, sequined gown in pomegranate pink—really was the most beautiful thing I'd ever worn in my life. Mom and Dad said this was an occassion to splurge. After all, Mr. Von Krupcake was taking us all to Hollywood. (Mr. Ansel Aaron made sure of that!) Ms. Razzberry Pink had a friend who was a dressmaker, and she whipped up this dress in two weeks. I was in heaven. I was dressed in pink and at the red carpet premiere of *Boston Holiday* after all. It was a very big deal. And even though I didn't have a star on the Walk of Fame *quite* yet, I knew that somewhere on Hollywood Boulevard there was a future spot reserved for Ms. Maeve Kaplan-Taylor.

Film camp didn't just go out with a bang—this was an explosion. Mr. Von Krupcake, true to his word, had arranged a bona fide movie premiere, complete with all the glitter. I'm talking cameras, limousines, gowns, tuxedos, and of course . . . a red carpet. Plus, we were allowed to invite our whole families. I had to admit, it was really generous of Mr. Von Krupcake. I wished we got to bring our best friends too, but alas, my darlings, the BSG, would have to miss out on this adventure. Of course, I promised to tell them every tiny detail.

I wanted to run around the red carpet and see all my film

camp friends, but the outside of the theater was so crowded I had to use all my powers of concentration just to keep track of my own family. Mom and Dad were working on keeping track too. I could tell, because they couldn't take their eyes off each other. Then again, Mom did look beautiful in her dress . . . which was plum. And Dad did look handsome too . . . in his tuxedo. (Who says dreams can't come true?)

"Attention, ladies and gentlemen!" Artemia stood in the middle of the carpet. The crowd—breathless—drew back around her. She wore a smashing gown made of ruby red satin. Her sleek, auburn hair was twisted into a bun using two chopsticks with diamond butterflies on the ends. I noticed she had a tiny microphone clipped behind her ear. "This is it. The moment you've all been waiting for."

Where's Apollo? I wondered. I stood on my tiptoes and scanned the faces, but the carpet was so packed, it was impossible for me to spot any of my friends. Everyone just looked like one gorgeous movie star after another. If only Apollo were wearing his favorite Dodgers hat, finding him would be no problem.

Artemia went on, "I am pleased to welcome you to the world premiere, first-ever public screening, of the New York Film Academy's production of *Boston Holiday*! Now, in an orderly fashion, please make your way into the theater."

Everyone cheered and began to walk toward the grand marble entrance of the building. But then, suddenly, the people stopped and turned around. A white stretch limousine rolled up to the front of the red carpet, followed by not one, not two, but THREE news trucks full of reporters.

Sam tugged at my hand. "Bet I know who this is . . ."

I put my hands on my hips. Sure, I was no math genius or anything, but come on! That's a bet I'd never take. "Okay, Sam, do you really think I'm that—ow!" Someone stepped on my poor big toe. A mob of kids, like a herd of wild animals, charged past me toward the limo. Dad lifted Sam into the air to get a better look. By the time Sam had gotten a glimpse of what was going on, the word was already out: Justin DePre, winner of the hit reality TV show *U.S. Superstar*, was attending *our very own* red carpet premiere.

"I see him! I see him!" Sam cried. "Hey, Maeve, he's signing autographs."

"Oh, no fair," I murmured, wishing to rewind five years to when I was still small enough to be lifted onto Dad's shoulders. Justin DePre was fourteen years old and beyond adorable. And when I say adorable, I would be talking Justin's-*CrushMagazine*-cover-is-on-my-math-binder adorable. (I needed the cutest of boys to make my math ANYTHING look good!) Justin's yellow spiked hair was his trademark, along with his swoon-worthy hit single, "Secret Study Buddies." I could completely understand why everyone would be freaking out about Justin DePre being here. *But just why IS he here?* That was the part I couldn't quite figure out.

"Maeve," Sam shouted down to me, "Guess who he came with . . ."

I didn't have to guess. I already knew.

Cameras flashed wildly and reporters swarmed the dazzling teen star and his glossy blond date, Madeline

Von Krupcake. She paraded proudly down the red carpet arm and arm with Justin DePre, waving gracefully, blowing kisses, and striking poses for the photographers.

"Madeline, how long have you and Justin been an item?"

"Madeline, is it true that you're starring in Justin's 'U Ain't Crawling Back 2 Me' music video?"

"Madeline, can you comment about the rumors that you stole Justin from socialite Venice Doubletree? Is it true that you and Venice are no longer friends?"

Madeline waited for the hubbub to simmer down before she answered. "Justin DePre and I are dear old friends," she looked at Justin mysteriously. (I wondered how their paths could have possibly *ever* crossed with Maddie growing up Boston, and Justin being from a small cheese farm in Wisconsin. Old friends? Mmm . . . the power of Maddiecakes. I wondered if Justin was a fan.)

Maddie went on "As far as the rumors that I am to star in the 'U Ain't Crawling Back 2 Me' video . . . my publicist and I have no comment." Maddie grabbed Justin's hand and tried to squeeze through the crowd and into the theater. But with all the kids shoving paper at Justin DePre to sign and the reporters screeching, "Maddie, Justin! Over here, over here," the two star-studded sensations were positively stuck.

Lucky for me, this was one red carpet occasion when I would be spared from the pesky paparazzi. With the rest of the kids and families, we snuck right by the huge crowd around Maddie and Justin. As I walked away I could hear Maddie's perfect-for-stage voice boom, "Venice Doubletree is a spoiled, double-crossing princess and she is NO friend of mine."

Sam and I looked at each other and shook our heads.

The theater filled up quickly, but we got fabulous seats right smack in the middle. I thought maybe Apollo would be by the stage adjusting the lights or something. I squinted and examined the entire room. Still, he was nowhere to be found.

I sat in between Mom and Dad. Sam insisted on taking the aisle seat, which was probably best. (He had a habit of leaving movies at least three times in the middle to get something.)

"Are you excited, sweetie?" Mom asked.

"The word 'yes' doesn't begin to describe!" I answered. "This might be one of the top three most exciting things *ever* to happen in the history of Maeve."

Dad grinned. "What are the other things?"

I shrugged. "Don't know yet. But I'm reserving places for two at least. I'm going to have a very exciting life, Dad."

He nodded. "I don't doubt it for a second."

The lights grew dim and I squeezed Mom's and Dad's hands. A large, white castle appeared on the screen. The narrator (Apollo) began, "Once upon a time, in a faraway land called Tazmundo, there was a princess who had everything. Everything, that is . . . but adventure!"

The castle turned into the Boston skyline and cut to Sufoo (ME!!!) running through Chinatown carrying a bundle of fabric.

"And so," continued the narrator, "our story begins . . ."

Red Fooey

Okay, I admit—I *was* crying a tiny bit at the end of *Boston Holiday*. It was just so tragic that Grego and Sophia could never be together, on account of Sophia being the future Queen of Tazmundo, and Grego being a kung fu instructor who didn't want to give up his U.S. citizenship. "But Grego, no matter what happens . . ." Princess Sophia uttered tearfully, from her royal convertible, ". . . we'll always have Boston. And this." Princess Sophia released a pink parasol, and her car rode down Newbury Street and into the sunset, with Grego and Sufoo left in the distance.

For a second, I forgot I was watching a movie. That is, until the clapping and cheering began. Dad tapped me on the shoulder and turned me around. "Maeve! Look!" People were shooting out of their seats to give *Boston Holiday* a standing ovation. I had been a part of standing ovations before, but it felt really weird to be doing one for myself. Still, when people stand in the theater, the rule was you stood. Mom and Dad were practically jumping, they were clapping so hard. I peered around them to see if Sam was standing too, but strangely, his chair was empty.

"Look! Look!" shouted a little kid in the front row. He pointed at the screen. "It's not over! Something's happening!"

Sure enough, there was something happening . . . a single red rectangle of light. I peered to the back of the theater and noticed two people huddled around the projector: Apollo and Sam. In the middle of the screen, in black inky print, flashed the words, "Red Fooey. Produced and directed by Sam Kaplan-Taylor. Edited by Apollo Aaron."

"I have a bad feeling about this . . ." I whispered to myself.

The song, "Everybody was 'Kung Fu Fighting,'" started to play, as a person dressed as a green, goopy monster did a kung fu kick for the camera. But it wasn't just any old green, goopy monster . . . it was me. Then the movie got even scarier. I watched, wide-eyed, as a straight-haired, much meaner version of me strutted proudly around the kitchen for the camera. Suddenly it all came flooding back—how horribly I'd acted at the beginning of camp.

"Oh nooooo . . ." I breathed.

Sam had caught everything on tape—from my spoiled rotten diva days to me snoring in the car at Boston Common. Clip after clip, I watched myself smear makeup on my tooth, fall on ice during rehearsal, and break into an Irish jig when I thought no one was looking. I had no idea my brother had been taping so much. I wanted to disappear on the spot.

Sam's mini documentary ended with a shot of me flying into the bush during the last day of filming and then the final cut where I successfully grabbed the umbrella. If the movie hadn't been "Maeve the Embarrassing," it would have actually been kind of funny. But as far as I was concerned, *Red Fooey* was far from a laughing matter.

Unfortunately, I was outnumbered. The entire theater was clapping and laughing hysterically. "Take a bow! Take a bow!"

One by one, each of the film camp kids got out of their seats and made their way to the front of the theater.

The more kids filled the front, the louder the clapping became. Even Artemia and Dad went up. They *had* to-people practically dragged them out of their seats. But I couldn't move . . . my feet felt like they were cemented to the floor.

Mom gave me a nudge. "Go on, Maeve. Get up there."

"I can't! Not after *Red Fooey* . . . it's way too embarrassing!"

At that moment, a powder blue tuxedo started bolting toward me from the back of the theater. It was David Dell. And he was shouting something. "We want Red Fooey! We want Red Fooey!"

My eyes grew wide. Oh no, it was contagious! "We want Red Fooey! We want Red Fooey!" the whole theater chanted.

David got to my row and stopped. "You heard the people. Bow!" He held out his hand and Mom gently pushed. In my pink pumps, I was easily push-able. David grabbed my hand, and I went flying down the aisle.

"There she is!" cried the same very loud little boy from the front row.

The theater whooped it up all over again, and I knew I was smiling the biggest smile. How could I not? It felt awesome to stand there with all of my new friends who'd worked so hard on the film.

The only camper who didn't make it up to the front was Maddie. She was stuck in back behind a wall of reporters. The clapping was so loud though, I don't think anyone really noticed.

But there was one person who was missing from the front, who really deserved to be there. "Where's Sam?" I asked David.

David's eyes suddenly got huge. "Um, Maeve . . . you better look out . . ."

The doors of the theater thundered open and I looked up. Sam was charging down the center aisle, headed straight at me. This was probably going to be his grand finale, when he tackled me down to get material for his next big hit: *Red Fooey 2—the Monster Returns*. But instead, Sam did something completely unexpected. He jumped into my arms and gave me a giant hug.

I had to smile. "How did you ever make such a hilarious movie?"

"What can I say? I had a really funny cast . . ." Sam grinned and looked back at Apollo, who was sauntering over from the side, away from the spotlight. "And a little tiny bit of help," he added in a whisper. I smiled at Apollo and I wasn't exactly sure, but I could've sworn he gave me a very quick wink.

At that very moment, as the Hollywood theater applauded, I couldn't deny it any longer. My little brother was a really talented *filmotographer*-person after all. "Hey, this is your moment. You should take a bow, Sam," I told him.

He shook his head, smiled, and grabbed my hand. "We both should."

And so we did.

To be continued . . .

And the winner is . . .

New York Film Academy Glossary

(with a few Maevisms)

Art Director—Person who is in charge of and oversees the artists and craftspeople who build the movie sets.
They've got to be artistic AND organized? Whoa.

Best Boy—Best Boy is like the second in charge of any group, most commonly the chief assistant to the Gaffer. Females are also known as "Best Boys."
Why can't I be a "Best Girl"? Oh well.

Body Double/Stunt Double—These peeps are used to take the place of the actor for a specific scene . . . like one with special effects or hard dance moves.
But don't worry—I perform all my own stunts always.

Boom Operator—You always see this sound crew dude around holding the microphone attached to the end of a long pole. But did you know the dude had such a funny name? The Boom Operator extends the boom microphone over the actors, out of sight of the camera.

Cinematographer—The person who is awesomely good at capturing images using visual recording devices (*that's fancy-pants talk for a camera*). The Cinematographer is also in charge of the lighting.
And don't yawn–that's a very important job!

Composer—This one is simple. Composers write the music for a movie.
One of my personal favorite movie scopes is Titanic. *Way to go James Horner, composer extraordinaire!*

Costume Designer—Person who is in charge of designing the costumes in a film.
My fashionista friend Katani would be very good at that job.

Dialog Coach—This person has to be very good at doing accents, because this dude has to help actors speak like the characters they are playing.
Think Henry Higgins in My Fair Lady . . .

Director—Um, this person's a pretty big deal. The Director has control over every single-bingle artistic aspect of the movie. I'm talking casting, editing, acting—the works.
Artemia Aaron rocks and that's all I have to say.

Dolly Grip—(*True confession–I mostly wanted to talk about this job because the name sounds funny.*) The dolly grip is responsible for positioning the dolly, a small truck that rolls along tracks and carries the camera, camera person, and sometimes THE DIRECTOR.

Editor—The person who edits the film.
What did you think an editor does . . . makes cookies?

Extra—Extras are people who don't have speaking roles and are usually used as fillers for a crowd scene.
Hey, everyone's got to start somewhere, right?

Gaffer—Person in charge of the electrical department.
(Fun fact: Gaffer literally translates to *old* man. *Come on . . . that's a hoot.*)

Grip—The person responsible for the maintenance and positioning of equipment on a set.
Maddie was a terrible Grip, I'd say.

Producer—Head honcho in charge of a movie production in all matters except for the creative parts, which are aaaaaall the Director. The Producer must also raise funds, hire key personnel, and arrange the distribution.

Screenwriters—Screenwriters create new screenplays to be filmed or adapt existing works into scripts for a movie, like someone did with *Harry Potter*.

Sound Designer—He or she is in charge of the audio portion of the movie . . . a really important job in the movies.

Wrangler—This is the dude in charge of all creatures in a movie who are EXTRA DIFFICULT to communicate with. Boston Holiday *didn't have a wrangler, but I bet* Dr. Doolittle *had more than one!*

Maeve on the Red Carpet trivialicious triVia

1. Where is Maeve's friend, Charlotte Ramsey, going for her winter vacation?
   A. Paris, France, *mais bien sur!*
   B. On tour with Justin Timberlake as the youngest-ever reporter for *Rolling Stone* magazine
   C. Montreal, Quebec
   D. Disney World

2. Maeve and Sam's mother surprises her kids with Chinese food and a new . . .
   A. Pink convertible Porsche
   B. Guinea pig
   C. Haircut
   D. Boyfriend

3. What does Sam really, really, really want to do for the film camp?
   A. Play Prince Harry in *Boston Holiday*
   B. Dress up as an Army dude and scare people randomly
   C. Choreograph the kung fu fighting scenes
   D. Be the filmotographer

4. According to Maddie, what is the ingredient that makes Maddiecakes so very special?
   A. Calcium and fiber
   B. Wheatgrass
   C. Vitamin L-O-V-E
   D. Hamburger meat

5. What do the kids at camp start calling Maddie and Maeve?
   A. Tweedle-dee and Tweedle-dum
   B. Princesses of Mean
   C. Paris and Nicole
   D. M&M (Isn't that fabulous?)

6. On audition day, what is Maddie's chosen mode of transportation?
   A. A white stretch Escalade
   B. The Oscar Mayer Wienermobile
   C. A horse-drawn carriage
   D. An elephant named Cinderella

7. When Maddie steals Maeve's _____ it is the final straw in their friendship.
   A. Muffin tops
   B. Fabulous movie idea
   C. Goose that lays golden eggs
   D. Imaginary friend, Lady Bird Muffleufagus

8. Why doesn't Maddie want David Dell to play the romantic male lead?
   A. His radiant handsomeness will outshine her.
   B. He's too short.
   C. He was disrespecting Maddie's momma, and no one disrespects her momma.
   D. No one knows why because Maddie is crying too hysterically to explain.

9. Who is Maddie's date to the Hollywood movie premiere of *Boston Holiday*?
   A. Fifty trained swans
   B. Apollo Aaron
   C. Justin DePre, winner of the hit reality TV show *U.S. Superstar*
   D. No one, because she was MEAN!!!

10. Sam's movie, featuring Maeve, is called . . .
    A. *Red Fooey*
    B. *Little Orphan Annie Part Deux*
    C. *Spidermaeve*
    D. *Big Sister and the Beast*

ANSWERS: 1. C. Montreal, Quebec **2.** C. Haircut **3.** D. Be the filmographer **4.** C. Vitamin L-O-V-E **5.** D. M&M (Isn't that fabulous?) **6. A.** A white stretch Escalade **7. B.** Fabulous movie idea **8. B.** He's too short **9. C.** Justin DePre, winner of the hit reality TV show *U.S. Superstar* **10. A.** *Red Fooey*

❀ 225 ❀

Share the Latest

BEACON STREET GIRLS

Adventure

Crush Alert

Romantic triangles and confusion abound as the BSG look forward to the Abigail Adams Junior High Valentine's Day dance.

Check out the Beacon Street Girls at

beaconstreetgirls.com

Aladdin M!X

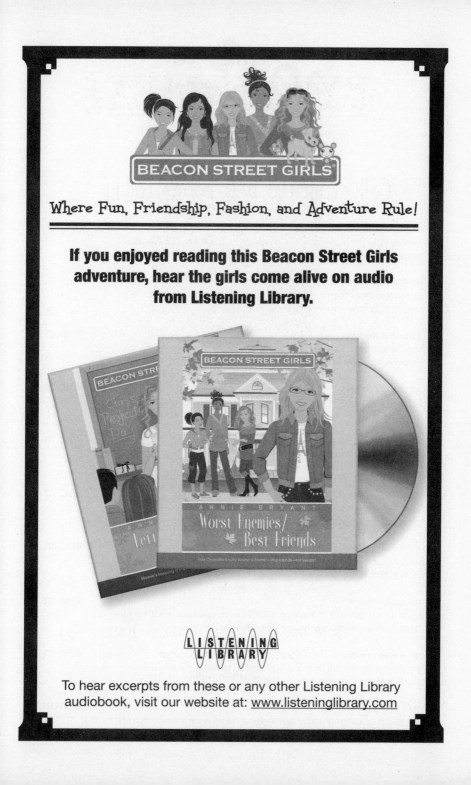

Collect all the BSG books today!

#1 Worst Enemies/Best Friends ☐ **READ IT!**
Yikes! As if being the new girl isn't bad enough . . . Charlotte just made the biggest cafeteria blunder in the history of Abigail Adams Junior High.

#2 Bad News/Good News ☐ **READ IT!**
Charlotte can't believe it. Her father wants to move away again, and the timing couldn't be worse for the Beacon Street Girls.

#3 Letters from the Heart ☐ **READ IT!**
Life seems perfect for Maeve and Avery . . . until they find out that in seventh grade, the world can turn upside down just like that.

#4 Out of Bounds ☐ **READ IT!**
Can the Beacon Street Girls bring the house down at Abigail Adams Junior High's Talent Show? Or will the Queens of Mean steal the show?

#5 Promises, Promises ☐ **READ IT!**
Tensions rise when two BSG find themselves in a tight race for seventh-grade president at Abigail Adams Junior High.

#6 Lake Rescue ☐ **READ IT!**
The seventh grade outdoor trip promises lots o' fun for the BSG—but will the adventure prove too much for one sensitive classmate?

#7 Freaked Out ☐ **READ IT!**
The party of the year is just around the corner. What happens when the party invitations are given out . . . but not to everyone?

#8 Lucky Charm ☐ **READ IT!**
Marty is missing! The BSG's frantic search for their beloved pup leads them to a very famous person and the game of a lifetime.

#9 Fashion Frenzy ☐ **READ IT!**
Katani and Maeve are off to the Big Apple for a supercool teen fashion show. Will tempers fray in close quarters?

#10 Just Kidding ☐ **READ IT!**
The BSG are looking forward to Spirit Week at Abigail Adams Junior High, until some mean—and untrue—gossip about Isabel dampens everyone's spirits.

#11 Ghost Town
The BSG's fun-filled week at a Montana dude ranch includes skiing, snow boarding, cowboys, and celebrity twins—plus a ghost town full of secrets.

☐ **READ IT!**

#12 Time's Up
Katani knows she can win the business contest. But with school and friends and family taking up all her time, has she gotten in over her head?

☐ **READ IT!**

#13 Green Algae and Bubble Gum Wars
Inspired by the Sally Ride Science Fair, the BSG go green, but getting stuck slimed by some gooey supergum proves to be a major annoyance!

☐ **READ IT!**

#14 Crush Alert
Romantic triangles and confusion abound as the BSG look forward to the Abigail Adams Junior High Valentine's Day dance.

☐ **READ IT!**

Also . . . Our Special Adventure Series:

Charlotte in Paris
Something mysterious happens when Charlotte returns to Paris to search for her long-lost cat and to visit her best Parisian friend, Sophie.

☐ **READ IT!**

Maeve on the Red Carpet
A cool film camp at the Movie House is a chance for Maeve to become a star, but newfound fame has a downside for the perky redhead.

☐ **READ IT!**

Freestyle with Avery
Avery Madden can't wait to go to Telluride, Colorado, to visit her dad! But there's one surprise that Avery's definitely not expecting.

☐ **READ IT!**

Katani's Jamaican Holiday
A lost necklace and a plot to sabotage her family's business threaten to turn Katani's dream beach vacation in Jamaica into stormy weather.

☐ **READ IT!**

Isabel's Texas Two-Step
A disastrous accident with a valuable work of art and a sister with a diva attitude give Isabel a bad case of the ups and downs on a special family trip.

☐ **READ IT!**